Dogs, Goats, Bulbs and Bombs

FEBRUARY 1943

Friday 26
(57-308)

Domino, Sam, Rusty & I were all quietly polishing the pretty little nick-nacks on the ornamental tables in the drawing-room (the last job of the spring-clean) when suddenly I heard the unmistakable sound of machine-gun fire, rather deep-throated but it came nearer - nearer still. Domino rushed out in the garden before I could stop him. The noise now was terrific. Four German fighter-bombers raced across our lawn at tree top height, machine-guns rattling as hard as they could. Domino rushing madly round the lawn below them barking furiously. I thought he would be killed for certain. I had Rusty in my arms and little Sammy frightened, crouching at my feet. Then before one had time to think the bombs had begun to rain down as well, the house swayed, the windows shook, the German guns spattered and roared. Some frightened children gathered round the gate into the lane so I called them in - They were very excited and talked without stopping. One had seen a bomb actually falling! He was thrilled!! The four planes vanished as quickly as they had come, but, over the town, bombing as they went. The devils - Anyway, after lunch I heard that another four came in from another direction and two American fighters brought two down over the sea ...

The diary entry for Friday 26 February 1943: one of the most dramatic and terrifying events recorded in the diaries. Esther witnessed four Focke Wulf 190 German fighter bombers race across her lawn, skimming the trees, machine gunning and dropping bombs in the area. Exmouth's last blitz.

Dogs, Goats, Bulbs and Bombs

ESTHER ROWLEY'S WARTIME DIARIES OF EXMOUTH AND EXETER

EDITED BY

JOHN FOLKES

First published 2010
Reprinted 2020

The History Press
97 St George's Place, Cheltenham,
Gloucestershire, GL50 3QB
www.thehistorypress.co.uk

British Library Cataloguing in Publication Data.
A catalogue record for this book is available from the British Library.

ISBN 978 0 7524 4883 1

Typesetting and origination by The History Press
Printed in Great Britain by TJ International Ltd, Padstow, Cornwall.

CONTENTS

ACKNOWLEDGEMENTS

Special thanks are given to my wife Margaret Folkes and my daughter Gill Walsh for their extensive contribution to the making of this book, while undergoing great stress in difficult circumstances. Margaret has given valuable assistance in the preparation of the introductory sections together with research and photography, while Gill has successfully completed typing the diary extracts, and has brilliantly managed to unearth the tangled web of Esther Rowley's family through extensive genealogical research.

Thanks are also due to the staff of the National Archives at Kew, the Devon Record Office, the West Country Studies Library, Exmouth Library, and to Roger Brien of the Devon and Exeter Institution.

Further thanks are due to Clare Broomfield and Sophie Burton of the National Monument Record Enquiry and Research Services, to Peter Baker, Chairman of Exeter Postcard Society, for help with photography, to Christine Trigger for specialised local knowledge of Exeter and finally to my editor at The History Press, Nicola Guy for her ongoing help, co-operation and friendliness.

ILLUSTRATION SOURCES

The photographs of the Chapel Street area of Exmouth following the air raid of 18 January 1941 appear courtesy of the *Express and Echo* and the East Devon District Council (Devon Record Office R7/4/C/106/7). The photograph of Market Street after the same raid appears by permission of the *Express and Echo*.

The photograph of Bicton Place appears courtesy of English Heritage, National Monuments Record.

GLOSSARY AND ABBREVIATIONS

Ack-ack – Military slang for an anti-aircraft gun or fire.

ADC – Aide de camp.

ARP – Air raid precautions. An organisation responsible for the maintenance of the Blackout but also, more importantly, a search and rescue service in the aftermath of air raids.

ATS – Auxiliary Territorial Service (Women's Section of the Army).

Billet-doux – A love letter (French).

Blackout – the extinguishing or concealing of lights that might be visible to enemy aircraft during an air raid at night.

Blotting my copybook – Putting a blot of ink on a book of models for handwriting, therefore a stain on one's character.

The Boche – Derogatory First World War name for Germans from the French word *alboche*.

BSA – Birmingham Small Arms Co. – Manufacturer of ammunition, guns and transport.

CB – Confined to barracks.

FANY – First Aid Nursing Yeomanry.

The flicks – Old slang name for the Cinema, from the flicker of early films.

Huns – Derogative term for Germans.

Hush hush – Secret, confidential.

Jerry – Slang word for a German

KG – Kitchen garden.

NCO – Non-Commissioned Officer.

OCTU – Officer Corps Training Unit.

RA – Royal Artillery.

RAF – Royal Air Force.

RAFVR – Royal Air Force Voluntary Reseve.

RC – Roman Catholic.

RE – Royal Engineers.

Salop – Shropshire.

Skep – A beehive made of straw.

Super – A type of honey-comb kit.

Smoker – A puffer to introduce smoke into a hive to extract the comb without bees.

Time bomb – A bomb with a detonating mechanism set for a particular time.

WAAF – Women's Auxiliary Air Force or a member of it.

WVS – Women's Voluntary Service.

Wren – An informal British name for a member of the Women's Royal Naval Service.

EDITOR'S NOTE

Although some of the views expressed by the diarist are far from the 'politically correct' perspective of the twenty-first century, they are of her time and typical of those held by many of Esther's contemporaries. If changed throughout, the power of her personality, which gives the diaries such variety, interest and authenticity, would be greatly diminished. Nevertheless, some remarks which could now cause offence to readers, or to the relatives of those mentioned in the diaries, have been excluded. The views remaining, however, do not represent those of the editor or of The History Press.

INTRODUCTION

Official and political documents are often used as indicators of past human behaviour and thought, but these tend to ignore the daily lives and mental attitudes of individuals and their aspirations for the future. Diaries alternatively, provide a rich source of information for those who seek to learn the reality of daily life as it was experienced by past generations. However, most diaries of any significant age are only available in the form of a printed book, while the original is held within a university library, or in a private collection. It is rare to encounter a diary of any literary merit as a manuscript which is available for sale, even one written in the earlier years of the twentieth century.

It was therefore with some degree of excitement that I noticed in the catalogue of a local auctioneer the rather modest entry: 'World War Two Diaries: four handwritten diaries 1941-48 by a local woman with detailed entries covering blitz etc with many local references.'

Viewing the four diaries – three approximately eight inches by five and a quarter and the fourth a little smaller – I was impressed by the neatness of the handwriting and the vividness of some of the descriptive passages. Fortunately for me, at the auction which followed later, my enthusiasm was not shared by many of the other bidders and I was able to purchase them for a fairly modest expenditure.

The diaries spanned a period of eight years from Christmas 1940 to August 1948. The first three were in a page-a-day format and the fourth, covering 1944-48, in a year-by-year style designed as stated by the publishers for 'those who have neither the time nor the inclination to keep a full diary.' As a result the daily entries are naturally much shorter from 1944 onwards.

An airgraph – an early form of airmail – inserted in the 1942 diary, linked exactly to diary entries, and clearly identified the diarist as Miss Esther Rowley of 3 Cranford Avenue Exmouth. Research from other sources has since revealed the names of Esther's parents and her relations.

Published in their entirety, the diaries would form a very large, and often overdetailed book, as many of the entries are condensations of news reports from the Second World War that had appeared in the right-wing press of the period. Coverage has therefore been restricted to those sections of the diaries which were generated by the diarist herself, together with a few selected items from news reports of key moments in the war, in order to place the perspective of the diary within a framework of contemporary world events. Additionally, focus is centred on the period when the diarist lived in Cranford Avenue, Exmouth before her short-lived move to Drewsteignton, in April 1945. Esther Rowley returned to Exmouth the following year and by 1947 had settled at Lanes End, Littleham Road.

In 1940 the civilian population of Exmouth was unprepared for the reality of air attacks which did not discriminate between service personnel and defenceless men, women and children. Although the building of air-raid shelters began in July 1940, by 1943 it was reported that they had only been provided for 10 per cent of the population.

Observation points were set up for use by the Observer Corps but no one antici-pated the number or intensity, of the air raids, which at times threatened to overwhelm defence organisations in the town, between 1941 and 1943.

At the start of the war Exmouth was a relatively small seaside town with a popula-tion well under 20,000. It was seen as a safe haven area for evacuation and within a few days after 3 September 1939, the first contingent of nearly 800 evacuees had arrived. Each week saw a new influx until the position became critical. By October 1940, 150 arrived, after only twelve hours' notice, and 400 were expected the next day, as the bombing of London and other big cities intensified.

In Exmouth, as in other parts of England, the influx of evacuees was not univer-sally welcomed, especially by those who lived in the more elite areas of the town. Middle-class home-owners were shocked by the wretched conditions of many of the evacuee children. Those from poorer families were often unwashed, lice infested and shabbily dressed. Their appearance, together with their speech and general behaviour, provoked strongly adverse reactions from local people. Although willing householders had every room in their house occupied, compulsion was used against those who objected.

Esther complained when two boys were billeted on her in January 1941, as she was in the ATS and also had to care for her elderly mother. Her mother wrote to the bil-leting officer to say that she and her live-in housekeeper, also elderly, could not look after the boys. Their joint complaint proved successful as both boys were fairly rapidly re-housed, and even though she lived in a five-bedroom house, and had left the ATS later that year, she was never again approached by the billeting officer. She conceded that both boys had been well brought up by their father, a pub landlord in Penge and that the room where the boys had slept was none the worse for their fleeting visit.

In spite of this concession however, she soon exhibited snobbish intolerance towards evacuees in general, blaming them for contaminating cinemas and contribut-ing to the potential collapse of the town's drainage system.

The arrival of the evacuee boys at 3 Cranford Avenue coincided with one of the worst air raids that Exmouth experienced, as on 18 January, an extensive area of the town centred on Chapel Street, Tower Street and The Cross, was devastated by bomb blast and fire. The well-known grocer's, Wilson's, was one of the sixteen properties destroyed and fire spread rapidly through the drapery store Waltons, until it collapsed into a heap of smouldering ashes.

It was the first occasion on which the ARP had been called into action and they, and the police, were highly praised. However, the siren did not go off until after the bombs fell and this happened frequently between 1941 and 1943 – recorded both by Esther Rowley and confirmed by the recollections of residents after the war. Additionally, in a report on the incident, the district ARP organiser recorded that although about 100 soldiers were present, there were no officers there to coordinate their actions.

Twelve women and children were killed in the raid – seven of them were evacuees. Tragically five of these were from one family – the wife of a Salvation Army Officer and their four very young children.

Throughout 1941 there were a number of other raids. In March, five bombs fell on the Parade in the centre of town, demolishing a meat shop and a drapery store. There were four fatalities, but casualties would have been higher if the nearby Woolworths had been open, but fortunately the attack occurred after the store had closed for the day's business.

Six bombs fell on the Woodville Road area during the night of 28 May, demolishing three houses and killing nine people, including three small children. The local press described the area as 'working class' and Esther did not wake up while it took place. Eight people were taken to hospital.

By 1942, in addition to evacuees from other parts of the country, Exmouth now had its own evacuees as the number of families displaced by bombing increased, as many houses were destroyed or so badly damaged that they had to be demolished.

Casualties continued to mount and inevitably the most vulnerable became victims. On 12 February, in an attack around the Beacon, five elderly women were killed, three houses were demolished and some seventy houses had to be evacuated.

Although nearby Exeter was devastated on 4 May by a 'Baedeker Blitz', Exmouth appeared to have weathered the worst of the air raids and plans were already drawn up to reconstruct the bomb damaged areas of Chapel Street and The Cross.

However, in France, the German airforce had replaced the Messerschmitt with a new strike weapon, the Focke Wulf 190 A, that could carry a 550lb bomb in addition to its armament of machine guns and cannon. On 26 February 1943 eight FW 190s flew in over the sea towards the town. Splitting into two groups of four they cut their engines and glided at tree-top height, guns blazing and dropping bombs.

In the Strand, a crowded bus waited to depart on time from a bus stop. On hearing the siren, passengers crossed the road and rushed into the shops on the other side. A bomb struck one of the shops and the row of buildings collapsed, killing eighteen people. Two more died crossing the road.

In Raddenstile Lane, near Cranford Avenue, a house received a direct hit, killing the wife of the president of the local branch of the British Legion together with her two maids. At a guesthouse on the Beacon there was another fatality and on Albion Hill a man died as cannon fire struck the hut where he sheltered from the raid on an allotment.

In Exmouth's worst raid of the war in terms of casualties, twenty five men and women died, and another forty were taken to hospital. Because of the relatively large loss of life, extra grave-diggers were recruited from Sidmouth together with assistance from the Royal Marines.

There was at least some consolation for the devastated inhabitants of Exmouth – this proved to be the last air raid of the war and two of the FW 190s were brought down over the sea by the RAF's latest aircraft – the Hawker Typhoon the successor to the Battle of Britain fighter the Hurricane. The Typhoon quickly proved itself superior to the FW 190 both in speed and weaponry and greatly eased the threat from German aircraft on French airfields.

But the air raid of 26 February 1943 stalled Exmouth's struggling recovery and its drive towards the reconstruction of damaged properties

On 2 March an engineer and surveyor's report revealed the scale of the problem when he stated that he had ordered 200 crates of glass, twelve and a half tons of slates, 10,000 square yards of plaster board, one ton of putty and 6,000 asbestos tiles.

On 24 March it was reported that there were 794 evacuees billeted in the district, 600 of whom were children.

Esther Mary Rowley was born on 9 April 1909 in Spelsbury, Oxfordshire, the second daughter of James Farmer Rowley and Edith Augusta (neé Finch), who married in early 1897 in the Registration District of St Albans. She died in May 2003 aged ninety-four.

Esther's older sister Margaret (Meg) was born in 1901 also at Spelsbury. In the last quarter of 1939 she married Rawdon Frederic R. ('Tim') Reilly in the Devon Central Registration District (which includes Topsham). By 1941 she is living with him at Dundonald, Belfast. Meg died in 1982 aged eighty-one and 'Tim' in 1980 aged eighty. Tim's brother Reginald Oliver Stewart ('Reggie') married Alexa Mary ('Lexy') Fraser Tytler in the second quarter of 1931 in the Tiverton Registration District and in 1939 and throughout the diaries, they are living in Topsham. They both died in 1980. Esther also had a brother Roger, but he died in 1932.

James Farmer Rowley was born at Willey in Shropshire in 1865 and was for many years the rector of Sydenham Damerel, near Tavistock. He died in 1937 aged seventy-three in the Registration District of Launceston.

Esther's mother, Edith Augusta (known as 'Maimie' throughout the diaries) was born in Pangbourne, in Berkshire, on 16 August 1867 and died in 1952 aged eighty-five.

Both Esther's parents came from very large families – her father was one of fourteen children and her mother one of twelve. Almost all of them had died by the start of the diaries in 1940. However, two of her mother's sisters, her aunts, known as 'Amamy' and 'Beeloo' appear fairly frequently in the diaries. These are possibly Ada Florence (born 1866) and Alice Marion (born 1864). Esther's favourite uncle, known as 'Snuffy', was Arthur Thomas Finch (born in 1860), who died in 1954 aged ninety-four in the District of Chichester. He married Fanny ('Fancy') Mary Stuart Dunlop in 1906 in the District of Newbury, when he was the vicar of Kingsclere. She died in 1956 aged eighty-four in the District of Chichester.

The first diary is the largest and contains the most detail of Esther's day-to-day life. Beginning with Christmas 1940, the first entry reveals that the elite lifestyle of those lucky enough to live in the large detached houses in Cranford Avenue had hardly altered from the 1930s.

The first quarter of 1941 marked an iconic period in Esther's life when she was in the ATS during the day at the Record Office in Exeter, and at night, and at the weekends, at her home in Exmouth.

At a time when only one family in ten owned a car, Esther owned two, although in May 1941, she sold her sports car 'Bertie' to the Polish RAF and it was eventually owned by a pilot who was a count. When most car-owning families were unable to use their cars because of petrol rationing, Esther was able to use her fawn-coloured Standard, 'Clara' to commute from Exmouth to Exeter, because of her work in the ATS.

Army life on the whole is recorded with humour – attempting to run in threes on an icy surface without falling over and, finding that she and a friend had failed to hear the command to halt, and were out of sight of the rest of the platoon! Canteen lunches in Exeter were at times interspersed with visits to hotels, serving the un-rationed jugged hare with 'delicious soup'. She was however, irritated by the petty bureaucracy of the army and the attitude of those ranked above her.

At home in Exmouth, life was more serious as German air attacks increased and the passage of bombers flying overhead at night disturbed many nights sleep and progressively traumatised her elderly mother. Her other main concern at home was the illness and ultimate death of her puppy Julie which is sympathetically recorded.

At this stage she demonstrates her considerable observational and writing skills to describe natural events, such as snowfall in fluent prose which is at times poetic in its expression: 'snow always seems so hushed and almost deadly in its quietude.' This skill enriches the diaries in other years as she ably captures the subtle seasonal changes, and describes the wildlife she encounters in the countryside and in her garden.

At night, like many other people in the 1940s life in the winter evenings centred on the home, listening to the radio, reading or playing card games such as rummy, which Esther particularly enjoyed. She was also an enthusiastic philatelist.

In daylight at the weekend, her attention centred on her half acre of garden, aided by her elderly, but very hard-working part-time gardener, William Madge, recorded only by his surname, in the middle-class manner of the time. The cash accounts at the end of the diary show that he received 8s a week for his labour – only 6d more than her expenditure on a book!

After leaving the ATS in May, to care for her mother who was becoming increasingly frail, her social life rapidly expanded as she played tennis at the nearby Tennis and Croquet Club, whose members included a number of high-ranking army officers, and enjoyed time at parties and pubs. Increasingly now she takes on new projects enthusiastically embracing the challenges of cooking – after she dismissed her live-in cook/housekeeper for incompetence – then beekeeping and especially gardening.

After the death of her puppy, she acquired the black spaniel retriever who became her constant companion throughout the war years, and beyond, who she named Domino after the monks of the Dominican order.

In June, in a vividly described diary entry Esther shows how war came dramatically close to 3 Cranford Avenue at about seven o'clock in the evening when a stricken British Lysander returning from patrol, was shot down in a one-sided fight with a Messerschmitt. The plane crashed into 'Deveron' a house just up the road, built by a former Mayor of London, which caught fire. Both the air crew died, but the occupants of the house, including the maids, survived.

Esther's neighbours waited anxiously for news of sons in the forces overseas and on one particularly sad day in September, Esther learned that Rupert Marshall, the nineteen-year-old son of her next door neighbours, a pilot in the RAFVR, who earlier in the year had been one of her rummy playing companions, had died of injuries received in battle.

In November a female spy – the German wife of an English soldier who had been living in one of the hotels in the Beacon – was shot without trial. However, the following year, Esther felt that German bombers were still finding targets too easily in Exmouth and was convinced that there was yet another spy at work.

In 1942, as Exmouth air raids continued, overseas the Japanese captured Singapore, a key base in the Far East for British and Imperial forces. David Leach, the twenty-two-year-old son of friends who she had known since he was five, was reported missing. Esther was convinced he would never return, and sadly she was proved right as he died on 5 April. 'All the nice ones are killed always,' she wrote in her despair as yet another of her friends was lost in the war which was then at a critical stage before the turning-point battles of El Alamein and Stalingrad, later in the year.

In May, in a particularly poignant passage, Esther describes the onset of the severe illness of her mother, which culminated in a stroke. Esther prays for her recovery and holds her hand as German bombers fly over the house on their way to bomb Exeter. Towards the end of the month, as her mother begins to recover and is left in the care of a nurse, Esther visits Exeter to see the devastation of the 'Baedeker Blitz' for herself. Her description of the damage evocatively portrays, in great detail, the violent transition to rubble of so many familiar shops and buildings, in a once peaceful and beautiful city.

At home, Esther discovers that beekeeping is harder than she thought, and when things go wrong it could prove to be very expensive. Breeding chickens also proved difficult as one of her hens killed all her chicks. Esther blamed this domestic disaster on 'the wartime meal with no nourishment'.

In July she received an airgraph from her friend Henry, a captain in the Royal Signals based in New Dehli in India. This airgraph helped to identify Esther Rowley as the diarist.

After a very stressful year, in November Esther very briefly left Exmouth for a visit to London. Her diary reveals just how luxurious and sophisticated a life-style could be still be enjoyed in wartime, in spite of the Blitz London had endured. Staying at a Service Women's Club in Sloane Street, she met up with friends from Devon for a whirlwind few days of entertainment and sightseeing. She took in three theatre visits, a ballet with top star Robert Helpmann and a night at the cinema to see the iconic wartime film *In Which We Serve*. She enjoyed tea at Harrods, lunches at the Savoy and at Gunters, an exclusive restaurant in the West End, owned by the father of her close friend Frances (Frankie) Putnam. She saw the Lord Mayor's Show, St Paul's Cathedral, the cells at the Old Bailey and then some of London's extensive bomb damage.

Early in January 1943, Frankie tells Esther that she had a narrow escape from death when her office was destroyed in an air raid in Exeter, but she had been in hospital with dysentery. The ATS huts in the Belmont Pleasure Ground where Esther had worked in 1941 were machine gunned in this raid and about thirty of the ATS personnel sustained injuries.

On 26 February the devastating effect of war returned to Cranford Avenue. In a dramatic incident, graphically described in detail, the house swayed, and the windows shook as four German fighter bombers raced across her lawn at tree-top height, machine-gunning and dropping bombs. Esther watched in horror as her dog Domino, raced out of the house into the garden, barking at the planes in terror as she held one of her cats in her arms. She called indoors a group of frightened children, gathered nearby, who were excitedly saying that they had seen a bomb falling. Domino survived, but twenty-five people died in Exmouth's worst air raid of the war in terms of casualties. A number of these were known to Esther personally.

By April her life had returned to near normality and her spirit was uplifted by the visit of the Archbishop of Canterbury to Exmouth's principal church – Holy Trinity. Interestingly Esther recalled a visit to St Peter's in Rome to see the Pope in 1939 and compares the two church leaders.

In May, seeking a new challenge, she embarks on a new enterprise, although already busy with beekeeping, her chickens and her garden. With her usual enthusiasm she describes her learning process as she tackles the tasks of rearing and milking goats, in pens in her garden at night, and tethered at her local tennis club during the day.

At the beginning of October, Esther and her mother reach a momentous decision and decide to sell 3 Cranford Avenue as they feel it is becoming too expensive and difficult to run, and that they now needed a paddock for their increasing herd of goats. They put the five-bedroom house, with its half-acre of garden on the market for its estimated price, a then substantial £3,250.

By Christmas, still at Cranford Avenue, Esther demonstrates her acquired skills as she cooks her best cockerel, and her guests enjoyed her homemade cake and mince pies served with cream from one of her goats.

At a time when many believe that Global temperatures have greatly increased over the past two decades it is interesting to learn that in February 1943 Esther was picking daffodils, and on March 11 a large wood was carpeted with bluebells. By April 14 the garden was getting very dry as, on a really warm day of sunshine and blue sky, it had not rained since the first week in February.

Esther's descriptions of the Devon countryside are both fluent and closely observed, as are her descriptions of her garden in Spring and her walks with her dogs across the fields encountering streams along the way, as they 'barked, begged, fought, paddled and swam'. They provide a suitably calming contrast to the ongoing stress of war which she increasingly experienced.

By 1944 and 1945, as a result of the shortened space for comment, diary entries are much more brief and concise. While the immediate threat of war has faded, after air attacks on Exmouth have ceased, the conflict is still very much in Esther's mind as she walks with her friend to see thirteen invasion barges in Exmouth docks in January 1944. In May, with another friend, she saw the estuary full of craft 'wonderfully hidden away on the far side of the river under the woods of Powderham'. It is interesting to learn that the invasion of France seems to have been such an open secret, and that the barges were not closely guarded. Even shopkeepers advised her 'to buy extra things as when the invasion starts transport will be very limited'. In August, two months after D Day, she, in great distress, learns that one of her close friends has been killed in Normandy.

Although still at 3 Cranford Avenue, she and her mother decide to buy Silkhouse in Drewsteignton and by October, she and her sister move fruit trees and shrubs into the garden. In Exmouth throughout the war she is still excited by goat keeping and, in spite of her new hectic lifestyle, she still finds time for partying.

In January 1945 both goats and dogs enjoy the snow and one goat even travels by train to Sidmouth, where the snow is six inches deep, to be mated. The cold is intense in January as Exeter had its coldest night since 1813 with 24 degrees of frost, bottles of milk freeze on the Exmouth doorsteps, and in Topsham the mail is delivered by sledge.

In February, Esther decided to ride, and vowed to give up smoking. Later she encountered her sister's godson and his family on holiday in Budleigh Salterton from their home in London, while their windows are being repaired after an attack by V1s (doodlebugs).

As the war in Europe nears its end Esther finally left Cranford Avenue, in April, packing up her menagerie of fowls, chicks, ducks, bees, cats and goats, and travelling with her favourite dog Domino, in another van. Further vans followed with indoor and outdoor stuff, and soon Esther is introducing herself to the local tradesmen in Drewsteignton and Chagford.

Esther Rowley's character, as revealed by the diaries, is complex and changeable. On first analysis she appears to be an obvious extrovert with strongly held, and forcefully expressed, views on a variety of issues, from the influx of evacuees, non-British people especially, naturally at a time of war, those who were then enemies of Britain, and those who were to the left of her politically. She was a keen tennis player and a partygoer with a wide circle of both male and female friends, a driver, initially of a sports car, a regular drinker and a confirmed smoker – sixty a week in 1943. She frequently sought new challenges and embraced each with great enthusiasm.

And yet it becomes clear that she has not had, or was at that time, involved in a serious or deep relationship and she tends to appear to be ingenuous in male company.

Although attracted by men, and seemingly attractive to them, she probably found it difficult to adjust to a time when, due to the ephemerality of a wartime existence and sudden death on the battlefield or in an air raid, there was an erosion of previously accepted morals and mores. As a vicar's daughter, marriage was for her the only relationship which was acceptable and any other type of liaison was therefore seen as regrettable and one to be condemned or pitied. In addition she was at the time in her thirties, when most of the men she encountered were in the services, a decade younger than her, and very likely to die in action overseas, while those who remained at home were a decade or more older than her, and already married.

Throughout the diaries she writes movingly on the loss of young friends and the devastating effect on their parents. Each one greatly missed, especially Jasper (Jappy) Rowland, a captain in the Devonshire Regiment, killed in Normandy in July 1944. But at least one good friend survived the war as Henry, the airgraph and letter correspondent in India, returned from his duties at the Royal Signals headquarters in Dehli, fit and well to stay for a short time with Esther after the war.

Esther appears to be more relaxed when she is in the company of a group of people rather than with one person, and certainly more with animals, where she can freely express her emotions and speak in terms of endearment. All her animals from cats and dogs to goats, chickens and ducks are named, and their lives and deaths are described in a manner that is sometimes over anthropomorphic.

Additionally, she exhibits many instances of ambivalent behaviour especially towards men, finding them difficult to work with, but useful if they carry out physical building or maintenance tasks on her behalf. She is even ambivalent towards her favourite dog when he understandingly resists her attempts to acquire another dog as well as him. And also in clothes: in 1941 she buys a number of expensive coats, skirts and sandals, but then spends a morning mending four pairs of knickers!

Although amused by the humour of others, from the friendly joviality of her ATS friends to the colourful stories of her friend Rawdon – which in contrast offend her mother – and the farcical attempts at tree felling she witnesses in her garden, she admits she finds it easier to get amusement from the remarks and actions of others than to generate humour herself.

Her beautifully written and closely observed descriptions of the local countryside, its flora and fauna and its changing seasonal weather patterns, contrast with her equal ability to describe the dramatic events of war, she witnessed close at hand.

Personal recollections may be flawed, as can any form of historical evidence, so they must be analysed, compared and verified by the use of other contemporary primary sources in order to provide an accurate and authentic view of past events.

Esther Rowley's diaries generally successfully withstand this detailed scrutiny and even when they differ from some other sources, the strong corroborative evidence she provides, suggests that her entries can sometimes provide a powerful new insight into the history of the period.

I did, however, discover some major errors to her entry for 22 August 1941. Describing a visit to a cinema in Exeter, which did not include the name of the film, she stated that it starred Diana Churchill, daughter of the Prime Minister, and that she saw it at the Plaza Cinema. However, Winston Churchill's daughter Diana was not a film star – the film star of that name was no relation. The film Esther saw was called *Spring Meeting* and starred the other Churchill daughter, Sarah. In addition, it was not shown at the Plaza, which was destroyed the following year in Exeter's Baedeker Blitz, but at the Savoy, on the opposite side of the road, which although damaged in 1942, survived the war.

Esther expresses herself in a style that is at times forceful, sometimes over enthusiastic, but always interesting. Her use of English is excellent and at times lyrical and poetic, but her spelling is eclectic and phonetic. Most of the errors have been corrected but it has not been possible to check the name of every one of the many people she mentions, especially as a number of them are only referred to by nickname. In a few instances I have deliberately included an incorrectly spelt word of an object or a place if this indicates her pronunciation, and therefore almost provides the authentic sound of her voice.

The diaries are rich with detailed minutiae of the period, from the unavailability of seed to feed garden birds, the shortage of dog biscuits, the best food for cats before specially prepared cat food existed, to the use of dusty crumbs of Ryvita blown up in air raids, as ideal food for young chickens.

For a socialising wartime woman there were shortages of powder and lipstick and a great increase in the price of stockings. Clothes were rationed from June 1941 but after this were recycled among friends and relatives. Esther greatly added to her collection by a shopping spree in the early part of that year.

In an age before the credit card, credit was obtained by opening a 'book' – a credit account, with local shops and suppliers.

New books were expensive, but there were many good new and second-hand bookshops and an increased interest in reading and literature as people's lives centred on the home.

A car licence cost £15 a year and a hand car wash 2s 6d, while five gallons of petrol sold at 10s 2½d.

Churches were packed with people but had little artificial heating because of a shortage of coal, while beaches were empty and often covered with barbed-wire.

Esther Rowley's diaries resonate with the party-going polyphony of the many bright and diverting people who helped her to ameliorate the tension of war and to soften the pain of the grief she felt for the loss of well-loved friends.

In November 1945, reflecting on the last word of the radio commentator at the Cenotaph, she wrote 'Victory seems a fearful conclusion when one thinks of the cost of all the boys and men one has known, as well as the countless thousands of others, who were killed for what purpose? Will we ever understand the bitterness of life?'

The diaries also reveal that while most people had aspirations for a better future at the end of the war there was some anxiety felt by many of middle class, with the emergence of rapid social and political change. Domestic service virtually disappeared, and the government of the country veered from the certainty of the pre-war Right to the unknown government of a post-war Left.

The diaries are a unique record of the day-to-day life of a remarkable Exmouth woman of intelligence and strong character, with many influential friends, who survived the challenges and uncertainty of an unforgettable period in the history of Britain. She outlived her family and contemporaries, to see not only a new century but a new millennium, but arguably her diaries mark the apogee of her long life.

John Folkes
September 2010

one

1940

Christmas at Cranford Avenue

Christmas Day

I am fortunate enough to be able to spend it at home having been given one day's leave, apart from the fact that my puppy, Julie, has had one fit and made a convenience of my bedroom, the drawing room and the dining room, the day has been a very pleasant one. So far we have had no air-raid sirens and the thoughts of war have been far away. Our noble King spoke to us on the wireless; he was fine and told us we must be less selfish in the future. He is indeed a great man. They broadcast greetings to all our allies after the King's speech. The fighting in Libya is going well; the Italians are being beaten to hell by the British Armies out there. The Greeks are winning on all sides, so the rotten Italians will soon wish they had never come in against the British Lion.

Maimie and I had tea with Mrs Everett and Mrs Dalrymple, the home-made cake was delicious. We are having pheasant for dinner as we thought turkey a waste of money in war time, it smells good while I write this by the glorious fire. We certainly have nothing to complain about, I must say; the room is full of bowls of Christmas Roses and pink and yellow roses and a huge one of my lovely violets: like late Spring.

two
❦

JANUARY TO MAY 1941
Army Days and Siren Nights

Wednesday 1 January

I opened the front door expecting to find a wet dark morning and to my horror I saw before me a white drive, the trees like ghosts before me and tumbling down the steps I found myself ploughing my way noiselessly through snow to the garage. Clara, the car, and I reached Exeter safely, picking up two boys who were on the way to Bedford to see their mother (they were 'hitch-hiking' all the way, so I put them on their way by dropping them near the Bath Road).

Had a busy day at the office but we caught up with the work a bit and was able to see to several old queries which one has to put by when one is too busy. Had lunch in the canteen and ate until I nearly burst: they do give us huge helpings to get through. It is very wonderful considering the rations. Everyone's in good spirits having been out at parties all last night.

When I returned to Exmouth the Avenue I live in was like a Christmas card glistening in the snow.

Thursday 2 January

… more snow in the night. Clara got me safely to the office, we took an hour getting there instead of our usual twenty-five minutes but it was better than walking or sliding a mile and a half in the pitch dark to catch a train. Most of the girls had fallen down at least once on their way this morning.

German planes over here tonight again but the siren did not go off. They did fearful harm in Manchester on Saturday night – they say there were 3,000 casualties – but they will never break the spirit of the English people!

Friday 3 January

The road's as hard as nails and so not slippery if you drive with care. The road's lined with snow frozen hard along the hedges. My bath water froze in the pipe instead of running away so I shall have to get a bucket and bail it out tomorrow. Margaret and I had lunch in the town and I bought a lovely Batsford book with some money Maimie gave me for the new year.

Patience (our Company Commander) gave us a shock at pay by suddenly informing us of a drill she has arranged for 12.30 tomorrow, so instead of going home to lunch we have all got to drill on the ice; I shall laugh if anyone falls down.

The news this morning was that Dublin has had an air raid and some people been killed there. I am surprised after the bloody way the Irish are behaving, only a day or two ago de Valera said he was joining the Axis against England so now I wonder how he will enjoy Germany's treatment.

We had a siren last night on account of a bad raid at Cardiff.

We are waiting for a German Invasion. When will they try again? Soon people seem to think.

Saturday 4 January

The drill this morning was really rather fun, we ran in threes 'at the double' Davidson and I leading failed to hear the command 'Halt' so ran on for miles until one of us suddenly looked round to see the platoon miles behind us! Marching was difficult owing to snow and icy surface, I nearly skidded several times, no one did fall down luckily, if they had I should have disgraced myself laughing!

The German planes were over us again last night, they were raiding Bristol again. Tonight, while I write, they are over with our planes. The siren went some time ago. What their objective is I do not know of course. Last night was a bad one for Bristol, they smashed seven churches there. Poor Southampton is mere ruins now. The High Street is gone except for The Bar, which is so ancient and magnificently built that it has withstood the bombs.

Sunday 5 January

Our RAF raided Brest yesterday, it seems so funny to think of Brest fighting against us; I remember talking to a French naval officer there some years ago when I happened to be in the docks watching the *Dunkerke* lying in dry dock. It has a magnificent harbour and breakwater.

Monday 6 January

The Tate Gallery was hit again last night in an Air Raid. They have smashed up the beautiful Guildhall completely of course – fortunately they have not yet touched St Paul's Cathedral.

Tuesday 7 January

The roads very bad, it has frozen again on the thaw of yesterday. The snow is still lying everywhere and it is fearfully cold but I am keeping warm. Thanks to my neuritis in my left shoulder I have arranged a screen round the back of my chair and rolled up in my rug with fur boots on. I am still alive in spite of all conditions. Last Saturday we had our waterworks raided at Newton Poppleford with incendiary bombs, the flare was so great that anyone could see to read a book on the Budleigh-Exmouth road.

London has had its longest alert today for some weeks, I hope nothing very awful is happening there. Broadcasting House has been badly hit and several of the BBC staff killed in the recent raids.

Wednesday 8 January

A bit of a thaw set in, some snow going in places, the road bad this morning but Clara managed it in spite of the surface being like glass. News not too bad, but the Germans are only lying low for the moment, in all probability when the weather conditions improve we shall be in for something. The raids on Manchester were awful – thousands of people blown to pieces. It will be a mess soon here in England. The air-raid sirens in Exeter were blown today as a trial in case they were frozen up; they were muffled but half the office heard it and donned tin hats and gas masks before they were told it was only a trial. I had lunch again in the canteen and ate a big one too; they give us a very good feed for one shilling, I must say. It is remarkable when food is so difficult to buy: Miss Rue who runs it is an exceedingly capable woman as well as delightful in herself. I posted a letter to Henry, it will be interesting to know when it reaches its destination, about six weeks or two months.

Thursday 9 January

Influenza has begun in the office; several of the ATS are already down with it, including three of our officers. A strong and bitterly cold wind is blowing strongly, it is freezing hard again but the wind has dried the roads completely so driving is easy in spite of the frozen conditions.

Poor little Julie is ill, Mr Blackwell says she has had suppressed distemper and now it is causing St Vita's Dance and was the cause of her fits. I hope she will be alright; it is a horrid thing, poor darling little dog. She is having medicine in the mornings and cod liver oil in her food at night.

We were woken up in the night by a terrific explosion outside the window, I heard the crash followed by a whistling noise and a dull thud and remember saying to myself, 'The Bloody Germans!' However, the house was quite untouched and no windows were broken. I heard the plane making off at a good speed after the dull thud. Maimie and Mrs Jones came in to see if Julie and I were awake, I was just but Julie was still in a sound sleep.

Friday 10 January

Nothing would start Clara, her self-starter stuck and nothing would make her go! Woe is me! The garage does not open till nine o'clock and I am supposed to be at my work at 8.30 a.m. Anyway, just as I was mournfully wondering when I could get help the front doorbell rang and on opening the hall one I found myself facing a tall young policeman, who had come to tell us that three bombs had fallen and two of them were 'time bombs' and they were less than fifty yards from the house, in Watery Lane! The lane was to be roped off and no one was to walk in it. Another half hour went by before I could get into the garage. Another policeman came to tell us about the bombs – he said the one which had exploded had torn up a tree and the others were big ones well buried in the bank below the house. He thought they would be fairly harmless. Then the postman came. He said the two bombs which had not gone off were probably dud ones made by the Czecho-Slovakians! They are doing a lot of that now as a trick against the Germans, they fill them with salt and then they will not explode. We are waiting to see and hear!

Saturday 11 January

As the ATS officers are all in bed with influenza, the result of last week's effort, we had no drill this morning, thank goodness, so got home for lunch instead of arriving frightfully late. I am afraid the girls will all be well enough by next Saturday to put us through our paces.

I gave Clara a terrific wash down after the frost; she was amazingly dirty and took me quite a long time to do. She repays one for a wash as her fawn colour looks all smeary when in need of one. The thaw really has set in at last, no more snow anyway down here, only in the distance on Haldon Hills, there is plenty of ice still on the Clyst by Clyst St Mary's bridge – and my little fish pool is frozen but I broke the ice this afternoon for the fish to get sufficient fresh air, and it broke easily. The hens are all laying now, we got eight eggs today, the little Buff pullets are doing their stuff well as are the older hens. They all 'love, honour and obey' the beautiful Cairngorm, it is amusing to watch them all playing around, he is certainly a wonderful cock bird to look at as well as his courtly habits.

Sunday 12 January

As we had colds Maimie and I did not go to church. I hoovered the drawing room and polished the dining room tables and dish covers to keep myself occupied. I have set-tled to alter the garden in so far as to have all the privet and dull bushes, ivy etc, rooted up under the wall opposite the drawing room windows; I am going to try climbing roses all along, they will be lovely. If the big trees should shade them too much I shall cut some of the lower branches to let the sun in. It is a great thrill, I do hope Madge will be able to get on with the job; it will mean a lot of work but if he gets another man to help it would not take so very long. I so dislike the thick ivy undergrowth and long to see it gone and other flowers instead, all along the edge by the path.

ARP men came to tell us not to use the lane as the bomb may be going off soon! They have dug it up and now are trying to take it away. I am glad I am not doing the job.

Little Julie not very well, she is a depressed little dog nowadays with her affliction.

Monday 13 January

Had a remarkable night. First of all Julie was very ill and had another fit, only a small one, in my room. She cried a lot and shook all over. Maimie and I sat up with her in my room till after twelve o'clock. Then I was woken up by the most awful noise, terrific! I listened, then heard our next-door neighbour calling her brother, 'take care, there is broken glass everywhere.' I got out of bed to find that my own bedroom window was no more, it was lying in tiny pieces on the lawn below! I then took a tour of house and found two windows in the drawing room and two in the kitchen were smashed to pieces, one of the drawing room ones being the big plate-glass middle one, ¼-inch thick. The conservatory and greenhouse were both minus a good deal of roof. Maimie looked very shaken, so we all sat by my fire and drank tea, little Ming came up, I found him sitting bolt upright in his chair in the kitchen, his great green eyes starting out of his head, so terrified. Poor little Julie was too doped to notice anything; she never moved when the bomb went off. She was very restless the rest of the night and I hardly got any sleep, and Ming had to be taken down to his pot.

Tuesday 14 January

I rang up the orderly room to tell them I was still too busy looking after Maimie and getting up broken glass in the house and garden. The lawn is a mass of big stones, one a very big one, which the bomb must have thrown up. All the houses in Cypress Road and Portland Avenue lost glass and some on the Budleigh Road. Mr Hellier was awfully kind and came to us early to put felt in all the broken windows, some of them have not yet been attended to, the cold of one's windows being smashed all the night is painful.

I told Madge about my ideas for the garden, he was so interested and we did out a plan for apple and pear trees on the lawn. He is going to get a man to help him clearing the north wall for the rambler roses. He says the trees will not hurt roses at all: it will be lovely when all the privet and bramble also ivy has been grubbed up. Madge says the dahlias would do well all along the wall in front of the roses; it will be a lovely show before I have finished.

Poor little Julie had a quiet night and has slept all day. I rang up Mr Blackwell and he said it was very good news that she was quiet and her eyes being bad meant that the distemper was at last coming out, poor darling little dog.

Wednesday 15 January

Maimie not at all well, the bomb explosion was too much for her for one thing and little Julie is worrying her very much, poor tiny dog, she is bad with this beastly distemper, she can hardly walk now, can only drag one foot after the other falling down every dozen steps. She lies crying all day on the sofa. I went back to the office and was met by much encouragement from the crowd, they are all very interested in my home experiences – Mr Heard says that I have been christened now by front-line fire and am a real soldier at last! Had lunch by myself and did some shopping but, being 'early closing day', could not get much.

Cardiff had a terrible raid at the weekend and Plymouth. Olive (our char girl, a charming girl) said she watched the Plymouth raid from her house which stands behind the hospital. She could see the planes flying in the glare of fire from their bombs. Twenty people were killed, seventy-five badly injured and a lot more hurt, so poor old Port of Devon is suffering a good bit but it does not get into the papers.

Thursday 16 January

I stayed at home again today as Maimie did not seem fit to leave she is quite knocked up with Julie being so ill. I walked down the town this morning to try and get hold of Mr Pratt who I bought her from, he is a genius with animals they say so I hope he will come up sometime, of course his 'pet' shop was shut so I had to leave a message.

Madge started cutting down the rubbish along the north wall, it looks more like a garden already.

Friday 17 January

Snowing again, ice everywhere and as cold as it could be. I went off to the office with every intention of trying to get tomorrow off as Maimie is looking completely knocked up and unfit to leave but I must go back to the damned old office. At pay parade I got a raspberry from Miss Thesiger about not turning up. In spite of ringing up the Orderly Room, I should have written a letter personally to her asking permission. I thought more than ever how bored I am with the ATS! One tries to do ones bit and joins the damned company and all one gets is constant kicks for the inconvenience of oneself and never a nice word said. That is what annoys me so much. If the officers bother to speak at all it is only to say something beastly. I am beginning to hate them all!

Poor little Julie still very ill, she is just lying on the sofa all day too bad to walk or even stand, poor little dog.

In spite of my raspberry at pay I got leave for tomorrow morning and Monday to try and put Maimie in a better state. I hope my presence will have the desired effect and she will look more herself soon.

Saturday 18 January

I was woken up at about two o'clock in the morning by a very violent shaking. In the morning was told the cause of it: three bombs dropped in Rolle Street and Chapel Street, killing several soldiers and about ten civilians. It was a terrible thing, one family completely wiped out and another woman and her twins killed.

After breakfast a ring at the bell! A girl with two evacuee boys. We had got to have them; it did not matter if I <u>was</u> in the ATS they were going to be left with us. Well, here they are; a nice little pair, brothers, one thirteen and the other ten. Maimie and

I then went down the town with the boys ration books to get some food for them. I could not drive down Rolle Street at all – the REs had got a pile of ammunition in the middle – so we parked the car and walked down a side street into Rolle Street opposite the remains of Walton's shop. It was a heap of rubble and they were still getting the bodies out. Every shop window in Rolle Street was broken to pieces and every house in Market and Chapel Street ruined. You never saw such an appalling mess in your life. The roofs were honeycombed with holes and windows blown in and doors too.

Sunday 19 January

Julie very bad. I had to get one of her doctors: Mr Pratt. He did not think too badly of her, said she was keeping up her strength well, and that she might stay like this for quite a long time. She now has to have a nappy! In case of accidents, poor pet!

The little boys very good, both keen to please and not be a trouble, cleaned their shoes and made their beds and help clear the table. Bobby the little one, is a dear little boy and Dennis is full of good sense. I like them both. Their father is a pub keeper in Penge and has certainly brought them up well. Mrs Llewellyn-Jones and Maimie despairing about them, they say the extra work and money will be tremendous but I do not agree altogether. I shall have to get Olive to come in another day a week and we shall have to manage somehow or other. I feel as if I was back at Matron's work again in school, shall have to settle down at night with a needle and wool to mend their clothes. I only know I shall be tremendously busy but I would rather have too much than too little to do. Life is now one rush from week to week.

Monday 20 January

Had a busy day at home. Thank heaven that Frankie persuaded me to take today because I had to go down the town about the evacuee boys' rations and buy some extra things, arrange what we are to do about them etc and etc. Had a good clean up of the house all the morning and decide to get another char to come on Monday mornings to help Mrs Llewellyn and Olive as the boys make a great deal more work of course. I can afford to pay for one to come once a week. I took Maimie to get some fruit trees to put in the garden, unfortunately it was a very wet afternoon but we chose our trees and they are being sent at once so Madge will be busy planting them tomorrow. They will be thrilling and look so pretty in the corner on the lawn. Mr Burridge, the foreman at Veitch's, so nice and took such an interest. He is sending us some really nice trees. Little Julie still very ill but a tiny bit better I hope. The boys told me a pony was lying dead in the lane. It had evidently fallen over the bank and broken its neck. I did not go down the lane as I could not bear to see a dead pony or any kind of horse. I love them all.

Tuesday 21 January

Pouring and pouring … The floods are up everywhere: even the park at Clyst St Mary is a sheet of muddy water the spring having burst out. Clyst St Mary bridge was well up in the water. I had a busy day in the office; there was a lot of work to do, putting straight the Monday work poor Bill could not cope with when I was away. Everyone very nice and they all asked after Maimie after the bombing and were very sympathetic. Had lunch with Frankie at our funny little café. We had not been there long when Barbara joined us and came back with us. Frankie rather solemn today. I had an interview with Miss Thesiger on the evacuee subject. She thinks it is a shame to make me have them when I am already in the ATS but she does not think she can do much to help me. The army versus the civilians is a bad thing if one can think of any other way out. I collected my torch and wallet from the police station which took a good time. It rained in sheets all the lunch hour and the girls all came back from their hostels soaked through. I was lucky to have dear Clara to keep me dry instead of my own legs to take me to feed.

Wednesday 22 January

Had lunch again in the city with Frankie and Margaret. We all ate an enormous meal being thoroughly hungry. Maimie wrote to the billeting officer and told him we could not go on having the evacuee boys. Mrs Llewellyn cannot do the work and Maimie cannot have the extra worry of them. After all, they are both old ladies and the idea of them looking after two school boys is in itself fantastic. After all I am doing <u>something</u> for the country by my work in the ATS. So the house is doing its bit already. All my friends in the company agree that it is an impossible situation.

Julie still very ill and Maimie getting very weary with the constant worry over her. Poor tiny dog, she cannot lift her head from the pillow at all – only lies there quietly all day.

Thursday 23 January

A thick white fog this morning but I managed to get myself into Exeter safely complete with Clara and was up to time too. The floods had gone down a bit but the fog was a very wet one.

Little Julie still very ill. She can't move her head from the pillow – just lies sleeping all day and night.

My fruit trees arrived from Veitch's, they are lovely big five-year-old trees, very strong and much taller than I am. Madge planted them all and they look very nice: eight on the lawn and three in the kitchen garden. The lawn is very much improved by them and really looks charming, they are near the rose beds in a large clump and will be a picture when they flower. The three in the KG are planted up the path beside the asparagus bed and frames and make the garden look much more exciting and not so flat.

Mrs Llewellyn-Jones' son came here on leave, he is going to help us about the boys and if necessary will interview the billeting officer for us, which is very kind and will be a great help. I spent the whole evening talking to him instead of doing odd jobs as I had intended! But he is interesting and full of chat.

Friday 24 January

Had lunch with Miss Nichols, she chatted a lot and seems to find the ATS rather a general disappointment – of course it is a mistake trying to mix up the civilian staff with the army and ATS. That is the bottom of the trouble in my opinion. The Record Office should be run by all of one or other and not combined. The rules for one do not coincide with the other, consequently an everlasting clash. Poor Miss Nichols, she gets the brunt of all the difficulties on her head but on the other hand she, as a sergeant, is in a position to do a lot of good among the girls under her.

Poor darling tiny Julie very ill. The vet does not think there is any hope left now. She is so good poor darling little dog, I never saw a sweeter nature, so, so good and helpless. She just lies in her rugs all day and never moves or cries or anything, as good as gold.

Saturday 25 January

When I woke up there was an awful silence in the room. Darling little Julie was dead. She had died in her sleep and was lying in her rugs in the chair by my bed, had not moved or struggled at all. She looked so very peaceful and happy. Mrs Llewellyn-Jones so sweet, she is going to ring her son up to come and bury her this morning while I am at the office.

They buried her under the fir tree near Wuffy and Roy so she is not alone. It is a sweet place and so kind of Mr Jones.

The billeting officer has arranged to remove the two boys. He was very nice when Mr Jones went down to see him. He said he quite agreed that it was impossible for us to cope with them, so they are to go to someone who can take better care of them. It will take a lot of anxiety off us. Maimie is thoroughly unwell with one thing and another, I rang up Dr Murray yesterday, unfortunately I only spoke to his wife, but he is coming in to see her one day soon and I hope will give her a pick-me-up of some kind for she badly needs one.

Sunday 26 January

The house is dreadfully empty and cold without my little dog. I did housework all the morning till lunch time. It is better to keep busy and not let oneself think. It is the only thing to do. I 'spring cleaned' all the house and it does repay me, I must admit, although it was only a quick hoover, mop and dust.

Amamy wrote last week saying that Southampton was a ghastly and unbelievable sight. It does seem strange that there is no more High Street except for the Bar erected in Edward IV's reign, even more strange perhaps that this ancient gateway should have solidly withheld all the bombing. One cannot imagine how these things happen: one building falls in a heap of fragments while another remains with perhaps a few tiles loosened from the roof. Queer, but this World War is queer.

Monday 27 January

Another wet morning, a thick foggy rain but I found it quite easy to keep on the high road. Met Margaret at her house and we both arrived at the office in good time. I think it was a shade lighter this morning in spite of the weather. I was able to put out the headlight of the car before I reached the city which was nice.

Arriving home tonight, I found Mrs Hazell, complete with her car, removing our two little evacuees, Dennis and Bobby. The boys seemed quite happy to leave us. They are going to an old woman in a council house in Withycombe, where there are four other boys for them to play, so they will be much happier I feel really. I sent all their sheets to the wash and was thankful to find that they had been quite clean and the room none the worse for their fleeting visit. I cannot help feeling sorry for all these evacuees but our house is an impossible one. Mrs Llewellyn-Jones has not got the time or strength to look after them as well as Maimie, and Maimie is a wreck after even this short visitation. Anyhow we have a breathing space again while we find a second char.

Tuesday 28 January

We have a peaceful breakfast with the knowledge of having no boys to get off to school and the house to ourselves.

Mr Jones is a keen stamp collector and has thoroughly thrilled me once more by taking such an interest in my collection. I really am going to get hold of some more stamps before I am altogether too stony broke. I'm dying to finish various incomplete sets before I do anything else, so am going through my books with an eagle eye. It is nice to get ones mind off the ATS and the office and everything else sometimes.

Madge finished planting the fruit trees on the lawn and they look so nice, Maimie said he planted them extremely well.

Mr Jones spent the evening showing me his stamp collection. He has a very interesting English collection and pages of very nice red pennies – a stamp I always love, it is such a beautiful shade.

Wednesday 29 January

Olive came in and said she had not been able to come last week because her mother was very ill, poor girl she is so unlucky. Anyhow she is coming on Monday mornings as well as two afternoons a week which will be such a help and the house will not get half so out of hand. Next Monday she is going to come and scrub out the kitchen giving it a spring clean at the same time. It will be lovely to see the kitchen clean again. The boys' dirty shoes made the floor an inch deep in dirt and mud: I never saw such a horrid mess.

We have had no night raids in this country for over a week now, our system is evidently working.

Thursday 30 January

I bought some very nice stamps from Zoe Hutchings also a very nice album at the old price which was lucky. I love Miss Hutchings' queer little room up flights of stairs, it is all so unexpected. The stamps are muddled together in her tiny little room but by diligent search one finds what one wants. I am now mad on my collection!

The army really seems to be expecting an attack in the form of a German Invasion within the next two months. Bunny says they are expecting them to try and hold Devon and Cornwall, Margaret told me yesterday.

Friday 31 January

The only interesting thing in pay parade was when Patience told us to be nice to any French Free Forces we may meet at any time: apparently there are some women from France too, in the ATS … I should like to meet one and talk about France. It would be tremendously interesting to hear something of the state of affairs from a French person, especially if they were there at the time France capitulated.

We are making a lot of changes in our section and the 'Y list' is coming down to us, which means that we shall have to move up the hut as the Y list are to have our corner of the office. I am sorry our little corner is to be broken up because we all hit it off very well and the work went well, but these changes have to take place in spite of pleasant companions. Still, Bill Bailey and I get on together so we shall have to make the best of it wherever we are put in the hut. Army huts are always funny places and the red tape and nonsense very annoying at times; but we ATS are all very happy together in spite of the men being bloody at times – men are always a nuisance to work with, I hate them myself and will never work with men again!

Saturday 1 February

Got home in good time for lunch after which Maimie and I went out in the garden for a walk round. The snowdrops are out under the trees and look so lovely also the aconites are out. They also look very pretty. I always look forward to seeing the first flowers that herald spring, my winter crocus are in bud in big clumps outside the front door, they will soon be a picture. They are some of the loveliest mauve flowers I have ever seen, a clear, bright mauve in a lilac shade. Maimie and I picked a bunch of flowers to bring indoors, violets, snowdrops, pink polyanthus primrose, gentian, anemone and Christmas roses – a really beautiful bouquet. The bulbs are all up about an inch above the ground to remind me of the time when they will be in full bloom in another two months or so.

Hellier and his men came and put our new panes of glass in. We were so surprised at getting any real glass until after the war; we quite expected to have to be content with a sort of tack stuff I have seen used.

Sunday 2 February

Directly after breakfast snow began to fall. It fell in a strange assortment of funny-shaped flakes, some huge ones and others much smaller. It fell until six o'clock in the evening when there was a depth of five inches on all the paths. The garden was like fairyland; it was so lovely. The trees are white and look transparent like lace, except the firs which have a thick blanket lying on them. The lawn is dazzlingly white without one spot or speck anywhere. The trees beyond our garden all lacy and full of mystery; somehow one thinks of all the old legends and fairy stories of ones childhood days. Snow always seems so hushed and almost deadly in its quietude. I feel a sort of indescribable feeling of excitement far down in my inside – a feeling as if the thing I am waiting for may come out at any moment, it is a queer intensity in the air which seems to be hushed by an ominous silence which is only broken by that rustling of falling snow among the trees that one only hears after a heavy fall; it always awakes in me the feeling of expectant excitement of a funny danger not far off.

Monday 3 February

Had to catch a train to work in the morning; I did not risk taking Clara out in the snow. I was glad when I got outside the front gate to find the pavement and centre of the road thick sheet-ice formed by trodden down snow that had fallen in the night. With great difficulty I found my way to the railway station, the walk was more a slide than a walk but I never slipped down altogether in spite of sliding half my way down to the town. The train that was supposed to leave half an hour before mine was still in the station so my train was late and the bus in Exeter later still so I was LATE and no mistake, but Mr Champion was very nice about it, and said he would not expect me until he saw me tomorrow; so I shall not be worried all the way now he knows I have to take the train!

A siren has just gone and I am supposed to be a fire watcher but do not feel like crawling out into the garden on a night like this, so cold and horrid, in the middle of the night. I think I am going to do some of my stamp work unless bombs begin to fall!

Tuesday 4 February

The roads are even more slippery and the snow is still lying thickly over everything. It has only vanished where it has been swept away. Even the trees are still white this morning when I walked down to the station but on my return in the evening the trees were bare once more in spite of the roads being still thick with snow.

Wednesday 5 February

Still thick snow everywhere, except some of the trees, they have taken off their white mantle and look very bare and grotesque among all the lovely white billowy ones. It really is the most beautiful fall of snow that I can remember and the sun today is glistening on the ice and sparkling snow-covered houses made the city look a real picture. Even the army huts at the office where I work looked charming snuggling down in the park below the road. It reminded me of Service's poems about Canada and the log huts in the Yukon. Our garden is like fairyland at its best. I can almost see little fairies dancing up the snowy paths and singing amongst the silent trees. I shall always remember our garden, it was too wonderful to describe well but I was really struck by the poetry of the snow. Snow will never annoy me again when I remember the beauty and perfection of our garden.

Thursday 6 February

The snow suddenly began to vanish yesterday evening and now today it has gone, the wind is blowing from the west and it's warm air once more. I used the car again to go to the office with great thankfulness as my rheumatic knee is very painful for the walk down to the station. Clara started up well from her garage and, keeping well in the middle of the road, we got in safely. The snow is still piled up in dirty heaps along the sides of the roads and streets but the middle is perfectly alright. The colonel was as relieved as I was as he has a two-mile walk from Woodbury to Exmouth station and finds the hill down fearfully slippery in this weather.

Friday 7 February

Our company commander gave us one of her 'little chats' at pay parade today. She told me my hair was untidy, amongst other things. She had several of the girls up to the orderly room about their long hair!

It was much warmer and we quite enjoyed sitting in our awful cold hut working.

The colonel told us we had got to wear our gas masks occasionally for practice, because he says the Germans are sure to use gas if they eventually do try to invade England.

I am getting very interested in our new garden alteration. We are moving the ivy hedge away and going to plant four horizontal apple trees along behind the rose bed instead. It will mean that I shall have to find lots of pretty little edging plants to go up the side of the steps, and along both sides of the new path we are going to make between the roses and apples. It will make the garden really charming and a real improvement. I am continuing the path all along under the house past the greenhouse; before, the ivy hedge was trained across the path and up to the dining room window.

Saturday 8 February

Spent a thrilling afternoon in the garden. I made a path along under the house by the steps and dug the corner, getting up all the roots of the ivy. It does look nice now and when Madge gets the rest of the ivy hedge down it will be simply lovely. I am planting little rock plants, thyme and blue speedwell among the bricks of the slips and hope it will look really pretty by the spring. Also had an idea that the lawn grass growing up to the steps was very untidy so I cut it away a spade's width and planted some little plants and snowdrops, etc are up the side. It certainly is much better and will keep tidier than the grass which always straggled even with continual cutting.

In the evening after the siren had sounded the 'All Clear' I was fetched by Mr Marshall to play rummy with Rupert who is on leave before he gets his Spitfire, he has got his wings and is doing very well. We had great fun playing and I was lucky again! My luck with cards has quite changed – I never used to win any hand, but now I often hold a good hand.

Sunday 9 February

In the afternoon Mrs Tucker and Ambrose came over and took me out for a picnic on the ever beautiful Woodbury Common. Although it did rain the common was very delicious, the scents of bracken, heather and peat perfect.

Our Prime Minister, Mr Churchill spoke tonight. He made what I think is one of the finest speeches he has made. He made one proud to be English at any rate. His opinion of all our Generals at home and in the near East is very high. He says our Army of the Nile is magnificent. We may be invaded any time but we will stand the test and come out on top. He said he wanted the Americans to give us <u>all</u> the war material they can but <u>we</u> will do the fighting. He several times alluded to the King as our great Emperor indeed. Churchill was certainly at his best. It is a wonderful thing to have a man as strong at our head. He spoke very amusingly about the two dictators, especially Mussolini who he evidently has the greatest contempt for. I feel a sort of dull excitement; somehow we know something pretty big will happen soon now. I wonder when and what!

Tuesday 11 February

The ATS have now all got to be on guard all night round the hostels, fire watching. A dull business, especially in the winter, but it is quite a necessary precaution in these uncertain days.

I was asked a fortnight ago at Exmouth if I would do it so what with that and Maimie being so thoroughly seedy I do not see how I can do it in Exeter.

Wednesday 12 February

Three men have been to see Maimie already in answer to her advertisement about the greenhouse and I am hoping one of them will take it away, and we can use the conservatory for our seed boxes. The lean-to is so dilapidated and now nearly down thanks to Hitler's bomb of the other week.

Had lunch at our usual café with Frankie, Mac, Margaret, Barbara and my small self. We ate and smoked, not doing any shopping at all. A lot of funny camouflaged buses went down the High Street full of troops but otherwise everything was very dull as usual. The city is an amazingly uninteresting place as a rule, I must say!

Thursday 13 February

Barbara, Mac, Foley, Betty Supple + Hardiman + Margaret met at the Odeon at about 17.45 hrs. We decided to be comfortably extravagant for once, and went in the 2s 6d seats – so were able to be together. The film (Chaplin in *The Great Dictator*) was in my opinion extremely good – really imaginative, and a most brilliant satire on dictatorship. Bits of it were very funny, though one felt more inclined to cry than to laugh at most things. A wonderful news film showing the fighting in the desert (simply masses of Italian prisoners – only too pleased to be captured! – and thousands of vehicles and aeroplanes scattered about), also a picture of Churchill at – I think – Aldershot, reviewing mechanised troops. The audience was most enthusiastic.

We finished the evening at the Bude and Mac stood us all drinks.

Friday 14 February

Poured with rain as usual. Picked Barbara up at the traffic lights. She told me the morning's news. Japan is moving her navy and in all probability going to attack Singapore or somewhere out East. I suppose this will mean that America will come into the war without question! Perhaps Japan will not dare when the time comes!

Margaret and I went on guard tonight at the ATS Reception Station. We did not behave in quite the usual way that girls like us should. We spent an hour wandering round the garden. On arriving for our guard duty I was told I was the only guard who had walked outside during the week! So much for the guard! I also complained of the terrible blackout and one of the nurses was awfully nice about it and came out to see for herself. It seems queer that the Exeter Air Raid Wardens are not more particular. In Exmouth one would be severely fined showing even a glimmer of light on a dark night.

Maimie says she expects me to be at home to protect her at night, instead of being right away in Exeter where I am no use at home at all.

Saturday 15 February

The day of the War Weapons Week Parade. Fortunately I was not down for it! Instead I went to see Mona who is on leave for a week or two. I stopped at Buckfastleigh to ask the way of a very typical moorland countryman who happened to be walking down the road. I found that the bungalow was difficult to find. I went up about four miles at the back of Buckfastleigh. Went along through two moor gates until the road became nothing more than a cart track. I had to get out of the car to remove huge stones from the middle of the track. Eventually I stopped by a gate. There was the bungalow. I can never remember seeing a more beautiful view from any house. They look right down at Buckfast Abbey and the woods with the wild moor behind that in the distance.

Mona and the evacuee dog from Portsmouth met me at the door. The dog's a real darling. Mrs Wylie very cheerful and full of chat. I, Mona and 'the dog' went for a lovely walk up on the moor; it was simply glorious to breathe in the perfect air once more. We walked up to The Pupits and back. The view was glorious – unforgettable.

Mona gave me the beautiful black spaniel-retriever and he came home with me. He was as good as gold and well accustomed to motorcars. He cried a little when we first left Mona, he crawled over the back of the front seat and sat on the back seat with his paws on the back and his eyes glued to Mona's figure through the back window – when we had gone out of sight he came back and sat down beside me, poor pet. Arriving home, Maimie and Mrs Llewellyn-Jones admired him very much and he was quite happy. He slept in my room and was very good.

Sunday 16 February

Maimie and I have taken all day finding a name for the black beauty. I, at last, thought of Domino because on our first walk together I looked down at Buckfast Abbey and so we thought of monks of the Dominican order and from that I thought of Domino: so that is his name.

In the morning Domino and I went for a nice walk to Littleham village by the field path. He loved it and tore round the fields as happy as could be. He met some other dogs who he was quite friendly with, only smiling at them.

Monday 17 February

A dreadful day in the office, we all had that awful Monday morning feeling. It really is too awful going back to the bloody office after a lovely weekend at home in the garden in the fresh air. However, on my return home I was delighted to find that Madge had been and planted the new apple trees to make a hedge in place of the ivy one and he had cleared away the roots of the ivy, making a nice wide bed going along between the path and the apples. This year we are going to plant carrots or beetroots along there but in peace time I shall have it bedded out with wallflowers, stocks and other annuals to look lovely from the terrace also to smell nice.

Dear Domino was very pleased to see me back; he thought I had gone away and left him dumped at the house. Poor darling he is such a pet and was so good all night except to scratch, which he did often! So more flea removal!

Wednesday 19 February

A glorious early morning but by nine o'clock it was snowing hard. Great amusement in our canteen, the REs are doing an exhibition bridge-making show in Belmont Park so the men came and had lunch in our canteen, bringing huge galvanised containers of food with them. It is 'War Weapons Week' in Exeter and the services are putting up some sort of advertisement every day this week. Frankie amused me like everything by telling the RE soldiers how glad she was to see them because they are men, unlike our miserable Pay Corps men who look like a lot of dressed up ninnies. Frankie is a scream. She made them laugh like anything. The men were awfully interesting. We stood for quite a time watching them build a pontoon bridge – a wonderful exhibition of man power and strength. They all lifted this huge iron crane with one movement as one man – a really fine sight to watch.

When I got home Maimie told me that Domino, in his efforts to find me, had jumped out of her bedroom window. Fortunately he was unharmed as he must have landed on the soft lawn below.

Thursday 20 February

I sat up very late again: our second air-raid warning tonight. I was up till 11.30 last night, but tonight was much later. It was quite exciting outside in the garden; I went 'on guard' at intervals. The first time I went out, I stayed out for an hour or more as there was quite a lot of activity. The searchlights were combing the coast. The machine guns were going and bombs were dropping some way away. It appeared to be along the coast as far as I could see and hear. It is very difficult to locate the sounds of the bombs at night though I was all ears. Domino came with me and was very good, except when Mr Marshall came through the garden, then he barked furiously and growled. Mr Marshall appreciated him and said he was a splendid dog. Flares too were being dropped from the planes and their engines throbbed incessantly for quite an hour. Then all was quiet again, with only occasional planes flying over high up. I should like to hear the news and find out what was really up. I spent my time doing my stamp collection and sticking in some more I have bought until I went to sleep!

Friday 21 February

The roads are white again, but only a light sprinkling of snow so I used Clara and we arrived safely with no mishap. The morning was a particularly lovely one – to the east a brilliant sunrise and all the way round great rolling black clouds with bright pink ones glowing behind them in rose-coloured billows.

I went to buy some oatmeal at my shop in North Street, but found they had sold out. It has gone down to 3½*d* lb so the mob all eat it now. Mr Snow told me he had ordered it and it was promised on the 11th but was hung up on the line somewhere between here and Scotland.

Dear old Mr Rendle has lent me his stamp catalogue giving USA issues as mine is only colonial. He is such a nice man and so kind. I am simply longing to get back to work tonight and get deep in it.

Saturday 22 February

It rained in buckets all day and looked as if it would never stop. I took Domino down to the town to do some shopping. We went down by Madeira Walk and he thoroughly enjoyed the run all along under the Beacon by the sea, which was roaring and the waves beating up against the road. It was very stormy today. The gale the other night cut the Warren in half, so they say, so now I suppose the channel will be altered and the sea will be fiercer all along the front, because now they think the Warren will be completely washed away and so finish its work as a breakwater.

We tried to buy birdseed for our two little budgerigars but could only get 2lbs as they are running out of it. There is little hope of getting any more because canary seed comes from Italy and all seed from the Mediterranean so what are we all to do?!

Sunday 23 February

A glorious day after the rain of yesterday. I had my usual clean round the drawing room and went out to do some gardening. The ground is lovely and not too wet after so much wet. I planted out a lot of young wallflowers and then edged the new path with bricks from the greenhouse remains that were not taken away. I then got all the little bits of plants I could find from the rest of the garden to grow over the bricks. It will look nice when it is finished, but there is still a lot of work to be done.

Domino amused himself all the while by either playing on the lawn with Ming and Johnny or digging with me, usually digging up the plants as I put them in! He made me laugh like anything. I had to beat him yesterday for running after the hens but today he remembered and was very good, grinning at me and wagging his tail instead of rushing at poor Cairngorm.

Monday 24 February

Another terribly cold day. The roads very slippery as it had frozen on the top of a wet surface. Had lunch in the canteen and ate rabbit and creamy milk pudding. We all enjoyed it thoroughly and felt much refreshed. Somehow I was awfully hungry before eating.

I was told a nasty story of how Patience Thesiger was drunk last night. I could not believe it at first. If anyone had suggested such a thing to me I should have denied it indignantly. What a pity it will be if she often gets drunk. It will let us all down terribly and in my opinion be the finish of our Company, but let us hope it will not happen again – anyway in public!

What a life! It is a queer business altogether but if everyone was the same the world would be a very dull place so perhaps it is as well that some people do funny things and say extraordinary things to make some change.

I went to bed late again as there was so much air activity and I expected the siren to go, but it never did after all so I might as well have gone to my lovely comfy bed.

Tuesday 25 February

I was woken up again in the night by another big bomb falling near us. The flash nearly blinded me and the noise terrific. Poor Domino crept onto my bed, poor pet; he was a bit scared.

Two of these exploded, one on Cockle Sands and one in the docks and three delayed action, in Victoria Road, St Andrews Road and Point Terrace. I only hope they will be got rid of before they go off. The bomb I heard so distinctly must have been one of the two that exploded.

We had a game of changing all our places in the office today and a general spring clean. Bill and I moved up near the stove by a window looking out on the park, so we are quite happy and will soon settle down, but at the moment the table is a bit of a muddle having moved it all from the table we were sitting at. We now have Slee at our table too doing 'Y List'; she makes me laugh quite a lot; that is one thing about her, she is really lively and amusing.

Wednesday 26 February

A pleasant day in the office, everyone good tempered and plenty of work, but the time is flying by quickly as there is no time to think of home or anything other than work. I wish the men were always in a good humour, it makes such a difference when they are nice and the time goes twice as quickly.

Had lunch in the canteen and 'Yardy' said she would mention me in connection with guard here, as she agrees with me that my place is with Maimie when she is so old and delicate. It is kind of Miss Yarde to do this, as it will help me a lot.

The snow is still lying on the hills on Haldon Moor all around the Belvedere Tower but this evening the wind has got up to gale pitch and I smell rain in the air. I took Domino for a run on the golf links while Maimie sat and watched us in the car. The gale was glorious against my face and I felt so refreshed after the day in the smelly old office. Domino rushed about all over The Maer and nearly went mad with joy. The sea was very rough and the waves breaking right over the road which is thick in sand.

Thursday 27 February

No bombs were dropped at home yesterday although the German planes were flying over in shoals; after sitting up waiting to hear the siren sound the 'alert' I suddenly heard it wailing above the wind 'all clear', so it had gone on long before only I had not heard it through the gale and rain beating against the windows. It was a very rough night but the ice has left the wind and it is warmer, which I must admit I like.

I visited my stamp shop and found myself, to my dismay, leaving with a book of lovely Canadian issues I want badly. I had hoped that I should get away in time before I fell to the temptation, but no, so now during the week I shall have to decide on buying some of them as I know I have not got them.

Very busy in the office and found myself too damned tired to do any work after supper so I fell to sleep by mistake. But before it was dark I did manage to do some gardening. Tidied up the conservatory ready for the young tomato plants and got all the flowers and shrubs on one side. Still waiting for the new glass in the roof.

Friday 28 February

A strong warm wind blowing – a treat after all the snow and icy frosts we have had since Christmas. The sun has been out all the morning so far, I only wish I was out in it. If it is fine tomorrow afternoon I hope to garden like mad as there is a lot to be done now and I want to get it nice before the bulbs are in flower, it is such a lovely garden in the spring and I do not want to waste it by letting it be untidy. Madge is so busy with the alterations and planting and digging in the kitchen garden. He has more than he can do so I must get to work as much as I can myself.

Took Domino for a walk on the golf links, he loved it and tore round everywhere, poor little dog, he is so full of life and has such a dull day while I am away all day. I got some more stamps of Canada on Thursday so this evening I put them into my album and they are lovely, making up incomplete sets.

Saturday 1 March

Saturday in my home again at last, how I long for my Saturday afternoon all the week! It is a beautiful day for the beginning of spring. Warm and sunny but clouds are about. The gale has gone down, leaving a fresh wind.

I took Maimie shopping in the town; we got some cakes for tea tomorrow and dog biscuit for Domino. Poor little dog, he will be short, as biscuit will soon be off the market. I cannot bear to think of the dear dogs and no food for them. It is a cruel thing in my opinion. The birds are to go short as well as there is no bird seed. They will all die of hunger as far as I can see but there it is. How I hate all the rotten things about this awful war.

There were six bombs dropped this evening in the town and in Fair [sic] Park, so now we are having them every day. They fell while we were having our supper. The first one fell as I was shading the light in readiness!

Sunday 2 March

Had a busy day. I spring cleaned the drawing-room after breakfast; it was filthy as the chimney has been smoking badly. I then did my washing and hung it on the line while we went to church at twelve o'clock. Had a nice service and gave the Pattens a lift up on our way home. About five people were killed last night in the air raid and a lot of house damage was done.

I gardened all the afternoon and did quite a bit of planting, the ground being perfect for it. I got quite a few sweet peas potted but I was too busy to take poor little Domino for a walk.

Margaret and her mother and Betty Nichol-Thompson came to tea and we talked like mad things for two hours. Betty is coming for a walk with me one Sunday. She is a good walker and it will be great fun. Perhaps we might walk to Budleigh or somewhere along the cliffs.

I cannot remember if I mentioned that I had heard from Jappy the other day. He is such a pet, I really must write to him. He is pretty bored out in Gibraltar now as the 'fun' has not yet begun and they are just sitting on the Rock, very dull.

Monday 3 March

I went to one of the biggest stores in Exeter today and hopefully asked if they had any dog biscuits. The boy behind the counter raised his eyebrows in surprise and said 'no'. I then mildly suggested bird seed. He very firmly replied 'no' again. I then walked towards the door saying still hopefully, 'What about marmalade?' Two boys replied in chorus, '<u>No</u>! We have <u>none</u>!' So I went to Bobby's and got two pairs (the last two pairs in the shop, by the way) of very ordinary lisle stockings to wear in the weekends for walks and gardening. I had to pay 4s 11d each for them! Before the war they would have been no more than 2s 11d. We must go barefoot in the summer, I think, if our legs are going to cost so much to clothe.

Tuesday 4 March

On my arrival home I found Maimie had sprained her ankle, of course they had done nothing for it so I got all the bandages I could find and did it up as best as I could. It is a nuisance! Of course it is her bad ankle, the one she broke two years ago.

I went to the PT this evening and Peggy and I got a good laugh trying to do country dances. We had no idea of how to do them but got round somehow, always doing the wrong thing at the wrong moment. We must have looked awfully silly, but it was fun. Tonight we all go to drill at 5.30 so I shall have another late night home – shall be glad to get home and see how Maimie is. I think she will have to stay in bed all day, as she really cannot walk up and down stairs, especially by herself.

We had another air-raid alarm and the planes went over the house in droves. They machine gunned the Exeter people for the first time tonight but fortunately there were no casualties.

We seem to be getting into the limelight now with the Huns. I heard one burst of machine guns over our house last night, but could not gather if it was a German plane or English in pursuit.

Wednesday 5 March

Went on a shop gaze by myself and met Frankie and Barbara in Bobby's and quite made up my mind to buy in a whole lot of face powder and lipstick etc as they are not making any more after this lot is sold up. What a game it is. I also badly want a short coat to wear over odd skirts and frocks so I shall have to get busy tomorrow and get in a new supply to last for the duration.

We go drilling tonight and after I get back I really ought to take Domino for a walk on the golf links or somewhere. I hope it will not rain this evening because if it does I shall have to dry the car which will take up all my time before supper.

Maimie's ankle better and not quite so swollen. I spent the evening getting the spare room ready. I had not done anything to it since the evacuee boys were with us, so it was rather nice to get it pretty again with the bedspreads on and the lovely coverlets Maimie made. I was quite pleased with the room by the time I had finished.

Thursday 6 March

Today is a lovely one as regards the sunshine. The birds sang while I dressed and the beautiful wood pigeons cooed in the trees at the bottom of the garden. It was a bit foggy coming along but not freezing so the wind screen kept clear.

The office seems unutterably fuggy and oppressive on a day like this. I find the stoves awfully trying, I must admit, and shall be more than delighted when we give them up later on.

We had a peaceful night with no planes or sirens so feel as if the war has suddenly stopped. No doubt they got it badly somewhere else instead. By the time I had dried the car it was too late to take Domino for a walk so I finished up the spare room.

One of Olive's boy friends was killed by the machine guns the night they came for Exeter. Poor Exmouth is having bad luck.

Friday 7 March

Air raid warning! Damn! It is so boring. The noise and everything. We are to go in the cellar soon; it will be so cold and dark up there. I hate sitting in the old cellar it is an awful nuisance.

Fortunately the 'all clear' went before two o'clock, so we escaped the cellar, also we got paid which was good for me anyway as I was down to my last penny as usual. It was a pleasure being paid today by Mrs Courtney, who did not give us a raspberry and just said one or two things and smiled at us. I am absolutely fed up with the way Miss Thesiger only speaks to us if she is ticking us all off. It has become very boring and disagreeable after so long. I think it would be better to tell us off once a month good and proper and not do it <u>every</u> week. It is easy for me to talk I know, but all the same, pay day should not be dreaded and the pay parade made into a nightmare.

Terribly cold again today. When I got home it started snowing quite hard and the wind awful, blowing all the soot down the drawing room chimney. The room terribly dirty.

Saturday 8 March

The whole house is smelling terribly of soot. The drawing room's unusable, so I had to put Gwen off for her weekend with us, which is rather sickening in my opinion. On my return home Mrs Llewellyn-Jones had decided to leave us rather than keep the dust down. So there we are. Hunting for maids once more. Mrs Llewellyn has made up her mind for some extraordinary reason to leave the house day after day to get more and more filthy, so I shall be glad when we get someone cleaner. This sort of thing is rotten. I can pick the dust off the floors in handfuls in spite of having a terrific go at cleaning every Sunday morning, but once a week is not enough. I was in a terrible rage this morning. To make things worse, Mrs Llewellyn told me that Domino had 'gone for her' in the larder. I do not believe it! She does not like him so says horrid things about him, which annoys me immensely. Anyway Maimie and I spent the afternoon in Registry Offices looking for maids and also showing Maimie the last bombing on the Parade. Poor old Exmouth is looking pretty awful now, all bombed and desolate right among the shops. We saw the big crater in Fair [*sic*] Park.

Sunday 9 March

I had a clean up in my bedroom and made it so nice and all shining with cleanness. It really looks pretty when it is dusted thoroughly. I also did Maimie's room. Tomorrow we are having a new char, an evacuee from Birmingham, poor thing. She has three small boys and has lost her husband so is feeling so stranded in Exmouth. I do hope she works well. I rather like the look of her.

After lunch we fetched Mrs Everett for a drive on Woodbury Common. I took Domino for a lovely walk up there while Mrs E. stayed with Maimie in the car. The common was looking so beautiful although the distance was rather misty. The clouds were very black and lying low over the hills all round, but it was quite warm and the sun came out at intervals. We all went back to tea with Mrs Everett. Pat and Jackie were there and we all played rummy and poker so amused ourselves thoroughly all the evening.

Monday 10 March

Another week. The office was quite fun today and the day went by quite quickly. I did some digging in the garden when I got home, much to Domino's disgust; he wanted me to take him for a walk.

The sweep has been but the electric light has failed, so the men gave us a temporary cable from Isca Lodge. Hellier has given us new glass in the conservatory and the backyard, so we are very smart once more. I must get some young tomato plants now to put in the greenhouse, they will do well there, I hope. I have never grown them in pots, always against a wall in the ground at the back of the greenhouse, but other people do well with them in pots so I am going to have a try.

Had lunch today with Mac and Margaret at the Queen's Hotel, it was very nice and we are going again today (I should say tomorrow). It was not expensive and the food nice so I am looking forward to another visit; this habit of cheap lunch gets a bit boring!

Tuesday 11 March

Had another lunch party at The Queen's. Mac, Peggy, Anne, Gwen and myself. We ate sumptuously on jugged hare and delicious soup. Mac insisted on giving us all a cocktail and lager, so by the time we all went back to the office we were well away and feeling on top of the world. We have decided to it more often and blow all the expense!

Had a dull day at the office – not enough to do!

When I got home Madge and his son had been and dug up nearly all the ivy and roots under the long wall, so I started planting the cyclamen and crocus etc under the big trees. It really is very thrilling and will look grand when Madge has tidied up the wood from the lawn.

We had another air-raid siren, a long one, but I was so tired and few planes came over Exmouth so I went to bed and forgot it, which was not the right thing to do but one cannot sit up all night unless there is much local activity. I wonder where they went – up the country I imagine.

Wednesday 12 March

I really must go shopping at the lunch hour today and fetch a clock I left at Brufords about six months ago. They will soon give it to someone else. Fearfully cold this morning so I am shivering, but the sun now is heavenly.

Frankie, Margaret and I had lunch at our usual little café but they have put the price up, so Frankie has arranged for us to lunch every day at Colson's, which will be much nicer and we are wondering why on earth we did not fix it up long ago. Colson's is a really nice place, everything clean and smart people there, so we shall have some fun there instead of our dirty little Swiss Café.

I arranged to have the car thoroughly washed and the bottom oiled and all bolts tightened etc, it is to be done tomorrow. I am longing to have her done as I feel she is in need of a little help, poor Clara! She is a lovely car and I don't want anything to happen to her so I am doing her up before she refuses to go (I hope)!

In spite of the awful cold I did some more planting when I got home but was later than usual because of our weekly drill.

Thursday 13 March

Had another air raid last night, it was on until three o'clock but Maimie and I went to bed at one o'clock. Before retiring, however, we had a certain amount of excitement: a battle took place between a German bomber and one of our fighters right over the house. They were both going 'all out' with machine guns rattling like mad. Also several bombs were dropped.

Saturday 15 March

Took Maimie and Domino on to Woodbury Common for a breather and had such fun. I stopped the car by the side on the moor along the road to East Budleigh and was just starting on a walk when suddenly, the hounds! It <u>was</u> lovely. The East Devon pack came down to draw a wood, so Maimie got out of the car and we sat on the hillside overlooking the fir wood below, but they were unlucky, so came up again. All the hounds came up and smelt poor Domino, who trembled a bit; he did not quite know what was going to happen to him, so many foxhounds and only one small retriever. But they were all very friendly after their day's run and only grinned at him before throwing themselves down in the heather round the whip while he had a glass of beer.

After the hunt had disappeared, on the way home Domino and I went for a beautiful walk amongst the heather and woods. We found a nice young honeysuckle which I dug up to plant up one of our entrances in the new wild garden.

Sunday 16 March

A glorious and wonderful morning. The birds singing in the trees and the pigeons cooing, the magpies playing in the oak and the rooks cawing as they flew round overhead carrying twigs and shouting at one another over their pet trees where they thought they would build a nest. It was as warm as summer, the sun blazing and no wind to remind one of winter.

Maimie and I spent the morning in the garden and I nearly finished the new border along the wall. I do hope it will be a real success later when the flowers come out.

After lunch we rang Mrs Everett up and took her up on to Woodbury Common. We went up on to Black Hill where I left the car and took Domino for a long walk down towards the castle, leaving Maimie gossiping with Mrs Everett who we went back to tea with and had another game of poker with Pat and Jackie. Domino disgraced himself; I gave him a dose this morning so, poor pet, he lay doing the most awful smells at our feet while we played cards, until at last we had to put him in the garden where I left him till we went.

Monday 17 March

With Pat's blouse as an inspiration, I got a really pretty cherry red one at Maynes for 10s 11d, so cheap and it fits beautifully round the neck and shoulders. Frankie came with me and got one as well. We had a delicious egg for lunch at Colson's and thoroughly enjoyed our lunch.

This is really 'Hush! Hush!' but the whole of Exmouth knows: we have got a whole lot of anti-aircraft guns and searchlights arrived today, so now when the planes come over we will put up a barrage. They came over again last night on their way to Bristol, where they did a lot of damage with many casualties; perhaps we shall be able to bring some down before they get so far up the country in future. Harry Everett has been having a terrific time in Portsmouth, they bombed his barracks and one time bomb fell 6ft from his colonel and 50ft from him – a mercy it did not explode. Portsmouth is in a very poor way now, I am afraid, and there is hardly anything left of Southampton either.

Tuesday 18 March

I chose a very pretty cherry tweed coat as an odd coat and left it to be slightly altered. I hope it will be ready to wear by the weekend. I am trying to decide on a skirt to look nice in the summer. I rather want a mauve one or a light forget-me-not blue or something light. It is quite exciting trying to find some suitable coloured material. Have decided on pretty coloured tweeds to wear in the summer as I do not find cotton frocks warm enough now I am in thick uniform all the week. But one can really find such pretty woolly materials now in the shops. By next year I should think we shall be running short of variety but now there are so many to choose from. We all so long to find pretty frocks now we are all wearing khaki so interminably. When shall we be free again and the war finished!? Nobody knows!

They are conscripting all girls between the ages of nineteen and twenty-one in April, so we are just beginning to take things seriously and weed out every man in the country, even the ones in 'so called' reserved professions.

Wednesday 19 March

Had a large and fat-making lunch with Frankie and Mac. It was nice to sit down and eat. We were all very hungry. Colson's is a pleasant place and one usually sees someone who one knows, which is nice and cheering as life now is rather a grim affair!

They had an anti-aircraft gun practise at Exmouth yesterday and were busy. Domino did not like the noise very much and sat on Maimie's lap.

The battle of the Atlantic is still going on. If they are not careful the Germans will get a raspberry from America!

We seem to be losing rather a lot of ships, but the papers are not allowed to say very much.

They had a very bad air raid on Merseyside and Hull and over 1,000 people were killed not to say anything of those injured. The war is certainly a depressing concern but one day, when we get the chance, the fun will begin and then the Boche will yell I bet.

I started tidying the rock garden and weeding it out; the little plants are coming up quickly.

Thursday 20 March

A wonderful spring morning, the lawn white with frost and the sun shining and birds singing. Too good to waste in an office all day, but never mind – one must do something I suppose!

I have been asked to parade in D Company for the War Weapons Week at Exmouth; Gwen, Barbara and Betty, also Margaret are coming. It will be great fun and I am looking forward to it.

Gwen is terribly thrilled because she is coming home with me tomorrow evening for the weekend. She is supposed to be fire watching in her hostel but Mrs Courtney has excused her as she is coming to us. I do hope the weather will be lovely and we shall be able to walk and play about all Sunday and Saturday afternoon.

I washed my hair and no sooner was settled on the floor in front of the fire than the siren went and the German planes began coming over by the dozens. Of course I did not fire watch as my hair was soaking and it was a very cold night with a hard frost. Fortunately they did not drop any bombs near us as they went over so my absence was okay.

Friday 21 March

Another very white frost and a thick foggy mist over the sea and as far inland as the city of Exeter but there it cleared up quite considerably. I fetched Margaret, who had her hair permanently waved last night. I really am going to have mine done one day next month.

Rushed into the city with Betty to do some shopping, we managed to get some quite nice bits of food at the Somerset Stores, much the best grocer in Exeter. I got my cerise coat from Rowlands with much joy and am keen on trying to get a frock or skirts or something to wear with it. We then tore up to the Crescent to fetch Gwen and her case, plus three greatcoats and five tin hats.

We crowded them all in the car and raced to Margaret's house, where we left one tin hat and a shirt before continuing on our journey to drop Betty at a sherry party. At last we landed home complete with all the junk, to find an impatient little dog waiting for me with Maimie by the door.

Saturday 22 March

Gwen and I dressed with care and caution, only wearing issue uniform and our buttons shining like mad: ditto shoes. Got to the Park Hotel, the start of the parade, and 'fell in'. Eventually started on our march through the town; all Exmouth turned out to see the fun and laugh at us! Actually we got quite a few cheers from them! We were in B Company and they marched terribly badly, they never kept in step and the thing was awful. Of course, the armoured cars were difficult to keep time with as they did not go at the same speed all the time. Also we could not hear the band at all. The Marines headed the parade, then the RAs followed by the Devon Regiment and Armoured cars, motorbikes Bren guns etc. We went quite a distance all the way from the start. Fortunately the weather was fine and the roads dry, so we looked tidy and clean, which was some consolation, but the marching was very bad.

Sunday 23 March

Maimie made us wear uniform for church as it is a National Day of Prayer by order of the King. Afterwards we had sherry at Betty and Joan's. Joan was looking very smart in a grey coat and skirt. Before going into the house we all had a chat with the baby, who was smiling at the world contentedly from his pram.

Colonel Cowel came in for a drink, Joan Hazel and her husband, Pat Everett who was very nice to Maimie. It was all great fun and we both thoroughly enjoyed the chat and the sherry! Gwen was quite happy I think she too forgot the cares of being a corporal in the ATS. Poor Gwen, she does thoroughly dislike the life in her old khaki. I must say, I like the service and would be more than interested if I had no other cares in the world, like Gwen who has no home or worries of that sort, only her own life to live. I should put all I had into my work for the ATS if I was in her place. One can do a lot for it in one way and another and I wish I could do far more than I do, but never mind, I only can do my ATS during the day and the night must be devoted to my house, it is right that it should …

Monday 24 March

Gwen and I both loaded the car with luggage, tin hats and greatcoats galore; it took quite a long time to pack and even then the back was as full as it could be with golf clubs and shoes etc for our opening game tonight (however, it rained by the evening and I did not play at all).

By the time I got to Hospital Corner I saw poor Betty waiting for her lift, loaded down with coats and suitcases, plus a large picture to hang up in the NCOs sitting room at the hostel. Gwen was hugging a picture as well, a sweet coloured photograph of her baby niece. We got out of Exmouth and along the road till we came to Margaret's house where she was also waiting by the side of the road complete with a case and tin hat. Anyway, we all squeezed into the car and arrived at the office in very good time. As the car doors opened we all fell out, luggage and all. After a pleasant weekend we all felt very sad at returning but never mind, another weekend will come along soon! Gwen is so charming, we love having her in the house. I am longing for another visit.

Tuesday 25 March

Plymouth had its second very bad air raid on Thursday night when they came over us by the hundred. They have killed over 1,000 people and injured thousands. Union Street is practically wiped out by all accounts.

The Guildhall and the Theatre were both bombed to pieces, the Millbay dye works and a tremendous lot more that I do not know of yet. The Exeter bricklayers and builders have all been sent for at once to help with the awful mess and have gone down there in a mass.

When I think of the happy days I have had in Plymouth and now this brutal attack on it. It seems so dreadful and cruel.

The Exeter Hospital is full of the casualties which are much worse than the Coventry raid, so things are pretty bad. They got a Maternity Home at Plymouth and killed a lot of patients as far as I can understand.

I heard yesterday that the Plymouth streets are lined with soldiers with fixed bayonets, ready for the invasion; this I can hardly believe – they are probably preventing looting from the houses.

Wednesday 26 March

A wet day and evening drill was cancelled so I shall wash the car and dig in the garden if it clears up at all, but at the moment it looks very dark.

Mary, Frankie and I all ate Welsh rabbit today and thoroughly enjoyed it too.

I'm busy today in the office and have no time to talk to anyone or stop to think. I do like heaps to do. This place is hell with no work!

I got a little bunch of blue, violet and cerise felt flowers for Maimie, I thought them rather nice. They are made by crippled girls and Colson's has them. I want to get her some violet scent for Easter as she wears so much mauve and I think violet scent would just finish the effect. Mauve is definitely Maimie's colour; she looks so pretty in it. Her white hair and blue eyes are suited by that shade of soft parma violet.

When I got back the rain stopped and it turned into a perfectly lovely evening, the sun shining and the birds singing so I did an hour's gardening and got a quarter of the big herbaceous bed up the front drive weeded.

Thursday 27 March

The company all went to a dance at the Rougemont given by the staff; they had a grand time it seems from all accounts.

Frankie terribly thrilled by 250 marines being billeted on them at Farringdon House!

Tuesday 1 April

We had a terrifically rough night, the wind was blowing a gale from the south, but it was bitterly cold and noisy – Maimie and I went to bed late because we became interested in rearranging my bedroom pictures and books. I could do no gardening as it was so cold but on Sunday I pruned all the roses and planted up my young tomatoes from Canada, sent to Meg by Uncle Charlie. I also planted out all the old bulbs that had finished flowering in pots. I put them in clumps under the trees along the north wall.

Some children came and picked some of our daffs under the oak tree on Sunday but a nice-looking girl brought them back after tea to apologise and give me back the unfortunate little flowers, they were broken off, with tiny short stalks and crushed in the child's hot hand; but they are at this moment looking very lovely in a bowl on the dining room mantelpiece.

Wednesday 2 April

While I was dressing the siren went and by the time I was out in the garden a German plane came over with two RAF planes on its tail. They followed as far as Sandy Bay when they brought it down over the sea, I heard the muffled sort of thud as it hit the water. Good going for before breakfast. Olive told us that her father had seen the body of the German pilot brought into the docks in the afternoon. I must find out if they are able to salvage the plane or if it is too badly broken up. It was mentioned over the wireless at lunchtime which was quite a thrill for Devon.

After duty my platoon went on a route march along Barrack Road. It was rather good fun and I thoroughly enjoyed it – anything to be out of doors in the fresh air drinking in the spring. It was bitterly cold today but might have been considerably worse when one comes to think of it. Some of the girls were rather funny, I must admit, but on the whole we were much smarter than B Company on parade in Exmouth!

Thursday 3 April

I'm full of a new dream. But I'm sure it will be impossible. I was looking up some old photographs of Maimie's and came across some of 'Rowley Manor' an old timbered Elizabethan farm house in Salop. It used to belong to my family in the very old days and I am thinking how exciting it would be to buy it (probably for practically nothing) and make it beautiful once more. Of course this would be out of the question until after the war.

The snag is that the house stands in the real country miles from electric light and gas cookers so would it be perfect, or could it be put onto the main. I have quite forgotten how far it is from the main road. It is a wonderful old place with a glorious great timbered barn which stands a little way off from the house. Oh, it could be heaven! The only thing is the climate in Salop very cold and would all the flowers die in the winter time. I must have a wonderful garden full of glorious flowers wherever I live – our present home is a lovely place. The garden charming and will grow anything, so my dream would have to come up to a high standard.

Friday 4 April

I tried to get a book giving some idea of climate, geographical features of Salop but cannot find anything in Exeter. One cannot be altogether surprised I suppose by the way booksellers are only interested in the county in which they live. Anyhow I shall get Commin's to get me a really good book dealing with the county of Salop. I have ordered a guidebook by Ward Lock & Co. from Wheaton's shop in the hopes that it may give me a rough idea of the country, hills, soil etc.

Monday 7 April

Fearfully cold today, a black east wind, no sun and awful. After tea the sun came out a bit and I took Domino for a run on the golf links. He did so love it there. I don't think he stopped running round once all the time we were there. The distant hills looked beautiful and the sea cold in a green and cold way. I did not do any gardening because I have developed a cough and the wind was bitter, so I decided to give Domino a walk instead of getting frozen in the garden.

By the way, the garden is really worth a few words. The daffodils are all in full bloom so are the hyacinths and anemonies, also some of the aubretia is lovely now. My very lovely pasque anemone is in flower too by the lily pond, it looks so charming also one huge white hyacinth that stands by itself. I mowed the lawn by the pond on Saturday and clipped all the edges, it does really look pretty now. I almost finished weeding the wide bed under the hedge. The hyacinths there are beautiful also the delphiniums are nearly 2ft high along the back of the hedge.

Tuesday 8 April

I have developed a rotten cold in the head and shivered all day and feel rotten all through. I caught it from the girls, they all have got them; they catch them in the filthy picture houses in my opinion. I am completely put off going to the flicks by the fact that they are always full of evacuees from the slums so the seats must be dirty and the atmosphere soaked in unhealthy stale air. Hell. Hell.

I am in a bad mood. Having a cold for Easter is most annoying and just what one is led to expect from life's general routine. If one has got to have a cold, why must it be at Easter? Still, perhaps one may have some chance of getting better over the weekend.

I am trying to save money now too, but so far have not managed much. I think now with the bloody budget I must. 10*s* in the pound is not much fun to look forward to and I feel a little in the stocking might be useful at the end of this war. Will it end? Yes. Some day, when things are more difficult and the army slaughtered. Then, peace for a period!

Wednesday 9 April

My birthday. Meg and Tim have sent me a really beautiful cigarette case and powder compact in one. It is lovely, in brown leather and I can fit it into my tunic pocket which is so very convenient and altogether delightful. I can now powder my nose with one hand and offer my friends cigarettes with the other! Maimie gave me £3. I am going to try to save two of them.

I have just ordered a lovely book all about Salop; it is 10*s* 6*d*, but I really think it cannot be beaten. My dear Commins is getting it for me. They are such a delightful book shop, much the best in Exeter I think – a real old-fashioned shop with stacks of books and half dark, a musty smell and charming men who sell them.

My cold very bad. I feel rotten but have asked permission to get out of drill tonight. I shall go home and stagger to the fire and try to get warm. It is so cold out: a black east wind and no sun anywhere. Never mind, the world is still going round the same.

Thursday 10 April

Had to stay in bed and get Dr Grey as I have a temperature, he came along and saw me. I have mild flu and larynx swollen up so I am to stay in bed until Sunday; he thinks I shall be able to go back to the office on Tuesday. I do hope I shall, this is a rotten nuisance. I hate falling ill when I have a job of work to be done, fortunately we are still very slack in the office and so my absence will not matter very much as regards work. I hate what I call 'blotting my copybook' by being away sick. Still, I could not help catching this flu and would have done anything rather than that if possible!

Friday 11 April

Trying to keep interested although in bed! It is a difficult job to be sure. We had a pencil card from Meg saying 'they are still alright although very sleepy'; so evidently they have had an air raid in Belfast. The paper did mention one in N. Ireland, which we all knew meant Belfast.

I wrote to Meg and Tim thanking them for their lovely birthday present. I also took the bull by the horns and wrote to the rector of Worfield and Middleton Scriven asking them both various questions about one old house Rowley Manor and telling them that I definitely wanted to buy it if possible after the war. The two parsons will think me crazy but I do not care as one must have some ideas to look forward to. Heaven only knows what we shall be able to do by the time it does end. To begin with we shall be stony broke and to finish with we may get bombed before the war ends! But here is my idea for a future, whether it will come off remains to be seen. It is not in my hands.

Saturday 12 April

Woke up feeling much more myself. I started reading *With Lawrence in Arabia* by Noel Thomas — a vivid and most interesting book, giving remarkably good descriptions of Arabs and their ways, character and general habits. I must say that 'Lawrence' appears to have been amazingly clever, a very peculiar man but with wonderful foresight and understanding. He hated the Germans and was quite determined to send them out of Arabia and Damascus. He loved the British obviously like mad. He would do anything for the British cause against the German and Turk.

Dr Murray paid me a visit before lunch and told me I could go back to work on Tuesday alright. I was relieved to hear it as I hate the feeling of not doing my stuff in the evident of anything happening etc.

I had time after the doctor's visit to dress and come down to lunch which was fun, especially after two days in bed. Dear little Domino very glad to see me downstairs again; he did not like me being upstairs all the time.

Sunday 13 April

I could not go to church as my cough is still bad and the close atmosphere would start me off in all probability. It was annoying as Maimie likes to go on Easter Day but these things cannot be helped.

I went round the garden and out in the lane for a stroll to see the bomb craters at the bottom; which reminds me that five more bombs were dropped here yesterday night, they all landed on the beach fortunately doing us no harm except breaking half a dozen windows in the houses next to them. One made a big hole in the sand. I heard the shrill screaming as it came down and wondered where it was doing its damage. It was quite a relief to hear that no harm was done, last time so many houses and several people were injured or killed.

Monday 14 April

Did the family wash and some odd tidying up in the morning. After lunch we called on General and Mrs Nicholson, who were very chatty, also on the Bogles to tell Margaret that I shall be able to pick her up tomorrow morning for the office. They were delighted to see us and Margaret was busy making cakes in the mad maid's absence. Their garden was charming. The stylosa iris is well, also the new almond tree that Margaret gave her mother.

We then went up on to Woodbury Common to look at the fire caused by the incendiary bombs dropped there yesterday night. We did not notice anything to do with fire but the views were lovely and the common very beautiful. We drove along the road to Yettington and then took the East Budleigh road past the old church and along to Budleigh where we had to turn up by the railway station owing to all traffic being stopped along the Front by the sea. It is a pity. The run down on the front from the top of the town is so pretty especially at this time of year when the sea is so brilliantly blue and sparkling.

Tuesday 15 April

I went back to the office this morning to find Miss Nichols away sick and Peggy on leave so I have had the section to rule myself, it is fun and I have enjoyed it. The girls are all so nice and the men very charming too.

I was rather glad there were no air raids; they make such a fuss and commotion. All rushing to put the work straight; shutting windows and getting on eye shields before starting up to the cellar where we all sit bored stiff for the duration of the alert. It sometimes lasts such a long time but with the help of silly games we get through it smiling.

My cough better and the rest in bed has done me a lot of good. I feel much more cheerful and altogether more contented with life in general. I do think flu in the making is not a very exciting ailment and now it is over my general cheerful nature is coming out top after all!

Wednesday 16 April

We had quite an exciting night here, flares being dropped and the siren on all night until after daylight this morning. The town was entirely lit up at one time – one bomber was brought down – fifty-nine Germans have been brought down this month. Eight last night, two by anti-aircraft guns (one at Exeter). Northern Ireland was badly raided, including Belfast: where they bombed the town indiscriminately, both the shops and residential parts. Of course Belfast is one of the most important ports in the British Islands.

Food, taxes, clothes and everything going up in price like mad and nothing coming down until the end of the war as far as I can make out. So we shall have to make two bloody ends meet somehow!

Thursday 17 April

Miss Nichols wrote to me telling me that Ian Fletcher has been torpedoed on his way out to Ceylon. His boat was the SS *Britannia* and was travelling in a convoy. I suppose poor Ian is lost. He is missing.

Friday 18 April

The office news is that we are to work until 6.30 for the next three months. There go my evenings digging in the garden! I was issued with a very nice overcoat and must have it shortened next week.

I told Barbara about Ian and she was glad I told her before she rang up Maggy tonight.

Miss Thesiger told us at pay that a number of sub/leaders from the Company were being transferred in the near future. So far Gwen, Peggy, Anne and I think Barbara are all on the go. I shall be lonely without them.

I am still getting on alright in the Section, all on my own. Actually I like it. The girls have all been very nice and we have had no mishaps so far. It has been a good experience for me too to have it all in my own hands.

Next week they are starting the two-watch nights at the hostels instead of the three. I think it will be better for the girls on the whole as they will get more sleep in the long run.

Saturday 19 April

Gwen came home for the weekend. I picked her up with Betty and then we went to fetch Paul and his little dog Dusty. We all scrambled into the car and came down to Exmouth, where I dropped Paul and Gwen at her house where they remained to tidy it up before the next let. Poor Gwen, she is in a terrible state of nerves, she had an awful row with Miss Thesiger this morning and is reduced to pulp now. She cannot go on like this much longer.

Maimie and I took Domino to Cheriton Fitzpaine to see Mrs Leach. Domino was shut in the stable where he had a lovely time in the straw.

Mr Leach came back from three days in London while we were there. He got full into the Blitz and said it was awful. He went along Victoria Street, it was badly hit. Also he said St Thomas's Hospital, Vauxhall and from Clapham to Waterloo was very bad, including the railway line.

He said Westminster Hall was hit which is sickening. The paper this morning said that St Paul's Cathedral had had it again, also Chelsea Old Church. George says Admiralty Arch is down. There will be nothing left soon!

Sunday 20 April

Gwen and I went up to the house and cleaned it all the morning and afternoon. We hoovered and mopped and dusted it from top to toe. I polished all the lovely old

Sheffield Plate candlesticks. Gwen washed the crockery and tidied up in all directions. It was great work done and took the day to do. We did not finish until late in the evening and got home for supper after doing a good work. Dusty and Domino played about together all over the house.

We had General and Mrs Nicholson for tea, also Colonel Cowel and Paul. It went off quite well and everyone was happy which was one great thing. I gave Mrs Nicholson some rather lovely anemones which she was so pleased with. Paul and the General talked hunting so were as happy as sand boys. Gwen looks better today. After supper we all persuaded her to have a chat to Miss Thesiger about coming out of the ATS before Military Law comes into force at the beginning of next month. We are sure that if Gwen stays in the ATS she is heading for a breakdown.

Monday 21 April

Gwen had her interview with Miss Thesiger and Miss T. was very nice to her and told her to go and see our doctor this evening.

Mac had another interview and Miss Thesiger was pretty rude but she is going to the doctor as well; so we must wait and see.

I went in and saw Dr Murray tonight. I first saw his wife who was delightful and most helpful. The doctor himself then came in and told me that in his opinion it was time I got my discharge from the ATS and came home to keep an eye on Mother. He said he would write any medical certificate they liked to ask for and was of opinion that I could be doing just as good war work away from the ATS. Still, taking off my khaki will be irksome and upset me a bit. But on the other hand I feel I am not doing my stuff where Maimie is concerned so shall be glad to be away and be able to live at home. I shall get a job near and be able to bike to it instead of using so much petrol.

Tuesday 22 April

Dr Mabel Gates told Gwen that she was absolutely exhausted and that every nerve in her was strained to the last possible degree and that Miss Thesiger had caused her to become so nervy by shouting at her. It is a great pity our Company Commander always shrieks so loudly at us all! I must admit that it reduces me to pulp and I am a strong girl so no wonder some of the weaker ones go under.

Mrs 'Mac' also saw the doctor who told her, she was too old and her heart was bad, she had blood pressure. So Mrs 'Mac' will be discharged for her health.

Peggy is hoping to get a commission shortly, Barbara has something up her sleeve and Margaret has been offered stripes if she goes into a hostel; so there are a lot of changes coming soon. Anne has another job; she is in the recruiting office instead of our office so I never see her except on her bicycle sometimes. Betty will be all alone soon to sit in her hostel and look after the company. She will be very lonely.

Wednesday 23 April

I had my interview with Miss Thesiger this morning about getting discharged, to come home to look after Maimie. She was most awfully nice and seemed to agree. She told me she thought my place was with my Mother and I must get the doctor to write a letter to that effect. It all went well anyway and I was relieved. It has been in my mind for some time and I have expected to have to get out one day. Miss Thesiger asked me to go on the reserve for three months. My friends all say do <u>not</u> do anything so foolish. Mr Ware and Barbara agreed and he said I could find another job quite as useful without being in an ATS.

I cannot help feeling a bit funny at the idea of being out of the service altogether. It will be very queer and not very nice in my opinion, but I must only think that I have tried and done my best – and I cannot do more.

Hitler is threatening Gibraltar now. He is 'ready and the time has come'. So Heaven help Jappy and all his battalion out there.

Thursday 24 April

American newspapers are in favour of coming into the war and fighting. I wonder if they will? They must be getting stronger every day arming as they have been since the war began.

We were paid today; we have an inspection tomorrow so there will not be the time. I had lunch with Mac, and Patience was sitting at the next table, rather overpowering but fortunately she did not see either of us.

At pay she was in a nasty temper, telling us all off again! Never mind. I began to feel quite glad I was going. If she had been nice I should have felt so different. One thing is the more bad tempered she is the less I shall mind going away. So it will be much easier.

Friday 25 April

We had a frightful inspection by Mrs Knox a 'Controller'. A very smart-looking woman in herself but not too pleasant from all accounts! She gave our officers hell. Ticked them off right and left, until eventually, when it was time for inspection, Patience was so het up that she gave the wrong order – telling us to stand 'at ease' when we were already in that position!

It was a dreadful day and one I hope not to have repeated. Everything seemed to go wrong and we were caught on the run which was an awful moment but not our fault. Peggy and I felt terrible but we were only carrying out orders.

I fetched Marjorie at 6.30 at the Bus Depot and was charmed to see her. She was very smart in navy blue with an off-white overcoat on top. She looked very well and younger than ever. She does not seem to age much. Marjorie was absolutely in love with the City of Exeter, she wandered about it most of the day and had done a lot of shopping as well. She thinks a flat in the Close ideal.

Saturday 26 April

I brought Betty and Margaret back to their homes and they both felt very thrilled. I was delighted to see Marjorie and we all went out after lunch in the town where we did some shopping and showed Marjorie the bombed areas of Exmouth. It does look desolate. I had not seen it myself for a long time. Poor Plymouth is in an awful state and all the casualties are being brought to hospitals here by the bus load. A tragedy and it will be even more awful I suppose by the time it is ended. It is so lovely to see Marjorie again, it is so long since we met. She came over for the day to see Meg when she was home in December.

Today much to Frankie's delight a Polish Squadron arrived with fifteen officers billeted on her Mother. She says they are lovely. Beautiful and charming in every way. They fly in black planes so let us hope they will do their stuff good and proper. The Poles are utterly ruthless in this war we know – as they have been treated so terribly can one blame them for <u>anything</u>?

Sunday 27 April

We sat about all the morning in the sunny conservatory and read and discussed many topics before lunch. I managed to get a large wash done as well, hung it up in the garden and left it till it was dry.

After lunch we all went for a drive. We went over Aylesbeare Common past Miss Kelly's house to Ottery St Mary where we stopped to look at the very beautiful church. I and Domino strolled round the churchyard stopping to look over the wall to look into the Coleridge's garden. It struck me as one of the most peaceful places I had been in for ages. The big red-brick Manor house and large beautiful garden, clipped trees on the mown lawns and huge beeches in the distance, while the stables and roofs were covered with cooing pigeons, sunning themselves and spreading out their wings to catch the best of the sun. It is the home of the Coleridges since before Maimie was a girl, so it has that particular charm that the real old home has but now it is becoming almost unique.

Monday 28 April

Another Monday morning. I left Marjorie asleep and picked up Betty and Margaret on our way to Exeter. I am beginning to feel rather desolate at the thought of going away from the Company and feel rather silly about it. Never mind. These things must be. But somehow I have quite begun to feel a sort of second mother to the girls in my section and hate to leave them, but I feel confident that I am doing my best by leaving them.

Today I decided that I shall try and get a job in the canteen if Miss Rue can give me one; I could then see all the girls and keep in touch with them.

Had lunch with Mac, Frankie and Margaret – Mac gave me lunch and we all sat talking till it was time to make a rush for the office.

I met Mr Leach in the street and told him I was getting out of the ATS, he was horrified and did not approve of my quitting khaki. Men seldom see two sides of a question. I did not see Mr Leach long enough to explain my reason except to say that Maimie was not well.

Tuesday 29 April

I received a chit from my Company Commander telling me that I was to be discharged next Monday and everything is in order and I am to bring my uniform back on Monday or Tuesday. What a party. I do feel desolated. I found myself weeping when I read the news but after all I have been in the ATS for nineteen months and Miss Thesiger says I can keep my silver brooch, which is a great thing as the brooch was only given to volunteers who joined before war broke out. So I am very happy. It would have been horrible to give it up. Miss Thesiger has written me a splendid testimonial, I gather from the orderly room sergeant that it is the best that I could have had. I am so glad she liked me and realised that I did try to do my job; it is a comfort to know that my efforts have been appreciated as far as they went. Frankie is very sad at losing me. So is Margaret. Little Bill had tears in her eyes and could not speak when I told her that I was leaving the company. Colonel Seales told me how sorry he was to lose me too.

Wednesday 30 April

Plymouth has been raided again. Last night was a very bad raid, it shook our house and kept us sitting up till the 'all clear' went at 2.30. The people of Plymouth are sleeping by the thousands in the fields and under the hedges for miles around in the country. They are going to evacuate the city altogether. There have been thousands of casualties already; several hundred sailors were killed when a direct hit landed on their shelter. Many people were killed last night.

Thursday 1 May

Margaret Fletcher came over to tea with Maimie yesterday; she seemed so nice and chatty. They have not heard anything of Ian and old Mrs F. is ill with the worry, walks round the house looking like a ghost saying over and over again 'Has he been saved?' It seems very terrible.

Madeline is peculiarly careless about the whole affair, I cannot understand her standpoint. She will have it that Ian is safe and that his mother has a feeling that he will walk into the house one day as if nothing has happened.

Personally I feel that it is most unlikely that he is saved, especially as so few are now when the ships are torpedoed. Some months ago now a man told me that when he was coming over to England in a convoy, one of the other ships was torpedoed in front of them; and they had to pass and see the people drowning all round and were not permitted to stop on any account to pick anyone up. I suppose if they once stop the engines and really stop it runs them into far too much risk of being caught and sunk themselves.

Friday 2 May

My last Pay Parade. I nearly cried but that is silly – but somehow I have been paid by Miss Thesiger for so long and it seemed awful to be the last time to stand there till my turn, then salute and smile etc and etc.

After tea I was sitting writing at my table when suddenly Peggy put a large flat parcel down on the table in front of me and all the girls came round my table. What was my surprise to find they had given me a lovely parting present. So sweet of them all. They chose for me a beautiful Morocco writing case from Brufords in green leather with zip fastener.

Saturday 3 May

My last morning as Sub/Leader in the Casualty Section at the Record Office, Exeter. I felt so sad somehow to think I should never be able to help the girls again, but still, there are other sub/l who will be able to do all the funny little things for them instead of me.

They all came up to say goodbye before they went away at 12.30 and I promised to see them all next Friday in the canteen when I am helping Miss Rue in the mornings once a week. The girls are all delighted to think they will see me again and it is so nice to think I shall be seeing them all again.

I had lunch with Frankie and Margaret at Colsons before tearing back to get ready for the Recruiting Parade and March from Belmont Park to Exe Bridge. It went very well in spite of the music changing time at intervals which at first was difficult. Betty told me when 'at attention' that she was to report in London tomorrow afternoon! I promptly told her that I would go back and help her pack her things at the Crescent and bring them back to Exmouth.

Sunday 4 May

When I got up this morning I could not help thinking of poor Betty sitting in a cold train on her way up to Town. I wished I was her. But I wonder if I really wished it. Our little garden is so pretty and there is plenty of work for me to give myself a full time day at home. I hope Maimie will look better for having me at home, she certainly is looking very unwell in my opinion. Dr Murray seemed to think that she would perk up if I was with her, so she would not be able to worry so much about all the silly little things of life.

Miss Thomas rang me up about driving her car, so I went to see her on my way back from church. She was so sweet and fixed up with me to drive her to Exeter once a fortnight and occasionally in the evenings in the summer time. She said if I got a better job I was not to think of her, but I think I shall only try to get two days a week as chauffeur-gardener somewhere to get some pocket money and pay Madge etc. I must do some spring cleaning here first.

Monday 5 May

Maimie and I decided to do some shopping in the city of Exeter. We went to Colsons where I tried on several summer coats, eventually buying an ice blue one of beautiful cut and material. It cost me eight guineas. I then tore into the hat department where I put on lots of grotesque and very peculiar hats of all sizes and shapes. At last the charming dame who served me brought me a really pretty one, in a soft deep saxe blue with a wide fuchsia ribbon tied in a soft bow at the back, only one guinea and suited me like anything, it has a very pretty rim, dipping slightly in the front.

We then had tea at Bobby's before going to the orderly room with all my uniform. I was greeted with cries of 'oh, how nice you look in mufti' from all the girls and Frankie took down a list of all my things and I am to pay 2½d for some of the things I have 'lost' such as my titles, hat and badge, coat and one pair of stripes! The officers are quite amused at my habit of losing these items! They were all very pleasant and full of fun.

Tuesday 6 May

I turned to and started the abominable job of spring cleaning. I got the landing, stair and hall carpets up and spent the entire day washing the paint while Domino looked on very disconsolately, he does hate my being in the house and prefers me when I dig and weed out of doors when he can run round playing on the lawn. The paint work looks all the better for my day's work. It had not been done since the war began so was dirty.

Madge beat the carpets for me on the lawn and in the evening I put them down, the staircase one went down pretty well but they are always rather tiresome.

The hall paint took me about four hours to finish but worth the time.

The two recent raids over London have killed 2,500 people, and many of the beautiful buildings are now only ruins. There will be nothing left of the grand and glorious capital soon at this rate. It seems to be getting more serious now and the damage more vital every raid.

Wednesday 7 May

Spent the afternoon mowing the lawn and cutting edges. Got the lawn by the pond very nice, but the big one is in a terrible state, it really wants a scythe on it already. I wish I could get hold of a motor machine. I managed to cut round one of the rose beds but the others are awful and will have to wait till I can get some means of cutting the lawn. The daffodils and narcissus are over but the tulips are just beginning and they will be lovely everywhere. My Suttons forget-me-nots are beautiful, large clusters of rich and brilliant flowers. The polyanthus is finding the drought rather hopeless, they naturally like damp soil and now the earth is quite powdery and dry as anything.

Sergeant Jones very full of the joys of spring; he has spent the day in Exeter getting a new uniform made and all his kit together. It is all very exciting for him.

Thursday 8 May

Mr Jones very kindly helped me get Bertie ready for sale. We could not get him going but he is cleaner and tomorrow I shall have to get him taken to a garage to be put into working order!

Last night during the alert they bombed the hospital at Teignmouth. The night before they tried to get the Marine Camp here but missed it! Frankie told me that the Polish flying officer I met called Eugene ----- had to bail out last night as his plane was shot and caught on fire. So the local news is quite thrilling. One of the tiny thatched cottages at Exton is a lump of rubble but I believe none of the occupants were injured.

I had a letter from the Squire of Worfield, the vicar being on active service; he told me that Rowley Manor had recently been bought by a farmer and he did not think I should be able to buy it.

Friday 9 May

I took Clara into Exeter taking Sergeant Jones with me as he had to go in to see about his uniform. We stopped at Best's Garage on the way, and arranged with Mr Best to have Bertie fetched and taken to his garage for an overhaul next Tuesday. I hope they will be able to do something with him, especially as Frankie still wants to buy it if her father's chauffeur will pass it. I then went to Exeter and to Chandlers, the photographer, where I saw my photo. It was quite nice and I am having one of them framed for Maimie.

Then dashed to the canteen where I acquainted myself with all the other helpers and did various jobs with Miss Rue and dished out Horlicks and orange juice for the people. Everyone was very nice to me, especially all the ATS girls who came and talked to me and were very friendly. I rather longed to be in uniform, I must admit, when I saw them in theirs.

I saw Margaret, who is living with the Hardimans now and eating with them instead of with me. Saw Frankie and fixed up to go to Farringdon tomorrow.

Saturday 10 May

Started on the rose bed, getting most of it done but there is plenty still to do. The wind a wee bit warmer but still icy cold for 10 May.

I had a clean up in my bedroom but have not tidied it properly yet. Maimie had a PC from Meg saying that they are both alright and Tim saw a German bomber brought down over Belfast the other night.

After lunch I went off to tea with Frankie complete with my new ice-blue coat, it was greeted with screams of joy from Frankie and 'Baby' Davidson, who is staying the weekend with her. We strolled round the lovely grounds and basked in the sun and smelt the flowers all over the place. Mr Putnam has sold the house, which seems awful, I must say.

We listened to the Polish troops belonging to the squadron talking to one another in Polish; it reminded me of the circus. Somehow the foreign language sounded so peculiar in the heart of the country. Eugene came and chatted to us. He was charming but the squadron was away on duty so we did not see any other officers.

Sunday 11 May

Last night London was badly bombed. The Houses of Parliament and Westminster Abbey were badly hit, also the British Museum. Westminster Hall had a fire. The House of Commons was on fire. Also Westminster Abbey roof was set alight. Casualties were heavy and the fire raged for hours.

We had tea with the Nicholsons – Mrs very pretty and friendly; the General delightful and so amusing. He was thrilled to bits by having his son arriving tonight on leave and told me lots of stories about the Great War when he had a brigade in France and his own son as his ADC.

Tuesday 13 May

The news this morning simply amazing: Rudolph Hess, Hitler's right-hand man has arrived in Scotland by air, having flown his own machine. He was discovered by a Scots shepherd and taken to a Glasgow Hospital as he had broken his ankle on his descent. I feel sure that his arrival here will mean some new development in the war. I cannot imagine how it will affect the nation, but one feels that there is some very big cause for such an extraordinary thing to have happened.

Last night we had some more bombs here. This time they exploded in the Pavilion gardens, breaking a lot of windows on the Beacon and smashing up two houses down on the seafront. The Beacon was very lucky to have got off so lightly; the bomb only missed it by a few feet and fell in the gardens down below. The Misses Thomas did not feel like coming out for a drive this evening after such a shaking up – they lost quite a number of their windows – so they are going tomorrow instead, all being well.

Wednesday 14 May

Gwen rang up last night asking us if she could stay with us for tonight so she arrived last night while I was being shown how to use the auto mower. She does not seem at all well, I must say. Her nerves have apparently gone to pieces; she is not at the moment herself in the least. In fact we are quite worried about her she is so thoroughly miserable and jumpy, it seems funny, when she used to be so very lively and full of the joys of spring.

I suppose like so many girls of 'getting on' age she is sorry she has not a husband to lean on and is getting all het up on the subject.

I mowed the whole lawn with its first cut which went off quite well though I had to set the machine high as the grass was precisely the same as a meadow and rough at that, a good number of stones still lying on it from the bomb explosion also sticks, sometimes branches, which had not been removed.

Thursday 15 May

Last night I took the two younger Misses Thomas for a drive on Woodbury Common; they seemed to enjoy it and I found their little car quite easy to drive, it is a self-change gear and a BSA. I used to drive it for them years ago when it was new.

The view up on the common is so very lovely. Soldiers have built huts and put up tents all over large tracts of the open country up there: I imagine they must be manning guns or something of the sort. I washed and polished the car when I had put it away after the pleasant drive. Today I went over the entire lawn with the new machine and it really looks lovely now, it is quite short and the roller is heavy enough to flatten it down at the same time as cutting. Madge was splendid helping me all the time. He cut off the long grass along all the banks and finished up all the places the big machine could not get at, which saved me hours of tiring work. Madge also had to kill and bury one of the hens. She has been ailing for a long time and so her time came to an end today, poor little hen.

Friday 16 May

I rushed into Exeter to shop before I went to the canteen. However, the queues for food were so immense I got the things later on in some poor tiny shops in Sidwell Street. I fetched my photograph from Chandler and framed it for Maimie. She really does like it a lot; it is very good of me and nice to have showing off my uniform.

I did the canteen and poured out coffee for all the girls and thoroughly enjoyed my day. It was great fun to see them all once more and have a chat.

When I got home I helped Olive spring clean Maimie's room from 3-6, leaving only polishing to be done.

After six o'clock I decided to take Maimie for a drive in the country, we picked on Mamhead Park for our destination. It was absolutely glorious, I had quite forgotten the perfection of the vast view from the park, it was a dream of colour and heavenly beauty with the vivid blue sea in the background.

Saturday 17 May

Tore down to the town laden with boxes and tins of flags for the sailors missions and arrived outside Boots, where I remained for hours. The wind was fresh and the air crisp and frosty. The shady side of the road was icy but the sunny side simply lovely and as hot as anything, really quite amazingly hot after standing for an hour in the shade.

When I returned home I felt rotten, but was cheered by Frankie, who came in to see me for a short while, full of beans and in mufti. She is all in a thrill for our party tomorrow; we are collecting a pair of handsome Marine officers then going to see Eugene, who is in the RAF Hospital in Torquay. It will be fun.

I lay down all the afternoon and when I woke up, Gwen, complete with Paul and suitcase, was standing under my window. They came in and we all had tea and chatted. Gwen insisted on Paul and me going down to the Beacon for dinner as the food ration is so short, it was awful fun. Domino escaped from the house and came as well!

Sunday 18 May

Gwen and I had sherry with Colonel and Mrs Cowel at their hotel and we met Beryl Shrubb and her husband – I had not seen them for absolute years. After lunch, Gwen went out for a motor drive while I went over to Farringdon to pick up Frankie. We then dropped in at Winslade for the two beautiful marines Geoffrey and Johnny. I like them both at once and the run down to Torquay was great, the weather heavenly. We went straight to see Eugene, who was waiting for us in the hall. He took us all round the garden and up to the cliffs up on the Warberries where we walked along by the sea, which was dazzlingly blue and the distance wonderfully clear. A marvellous view altogether. Then on to the Imperial, where we all ate a huge tea before sitting basking in the garden looking at the brilliant Torre Bay. We played an awful prank on Johnny who took it all quite seriously for two hours, when he at last found out that <u>we</u> had written the 'billidoo' after all! Got back very late but the day was such fun.

Monday 19 May

I <u>was</u> sleepy when I was called! I had to be up early because Gwen had to catch an early train to Exeter. Poor Gwen, she looked as old as the hills and as worried as an old crow and all because she was going back to duty. I wonder if she will get her discharge after all. I am beginning to think that the trouble with her is 'LOVE'! She is terribly sloppy over Paul and I really believe he is upsetting her much more than anything else. Well, we shall see how she goes on.

I feel awfully sleepy now and must away to my comfy bed. Got a certain amount of grass cutting done and hoeing paths.

One of my hens has died – Maimie found her dead in the run after tea with all her insides out, an awful sight, I cannot think what caused it to happen.

Tuesday 20 May

At dawn this morning the Germans made an air-borne attack on the isle of Crete, the Nazi troops wearing the battledress of the New Zealanders.

I suppose there will be a tremendous fight there. Crete is very important to hold I think.

Wednesday 21 May

Maimie, Mrs Llewellyn-Jones and I went in Clara to Torquay to see our respective relatives. Mrs Llewellyn got out at Kingskerswell and went on by bus as we went to see Marjorie at her new flat at Northernhayes; she has three rooms in the Searley's house and is so much happier with them instead of being alone in her bungalow.

All her old furniture looks awfully nice in the old house. Marjorie has a green drawing room, the doors and skirting painted in a lovely soft art shade of green, very pretty, with an old fireplace which I really did love.

From there we went on to see Aunt Margaret at 'The Wrekin'. We found her looking well but much older and deafer than ever before. She has quite lost her old dash and laughter now that Uncle Richard is dead. She seems to be so subdued and placid now. I expect it is something to do with her deafness, which has certainly got much more obvious and bothers her rather a lot. She had Miss Greene staying with her as her house has been bombed out; on Sunday night at one o'clock she was on the doorstep.

Thursday 22 May

I took Miss Thomas to Exeter this morning and found the queer little car quite easy to drive. We arrived about 10.30 a.m., just as it started to rain, but it was only a shower. I had an awful job to buy any cigarettes as all the big fashionable shops were completely empty and most of the owners very curt.

Friday 23 May

I went in to help in the ATS Canteen and was bored to tears, being really very tired and sleepy. It was so heavy and thundery today.

Olive is getting on very well with the spring cleaning. She did the spare room today and Mrs Llewellyn's yesterday. The paint looks so clean after its wash, which it has not had since the war.

Four more tiny chickens hatched out today, so I have put them on the tennis lawn in the coop that Madge has made me. My three older ones are getting quite big and are covered with feathers now.

Saturday 24 May

HMS *Hood* sunk early this morning off Greenland. Her magazine was hit and she sank immediately with a vice-admiral, captain and 1,300 men. She received a direct hit from the finest battleship of the German Navy, the *Bismarck*. Our other naval ships that were with HMS *Hood* are still in pursuit, the *Bismarck* being damaged.

Sunday 25 May

Maimie and I went to church in the morning, the congregation enormous as usual.

When I arrived home I decided to move both coops of chickens into the conservatory to keep them dry for the night anyway. The grass is so very wet and the ground is becoming so soggy for their little feet.

The garden looking really rather nice, the lilies of the valley and lilac are in full bloom, so the scent is delicious of both. My pink candy-tuft perennial edging along the path by the kitchen window is lovely this year. Last spring it was too young to flower much. The roses are in big bud and looking extremely well after my hand pruning in March.

Monday 26 May

We shopped in the morning quite successfully. We were able to get some wonderful stuff for the chicks at Norrington's; it is the dusty crumbs of ryveta which has been blown up in air raids, and is absolutely perfect for feeding chicks.

During lunch Colonel Cowel rang up asking me to see *All This and Heaven Too*.

Tuesday 27 May

Only 550 miles from Land's End, after a chase of over 1,000 miles, the *Bismarck* was sunk by HMS *Dorsetshire* at eleven o'clock this morning – so the sinking of HMS *Hood* has been avenged.

Wednesday 28 May

I took Maimie down the town shopping in the morning and heard all about the bombs that fell last night, I did not wake up myself but Mrs Llewellyn and Maimie both heard two bombs fall. Altogether six fell but only one did damage, it fell on three houses, completely wrecking them, killing nine people and injuring fifteen, so our town has been unlucky again.

Olive and I spring cleaned the drawing room we got on quite well for the first day but the dirt is awful, the paint terrible and the general thing very dusty. The fire makes so much dust and soot, but the room has not been done for over two years. We washed the floor, brushed all chairs with their covers off, cobwebbed the walls and ceiling and shook the curtains out. Now for the paintwork and polishing all the furniture. It is certainly much the biggest job of the house as the room really is a big one with plenty of paint in it – two large windows and three doors!

Thursday 29 May

Maimie, Mrs Everett and I went over to Ipplepen to see the little Misses Hodge and the Langworthys. The day was wet but very beautiful, so green and summery. We arrived and found both the Hodges in and so sweet. They showed us all over the dear old house; they have done up into a really delightful one. Their beautiful old furniture looked lovely in it and everything <u>so</u> clean. They told us that Mrs Langworthy had died. Mrs Everett loved the little Hodges so we were a very lively party. She admired all their lovely things so much.

We then went to see Dorothy and Diana, who were in and charmed to see us. They are so upset by losing their mother, poor girls. Their clothes were peculiar, both filthy dirty, one in long trousers and the other in breeches and filthy mackintosh. Diana wants to keep bees for the honey. The government will give me especial sugar allowance for bees.

Friday 30 May

I sold Bertie – my own little sports car which has been waiting in his shed for six months. Two young Polish RAF sergeants came over to see it and gave me £12 for him right away. They were very amusing and told me that they did not want to be rude but, 'your English mechanisms are not good, <u>we</u> can do anything with a car ...' The two brought with them a dear, dirty little aircraftsman who told me he had left his white bulldog in Warsaw. When they had got Bertie to go alright they started off, one driving him behind their car with the other two. They all saluted and told me they would bring the little car to see me when they had finished doing him up. The two sergeants were both tall, good looking and very nice chaps, who spoke and understand English well.

Olive and I finished spring cleaning the drawing room, that's to say we got it to look alright, but still have some paint work to wash and most of the furniture to polish. We altered the room round, much to Maimie's delight – she loves rearranging the rooms at all times.

Saturday 31 May

We decided on a joy drive in Clara, using up my last bit of ration petrol given to me by the Southern Command for my ATS work. So after considering the subject for some little time, I thought of Blackborough Hill near Cullompton. We took the road over Woodbury Common and Aylesbeare Common, along the main Exeter-Honiton road until we got to Fairmile, when I took the road to the left which took us to Plymtree, there we met the rector, a cousin of Mrs Llewellyn-Jones, she was so delighted to meet him unexpectedly. He showed us his very beautiful old church with its perfect screen and complete ancient oak pews. From here we took three lanes up to our destination. How wonderful it was, I found the gateway and drove through. Leaving the car, we walked into Paradise; the path wound along the side of this vast hill, on one side a mass of rhododendrons of different colours and to our left huge forest beeches, oaks, firs, sycamores and ash – underneath, huge ferns. A hazy but magnificent view in the distance.

three

JUNE TO DECEMBER 1941
Tennis, Gardening, Bees and a Sad Loss

Sunday 1 June

'The Glorious First'! This year our first real summer day. It has been simply wonderful all day, except for an hour at tea time when a thick mist enveloped everything from the sea. This cleared again by the time we had had our tea and the sun shone out once more and the garden was heaven once again.

I did not go to church as I finished mowing the lawn, which took me all the morning and wasn't I hot! I finished up in a cool bath before lunch, which was refreshing. After lunch I slept until tea time and afterwards Maimie tidied out her bureau in its new place by the fireplace in the drawing room. By the time it was done the fowls had to have their tea before I decided to plant out all my tiny stock plants and the eight young tomato plants against the hot wall where the lean-to greenhouse had been. So now I feel the garden is coming on. The rain during the week has made the ground nice and damp for young seedlings to grow well.

Monday 2 June

We have lost Greece! Damn. Another German victory. The isle of Crete is lost and so the last of Greece. The evacuation of Crete has been described as the most terrible ordeal that any men have ever had to undertake. The Dunkirk Evacuation was nothing in comparison to the horror of the twelve days in Crete. The German parachute soldiers landing there are all doped with a drug that makes them nerveless and ready for anything, but after the effect has worn off they suffer from a terrible depression (many of the prisoners we have captured are like this). When they die they turn a green colour, so Crete is an unpleasant place for the time being, covered with unburied green corpses!

Thursday 5 June

I wrote to Mr Paine about Rowley Manor, asking him to find out if the owner would sell it to me.

In the morning I took Miss Thomas to the city where I met Mrs Bogle who was thrilled by Bunny being appointed a staff captain, and on his way to the War Office today, it is wonderfully good.

It has not only been a wet day but a real hard downfall of heavy thunder rain, the poor tiny chicks are quite miserable in their wet and miserable runs while the hens continuously cluck in a temper as they are not allowed out for a run and scratch on the lawn.

Friday 6 June

Spent some considerable time in redoing the books in the spare room bookcase and the result of my efforts is nice; also put one or two pretty bits of china on the mantelpiece, which has improved the room considerably. Olive must finish washing the paint there today and then the room will be done. The house is certainly looking very nice now and the rooms all shine and smell of polish.

After lunch Maimie's beautiful Pussian [*sic*] ginger kitten arrived. We have christened him Tommy. He is wonderfully at home already. Ming does not like him at all; Domino is too full of interest but Tommy himself only sits and purrs and eats his food. He is a particularly pretty kitten and going to be a wonderful cat I should say from his appearance now. Domino is not allowed to touch him yet as he is a little frightened by such a large black dog.

Madeline ran in with some snaps of Ian, she says that Pauline was told that some of the people off the SS *Britannia* were picked up by the Germans. I hope Ian is not a prisoner!

Saturday 7 June

I wrote to Uncle Snuffy asking for his advice about my keeping bees in our lovely flowerful garden. I am feeling that honey would be a very great assistance in these days of rationed jam and marmalade. It will be interesting to hear what my pessimistic uncle says on the subject.

After supper Madeline and her sister Betty came in to fetch me out for a walk with Domino. We went all along the cliffs to Straight Point where we were amused to find that the Holiday Camp has become a camp of our Scots soldiers, the big bungalow being the officers mess. They all came out to have a look at us! Here we saw the huge craters caused by the bombs the other day along the side of the hill in a line towards Straight Point, starting in an orchard at the top by the Farm. The war seemed so far away until we suddenly came across these huge muddy craters in the fields.

Domino so loved his walk and behaved so well. He is no trouble when on a walk; he just loves every minute and is so happy rushing everywhere – sometimes perilously near the cliffs!

Sunday 8 June

Maimie and I went to church, Mr Heal preached a magnificent sermon and the service was really splendid throughout. We gave Mrs Everett a lift.

We sat out in the garden reading all the afternoon. Domino had to be tied by a string to my deckchair and when I fed the chicks, he came too, complete with the chair and my book in the chair.

The kitten played about under our chairs all the afternoon, he is getting accustomed to Dommie, who is very excitable about him.

Monday 9 June

We went down the town to do some shopping, got a few of the things we went down for, but of course the food-stuffs are very difficult to get now and if one is not registered the grocers will not give you anything at all. They are going to ration eggs and milk soon which will be trying, I must admit, especially as there is nothing else to eat. People who have got fowls are not allowed any eggs.

I got a 'Flit' syringe to frighten away the moths that have got about the house now. I have found a lot in Maimie's cupboard also my own room. Only hope it really will do its job and all the moths will vanish away.

Am pleased with the house now, it shines and smells lovely of fresh polish and the paint is looking so nice where Olive and I have washed it. I do like a spotless house and ours is getting on towards it now, we still have all the back premises to spring-clean and must get the sweep for the kitchen chimney which must need it badly by this time; then the whole house will be spotless!

Tuesday 10 June

I finished a letter to Jappy and wrote to Esme. Still cannot believe that Jappy is a captain – to me he is still a boy. He is only twenty-one, so I am so glad he is doing well as he is keen and wants to do well in the army.

Domino and I got some meat and dog biscuits in the town, also took the bike down to have it put right as it has a perpetual puncture. Dommie very good and followed my heels all the way. We went to the club where I paid my subscription to Mr Barrow who was very chatty. He gave me a cigarette while we talked. We fixed up for Maimie to be elected to be a member. On our way home we met Dr Murray who chatted, said mowing obviously suited me and he made me laugh as he usually does.

Madge mowed the bank and planted out a lot of the young greens. I mowed the whole lawn, did it without the box, so took half the time, got a few of the edges cut before the rain came on in the evening, it is fearfully thundery today ...

Wednesday 11 June

My first air battle! About seven o'clock in the evening I was weeding in my lovely garden near the lily pond. Domino was lying near the lawn. The siren went. Almost at once I heard a definite German engine vibrating through the air, then the angry buzz of several of our fighters. Bombs were dropped, one near and three some way off, then machine-gun fire – rattle, rattle – now they are over the garden – bang, bang – a fighter plane swoops unsteadily across the Marshall's roof towards the club. I hide with Domino under the thick hedge. The plane swerves, comes back rolling from side to side, gunfire screaming from it, over our trees – going down, down – nearer and nearer the ground, then a heavy sickening thud – silence. The plane had crashed on the top of a house just up the road, blackish brown smoke was pouring up into the sky. The machine gun was still unloading itself, bullets cracking ceaselessly. Ten minutes later soldiers, children, women, old men, air wardens, dogs and ourselves are all standing in the road watching the tragedy of a house ablaze.

Thursday 12 June

It has been revealed by the government what the 'Germans' in New Zealand uniforms were in Crete. They were New Zealand wounded soldiers captured while in hospital and made to walk in front of the German parachute troops, twelve were killed for lagging on the road, some had on only their pyjamas, others uniform. Eventually the New Zealand troops retook their hospital and killed or captured all the parachutists. They found the worst of their wounded lying face downwards in an olive grove having been there for five hours.

Had Uncle Snuffy's reply about bee keeping, very encouraging. So we phoned Mrs Everett to come to tea and then we all went down to see Mr Fisher at Budleigh Salterton, he was very helpful and gave me addresses to write to, so I have written to try and find out if I can get the bees, then the hive will come later. Mr Fisher said had he known a week ago he could have given me a swarm. Perhaps I shall have some luck yet! It is quite thrilling to start them going anyway.

Friday 13 June

Spent the day in the garden cutting away all the old bulb leaves which are looking awful in most of the flower beds. The iris beds round the lily pond are lovely now, one mass of bloom, mauve, magenta, greyish white, pale yellow, violet and bronze, a really glorious display of colour. Some of the anemonies are still in blossom round them too. The delphiniums are in big bud in the herbaceous border by the evergreen hedge. My Sutton forget-me-nots have been, are still being, admired by all. They do look pretty besides the thrift edging all up the drive and along the kitchen garden hedge. Our various kinds of catmint are coming out; they are all doing well and growing bigger every year. The red rhododendron is just coming into blossom, brilliant as ever, also full of fine new shoots. The garden is quite nice all round, my roses, which I pruned so much in the spring are better shaped and healthier than ever before, Madge complimented me on them himself; they are only just beginning to flower now, owing to the cold weather.

Saturday 14 June

Took Domino into the town where we did some necessary shopping. I was fortunate enough to get twenty Players cigarettes from dear Mr Griffiths. I was just on my last legs having been to every shop in the town with no success. We walked home over the Beacon and along the golf links by the sea. Dommie loved his run on the soft turf and in the sea breeze.

Frankie rang up to offer me one of her lovely little bantam cocks. He is a beautiful creature, half a pheasant so has real game black legs. He is accustomed to running wild in the garden and is very tame, always coming when he is called …

Sunday 15 June

Just sat about in the sun all day – managed to summon up enough energy to take the hens away from the chickens, to lay in the pen with the others: and to wash my hair: while I was drying it Colonel Cowel came in for a chat and loved sitting in the sun in the garden.

Mrs Everett and a girl called Mary Bootle came in after tea. She is the rector of Coppythorne's daughter and is staying with Mrs Dalrymple. She knows all the Reynolds and Cowies well and we talked for ages about all the Coppythorne news it seemed so funny to see anyone from there. I have not been in the New Forest for three years but still love the place dearly. I am going for a walk with her on Tuesday; we are taking the path by the coast towards Straight Point.

Colonel Cowel told me that we got one of the two Messerschmitts down, fifteen miles out in the channel, after the Lysander had crashed on the house up the road on Wednesday. I am glad we got the brute down and only wish I had seen it crash.

Monday 16 June

'Cut in' day at the club so I went up for a game of tennis. It was a perfect day and the courts played very well. My new and expensive racquet is lovely and the balls I got for 10s real beauties. I did enjoy myself and played quite decently especially towards the end of the afternoon.

There were quite a lot of people up there, partly I suppose because of the wonderful sunny afternoon. Summer has come at last it seems.

It seemed queer to think that a war was raging while I played tennis. Rupert Marshall came up and told me that he was on forty-eight-hours embarkation leave and going overseas, he thought Africa but did not know. I am sorry. It is so dreadful for the old people to have <u>all</u> their sons fighting overseas: Rupert is a full-blown fighter pilot now and looks topping in his RAF officer's uniform.

Whenever a young man is home at all now it is always embarkation leave. We only have the scruffy old men left in England. Young blood is best in this war it appears but it seems so hard on the boys. I wish they could take the older men who have had their fun and are ready to die …

Tuesday 17 June

I took Mary Bootle and Domino for a walk along the cliffs towards Straight point and she told me something which interested me. She said the Invasion of England off the Isle of Wight was genuine enough. The sea was full of Nazi bodies and our hospitals were full of them: most of them terribly burnt by our wonderful secret weapon which was blown up in the middle of them, while they were still on the sea nearing our shores. She thought <u>everyone</u> knew all about it! It shows our Hush! Hush! stuff is working in this country.

Wednesday 18 June

Derby Day at Newmarket: Fred Darling trained the winner and the second, so it was a good day for him. The weather perfect and the wartime crowd terrific but somehow it could not have been much run anywhere except on Epsom Downs. I listened to the race at Mrs Everett's on my way to a cinema with her and Mary Bootle. We saw a most amusing film at the Savoy with Frederick March in it. I laughed more than I have for ages at a film; the American humour was very funny, I must say. We all thoroughly enjoyed it but, I must say, that the glorious sunshine was awfully wasted in the cinema. Afterwards we all had tea at Clapps before returning home. Mrs Everett and I caught a bus up but Mary waited in the town for one to take her to Countess Weir, where she was meeting her aunt for supper in the City of Exeter. I spent the rest of the day gardening and playing with the kitten. After supper Mr Fisher rang up to say he had a swarm of bees for me.

Thursday 19 June

Biked over to Louisa Terrace where I collected Miss Thomas and her car and we went to Exeter. I told her all about the bees so she very kindly told me to take the car to Burgess and to buy the hive straight away, so I can get it home quickly without any waste of petrol, she is a dear. So off I went to Guinea Street where I remained for one hour, in the end getting the hive; I wanted and all the extras as well. The whole thing, including smokers and veil, came to £4 6s 1d.

I dropped Miss Thomas at her house and brought the hive home in triumph, really thrilling.

After supper Maimie and I went to see Mr Fisher and took him and Mrs F. to Otterton to see the bees, found them quite good so took them away in their box, I am so very excited! Mr Fisher and I let them out of their box and dropped them onto a board from which they all swarmed into the hive. We watched them all go in until there were none left. They seemed quite happy in their new home. I hope they will settle down alright.

Friday 20 June

Another heavenly morning. The bees were quite lively and busy. The roses a lovely show full of bloom this year. After lunch we rang up the Leaches, who asked us over the tea, so off we went and told them all about our Shropshire scheme; they thought it grand and not at all silly. Mr Paine wrote this morning, by the way. He went to see our old house Rowley and says it is lovely. All the rooms are panelled with the original Elizabethan oak and the staircase is solid oak. The owner, after some hesitation, said he would sell the house if he got enough for it to build a modern house, but not until after the war of course, so there we are. It all seems too good to be true and like a dream but I do so hope this dream will eventually be reality. I wonder if the war will end before our present house is bombed or the other one for that matter. Also whenever it ends what income will we get by the time they have taxed us enough. It all hangs in the balance but perhaps something really thrilling will happen …

Saturday 21 June

The bees have gone! I was suspicious when I got home last night as I could not hear them in the hive. This morning I looked for them and not a sign to be seen or heard. They must have swarmed again yesterday evening! Tommy Thomas's wife came selling flags and told me she had seen a swarm at 6.30 a.m. in Watery Lane. They must have been mine – Damn! I tore down the lane but of course not a sign. Rang up Mr Fisher who was horrified, he is going to try and find some more for me as soon as possible. I hope I shall get some more soon as it is getting late in the season now.

Decided to mow the lawn so did the big top one in the morning – the tennis lawn after tea and the iris garden one after supper. Mr Marshall came in to get some of the grass for his fowls and told us that Rupert started today for a most romantic and daring job as a pilot overseas. He has a marvellous report and has been especially chosen for this particular job – I wish it was not such a dangerous one, somehow I don't like it!

Sunday 22 June

Russia and Germany are at war. Early this morning at four o'clock the Nazi bombers rained bombs on the towns of Russia and the Nazi Army crossed the frontiers. This was done with no word, ultimatum or any of the ordinary formalities. The day before, the German Ambassador had assured Russia of their friendly feeling towards them!

Monday 23 June

We went shopping in the morning and Maimie got a very lovely dress, sweet shades of pinks and mauves small flowers sprayed on a soft light navy ground, so dainty and pretty. I fell for a very beautiful art blue lined skirt for an odd one to wear every day in the autumn and winter, am having the seat lined with strong lining material, it took eight coupons. I also got a delightful pair of sandals in fawn, inside calf.

Went to the tennis club in the afternoon, it really was lovely and I played tennis all the time. Mrs Carroll asked me back to tea with her and Veronica and her mother. Mr C. was home for tea so we all had a good laugh, the Carrolls are an amusing couple.

When we went back to the club I played several sets with Colonel Condon and got very hot and had some very good games.

Poor Domino has been alone all day as I have been away from home. He is thoroughly despondent and resigned, poor darling.

Tuesday 24 June

A glorious day. Brilliant, sunny and hot! I hoed the flower beds in the front of the house all the morning and found it quite hot. I have twenty water lilies in flower at once and over fifty in bud so the pond is looking really pretty. I had to cut down the poppies and most of the iris, which has rather dulled the effect of the two big herbaceous borders. The vegetables are all doing well and we are hoping to eat our new potatoes soon, also peas and beans.

After tea I called for the Misses Thomas to take them to see their cousins. They brought Miss MacPherson, the ideal Punch old maid – stiff, hard and frightfully prim and proper. We drove along over Countess Weir Bridge to Peamore Cottage, such a darling old place with the sweetest garden, I loved it all. Miss MacPherson and I walked down to the beautiful lake and sat among the pink rhododendrons for ages before returning to base after dropping the little Misses Thomas back. We all loved our evening very much in the peaceful Devon country far away.

Wednesday 25 June

Mr Fisher rang up to tell me that he had a swarm of bees for me – a big swarm this time belonging to Major Farley. So at eight o'clock, after a quick supper, Maimie and I went along to Budleigh to fetch Mr Fisher and he directed me to Major Farley's little bungalow. The major was very charming and good looking. He remembered Meg well at the Archery Club and insisted on giving me this wonderful swarm. He has six hives arranged among his potato patch among the apple trees: there are fields all round with plenty of pasture for bees to feed on. The swarm was in a skep, so we picked it all up and put it in the car with a counterpane thrown over it. Brought it home and, after putting in the syrup, we shook it into the hive, Mr Fisher said it was a lovely big swarm and weighed 5½ to 6lbs, so I can consider myself very lucky. It is a pity I did not find the other swarm but there it is and now I have a huge one and next week am to put on the super. How exciting life is getting once more. Uncle Snuffy wrote today.

Friday 27 June

Sitting painting in the drawing room when the Hodgson's gardener suddenly appeared to tell me that a swarm of bees had collected on a gooseberry tree in the Hodgson's garden, would I come down to take it away as it might be my lost swarm.

So I rushed round finding out boxes, veils, macks, boots and smoker and we started off down the lane – got to the house and the chauffeur told us it had gone! So we went to the next house and the people took us all round their garden but they were not to be found. By this time Maimie was getting very tired, so we sat ourselves down on the box in the lane on our dismal way home, when out of her garden door popped Miss Wrightson with her little West Highland Terrier. So she asked us to walk all round their large garden, which we did, but still with no success. But all the gardens we thus wandered in were simply lovely - all big and a blaze of colour, the roses exquisite.

I felt tired and Maimie worn out on our return but some days are down days, one must not expect too much thrill and another swarm would have meant buying another hive!

Saturday 28 June

We went shopping in the morning. I got some weekend cigarettes which are a comfort. I am only smoking five a day now but I find it an awful job having always smoked many more – never mind, it saves money anyhow!

After tea Maimie and I went to a small sherry party at Mrs Dalrymple's: it was quite fun. The garden was quite pleasant and, being a very hot day, it was nice sitting outside instead of being shut up in the house. Our hostess had done well for war time. She had good sherry, chocolates, masses of sandwiches and dainty little almond and nut things – very nice. It remains a mystery how she provided chocolates, I suppose by paying by the nose. But they were worth it! The Pattens were there with Pat, Mrs Shrubb and Beryl and General and Mrs Nicholson. She looked charming all in mauve.

Sunday 29 June

Maimie too tired to go to church so I mapped out an appalling day for myself – mending undies. So I sat down and mended four pairs of knickers and altered a cotton frock which has shrunk in the wash. A really awful day in my opinion.

Mrs Llewellyn's little grandson and his mother came up. The little boy is amusing and full of life. He kept me in fits. He seemed quite fearless and played with Domino without stopping. Once, Domino licked his face so he promptly knelt down in front of the dog and licked his nose in return. I wished I had a camera; it would have made a very funny picture. Keith also took great interest in all the chickens, the young ones on the lawn and the grown ups in the run. He called the bees 'The Stingers', which I think a good name especially as one has just stung Maimie and another rushed at me when I was walking on the upper path by the tomatoes, it is terribly thundery today so I think they are very fierce tonight.

I'm doing continual watering after supper now: all the seedling asters, stocks, echium, tomatoes and I root watered all the sweet peas coming into flower.

Monday 30 June

Put the super and queen excluder on the hive tonight. The swarm seem very flourishing and settled in well, they are very friendly and only very few were at all annoyed by my being near their hive.

Arranged to buy a new battery for Clara; £6 worth!

The Russian war still going on like mad. The German thrust is formidable but the Russian Army is so far withstanding it. The Germans are putting in their usual wedge and are trying to do a big thing in Poland.

Did not play tennis today. It was so thundery I felt thoroughly lazy and could not be bothered.

Tuesday 1 July

We had our first dish of new potatoes, they were delicious. Madge dug a whole basket of them and I was glad to see how big they all are.

After an inspiration on Maimie's part, I decided to ring up Marjorie and ask if she could come and take care of Maimie while I go up to Salop to see Rowley. So I duly rang up and Marjorie very sweet, we fixed up for her to come on the 15th of this month. I wrote to tell Mr Paine that I was coming. He has been so awfully kind writing and telling me his opinion of the house. He wrote lately saying he would like me to stay with him but for evacuees who occupy all his spare rooms. So nice of him. Now I am beginning to feel quite thrilled by everything. I hope everything will go off satisfactorily and the owner of Rowley will hold out some hope of our buying it after the war (unless we are bombed during it). I have a feeling that I am going to fall completely for the place; it is so old and full of ancient tradition.

Am going to write out a list of all the questions I shall have to ask regarding the house itself, the soil and aspect plus countless other things which are all so important when living anywhere.

Thursday 3 July

Madge did quite a bit of tidying up in the garden; he tied up all sorts of Michaelmas daisies and campanulas in the flower beds. He top dressed the artichokes and spread lawn mowings over the piece of ground that is to take the young broccoli when they are big enough.

The bees started buzzing so he again had to abandon the lily of the valley bed after putting in only half an hour. It is very cloudy tonight so I have not watered expecting rain. Got all the asters planted along the curved herbaceous bed …

Saturday 5 July

Another glorious day after a rather noisy night when I was woken up twice, once by hearing four loud bombs being dropped and once by a dog-fight going on overhead.

The bombs were on Budleigh Salterton and demolished four houses, killing two women and a child, injuring several other people.

I sat in the garden with Maimie, Domino and Rusty while I embroidered a wool cushion-cover with pink and red poppies. I took the opportunity of polishing up Clara and found that one of her front wheels is badly out of true so arranged for Mr Best to have her on Monday. Now I must mow the tennis court before bed time, it is deliciously cool now.

Sunday 6 July

Went to church in the morning, the congregation enormous as usual. Mr Heal preached a very fine sermon again. The new deacon was taking part.

Went to sleep all the afternoon in the garden. It was another perfect summer day. I also made notes about the Shropshire visit, re the old house and etc: I hope I shall remember to ask all the questions successfully.

After supper Colonel Cowel came in for a chat, he was very delightful and good looking as usual; sunburn suits him well I think. We gave him a bunch of roses for Mrs Cowel but unfortunately they were not our best as Maimie had picked them all yesterday evening.

Dear little Rusty very sweet all day, playing, eating or sleeping. He now triumphantly runs into the dining room with us when the gong rings. He is getting so grown up!

Monday 7 July

Played tennis all the afternoon and evening. The weather was absolutely perfect, really hot and the sun blazing, the courts as hard as nails and going quite brown and burnt up now. I played with Mr Marshall against Colonel Condon, a terrible game. Mr Marshall lost his temper and got het up because the colonel won! Pat up there, very pleasant. She had a lovely day with Mrs Everett and Jackie at Budleigh yesterday, where they bathed and boated.

Had a letter from Mr Paine, he has found a room for me which I must write to without fail today. It is getting very thrilling. Mr Paine is so very kind. He says he will come over to Worfield with me if he can get some petrol (which he is going to scrounge). I shall take a coupon with me.

For an hour at lunch time I heard heavy guns firing over the channel and a considerable number of our bombers went over to France at the same time; in the evening it was stated on the news that the RAF made there biggest bombing attack over France in daylight today.

Finished mowing the lawn after supper and hope the old neighbours got to sleep in time. I was busy till 10.30.

Tuesday 8 July

The roses flowering very well now also the sweet peas are in bloom. The brilliance of the big herbaceous beds over but they are still quite pretty. We ate our first dish of beans for supper, they were delicious too. Madge told me to put the cock by himself until he has finished his moult as it is better for him to be away from the hens, so I caught him and put him in the dog kennel. I also got the sick chicken some pigeon medicine at Norrington's, and hope it will improve the little bird's condition.

Wrote four letters, to Mr Paine, Mr Chester, the rooms and Marjorie, so let us hope the writing part of the Salop expedition is now over; writing is not my line of action.

Did the weekly washing and ironing today as I kept Monday for tennis since it is the day at the club – a foolish one in my opinion. Saturday would be much better for people doing war work etc: they simply cannot play on Mondays.

Rusty growing very fast, he is quite a big kitten now and rushes all over the house and garden by himself. Had his first game with Ming this afternoon.

Wednesday 9 July

Played tennis all the afternoon until tea time when we stopped. It was very hot but glorious of course. I find I feel the heat of the sun playing more than I ever have before. I suppose it is because I have not played at all for two years. After tea we let all the chicks out for two hours to run round the lawn as they liked. They loved it and scratched for grubs without stopping, tearing after each other madly and flying across the lawn to exercise their wings: the two broods are splendid birds, the one that is unwell is all the better for its pill and ate with the rest while they were loose.

Am cutting the grass under the fir tree this evening; it has grown tremendously in the last few weeks.

Last night there was some excitement (which I slept through as usual). The siren went and a German bomber flew over Exmouth and suddenly exploded into hundreds of fragments over Starcross, the people watching said that the explosion seemed to go on for some little time as the bombs on board caught alight. Maimie said she heard a remarkable noise like hailstones; these no doubt were the bullets and ammunition going off.

Thursday 10 July

I drove Miss Thomas, a friend and Dr Thomas into the city. We started quite early to get some shopping done before Miss Thomas's meeting at eleven o'clock. Exeter was very full and busy as usual. Quite a lot of food going. Got 7lbs of the finest oatmeal at Snow's much to my joy as the oatmeal here is horrid, not fresh and beautifully flavoured like his.

In the afternoon Domino and I set off for a bathe, our first: we got into the three o'clock bus at the club and joined Marjorie and Dolly with their little spaniel bitch, Shandy. The dogs were very good in the bus. Domino found himself rather big and had to make himself very small when other passengers tried to get out or into the bus. He was very amiable over it, although he must have been fed up some times I think. We all bathed at once and dear Domino was very nervous of the shingle and noise of the waves. Budleigh is always noisy owing to the pebbly beach. Next time we are going to Sandy Bay where he will not be so upset. Dear Domino, I think he had never really swum before; he did not seem to be at all at home in the water but he will soon get his confidence as he practises.

Friday 11 July

A very thundery day, we had a few claps after lunch but it only lasted a few moments. The weather so fearfully close that I fell asleep and slept the whole afternoon. After this lapse I did some hoeing and general tidying up all round the hen run.

Mona rang me after tea, she wanted to bathe tomorrow but as I am already bathing we had to postpone it this weekend. She is going on a week's leave from Sunday evening and wants me to go to a party in Torquay but I do not think it possible because of my visit to Salop and Marjorie coming, besides which I have no petrol to spare this month as I am trying to save it for Meg and Tim's visit when I shall need it all I expect.

I'm letting the chicks out to run in the garden every so often, that's to say every day. It does do them so much good. They all rush out when they are first let out stretching their wings and flying after one another like a lot of little crazy birds.

Rusty is growing and getting prettier every day; he is just reaching the stage when he is all over the place, you never quite know where to expect him next. He is starting to play with Ming now quite a lot.

Saturday 12 July

Went down the town to buy some cake for tomorrow when Frankie is coming over escorted by a marine officer (Geoffrey) and a Polish RAF officer (the one who bought my car Bertie) but I arrived in the town too late: all the cakes had been sold, so I had to be content with home-made scones and little rock buns. Shopping is certainly becoming a problem!

Have arranged to go to Bridgnorth next Wednesday, as I cannot get a room until then, otherwise I was hoping to travel up on Tuesday. I do hope the journey will be a successful one and not simply a waste of money and energy to say nothing of time. Anyhow, it will be very interesting to see Shropshire again, it is many years since I was there and then only a run through on my way to Westmorland, so there will be lots to see and remember of every small detail. I only hope I shall take it all in properly because as a rule I daydream too much to see everything.

Domino and I met Marjorie, Dolly and Shandy for a bathe, this time we walked to Sandy Bay along the lanes through Littleham and home over the cliffs. In spite of a thickish mist it was very hot and we had a lovely bathe and climb over the rocks under the Point.

Monday 14 July

Marjorie came by ferry and I fetched her in Clara, she arrived very punctually looking very charming in green, I never saw her look better and so happy. She loved
Rusty when he was introduced.

Wednesday 16 July

Marjorie walked with me down to the station when I started on the journey to Salop.
At the station we met Betty Nichol-Thompson on her way to South Wales where she
is staying with her sister. It made the journey so much pleasanter having Betty with
me. On my arrival at Shrewsbury I found that I had an hour to waste there before
catching the Bridgnorth train. It was a sunny and lovely evening so I walked up the
High Street and went into one or two bookshops before returning to the station.
The Shrewsbury-Bridgnorth railway line is a really charming one. It runs along the
valley of the Severn with the river along the side of the line with a steep woody bank
on one side and the other splendid views of the Wrekin and distant mountains. I felt
thrilled by the scenery; it is a remarkably lovely country and no mistake. Reached
Bridgnorth station in good time and met Mr Paine without any difficulty finding
him very nice and easy to get on with. He gave me a wire from Rowley to tell me
they were busy tomorrow (Thursday)! What am I to do! Let us sleep over it and think
again! We went up to Mrs Breakwell's farm and she showed me my room before we
went on up to the rectory.

Thursday 17 July

Mr Paine and his housekeeper met me at 11.30 for a trip to Bridgnorth, she had to
do some shopping and while she was doing this we looked round. Afterwards we got
in touch with the Chesters' daughter at Bridgnorth grammar school she rang her
mother up and we fixed up to run over tonight after supper. Then we picnicked in
the car before going for a beautiful drive up the Clee Hills going through Knighton.
The views magnificent up there, looking into the heart of Hereford and Worcester,
beyond Coventry and Birmingham and, to the west, the Welsh mountains. It was the
most extensive views I have seen. Had tea at the rectory and supper at Mrs Breakwell
before starting out once more for Rowley, Worfield.

Arrived at the house, walking up the lane and leaving the car at the bottom, we
found Mrs Chester very pleasant. She took us all over the house, indeed, I think I
have never been inside a house so old or genuinely lovely, there was nothing but the
original oak. The rooms are panelled and the floors polished oak with the original
pegs instead of nails. The staircase polished oak. The drawing room and bedroom
above had a patch and powder closet, the attics marvellous. The coat of arms above
the fireplace not ours. The staircase unique, it was superb.

Friday 18 July

Mrs Chester spent her time telling me of the improvements she is going to do after the war and she told me she was sorry I had wasted my time! Not at all hopeful. The trouble is that she apparently loves the old place herself, they have only been there fifteen months, Mr Chester's father farmed the place 1914-22. So Mr C. knows it very well. Mr Chester in conversation told Mr Paine that he would sell the house in a moment. It was so cold and draughty in the winter. So there I stand. Nowhere! Anyhow everything will have to wait until after the war. There was an oast house a little further up the lane on the opposite side and the remains of a huge tithe barn. The only thing against the place was that the drawing room and dining room windows have no view; they look up a sloping garden. At the back of the house there was a pretty view of the undulating hills and fields near by, while the church spire of Worfield looked a really romantic picture standing out against the woods. I must admit, I would give a lot to have this old relic of the Rowley family, it could be made perfect if the garden was reorganised and the vegetables could be moved away to the back of the garden to be replaced by flowers.

Saturday 19 July

I returned home yesterday. Mr Paine very kindly picked me up in his car to catch the 8.25 at Bridgnorth. The train was crowded with RAF men and girls. I had two hours in Shrewsbury so went along to see Rowley House, the home of my ancestors. It stands in what is now the municipal car park. This ancient house was built in 1590 and is now the museum for all the Roman remains from Wroxeter and the cases of these relics fill the oak-timbered rooms of Rowley House. I was glad to see what a good state of repair the house is in.

I reached home at seven o'clock, very glad to find myself back in my rose garden, the roses seemed to be so pink and like a perfect summer day in England. Marjorie went back yesterday evening before I arrived.

Today (Saturday) Maimie and I spent the day discussing our prospects. Will Mrs Chester ever sell the house? I cannot help feeling that it is possible that she is trying to raise my price by saying that she is not selling – I only wish I knew; I would be much happier in a way. I must admit, I shall be desperately disappointed if they do not sell to me at the end of the war.

Sunday 20 July

We did not go to church as I had a certain amount to do after being away a few days in the week. Mrs Everett came in for a chat yesterday evening she really wanted to know all about Rowley but also had a lot to tell us as Mrs Dalrymple's eldest step-son suddenly died in the week and she and Mrs Everett had to go to the funeral in Hampshire. It is a shock for Mrs Dalrymple as he was only ill for two days.

I did a lot in the garden today. I hoed up the two big herbaceous borders along each side of the drive, the astilbe bed, the rockery and the delphinium border: they are all fearfully dry so were quite easy to hoe. The drought is getting rather serious now, the soil is very, very dry right through and even my watering does not seem to do the good it ought to somehow.

I hope the farmers will have a good harvest we need it this year particularly as the Nazi are sinking so many of our ships but the Battle of the Atlantic is progressing in our favour according to the newspapers, so by next year perhaps our shipping will get a better time.

Monday 21 July

Went up to play tennis at the club and had a good afternoon and evening, it was great fun and I had a lot of games and sets. I find I like playing with Colonel Condon now, he is getting old and is charming to play with. In old days he was so frightfully critical and terrified me!

I was asked to tea with an awfully nice girl, Barbara – an evacuee from Jersey. She lives with her mother and father, the former I thought a particularly attractive woman. Barbara is going up to Oxford in October, how I envy her. How wonderful to be going to the heavenly atmosphere and get away from the war for a bit. She had a nice Oxford boy with her. He is going into the Irish Guards next year. It seemed sad to think that he was only having eighteen months at the university, but the good old army must go first in these days. After a delightful raspberry tea we returned to the club where we all played like mad again. It was a glorious evening and the tennis went on for quite a long time. Most of the people came up after tea.

Wednesday 23 July

The motor mower went wrong, the first offence. To begin with I ran over a stone hidden in some loose grass and broke the plate, then the motor refused to go on running for more than a few seconds so I had to drag the thing back to its shed and get out the hand mower, which was not set properly but after some difficulty I cut a piece but decided to leave the rest until tomorrow when Madge is here to help cut. He is going to mow the banks tomorrow and can show me how to set it.

The chicks out in the garden all day and thoroughly enjoyed themselves as usual. They are living on the lawn loose now; the running about is making them grow well.

Miss Price came in to ask us to tea and to see the kitten which she rather loved but said his ears were big and his tail was long. Poor little Rusty. During tea today Rusty was very sick, he ate his first mouse yesterday and brought some up with his dinner – he was very surprised at the job of being sick, he had never been before!

Thursday 24 July

Today the Bomber Command raided France, the biggest offensive since war began. We brought down thirty enemy aircraft and lost eleven bombers ourselves. The raid concentrated on Brest where we bombed shipping and the harbour, we scored hits on several German warships sheltering there.

I watched three squadrons go over our house on their way to France. They took ages going over and the air vibrated. It is wonderful to see them go out to their prey looking so lovely, shining in the sunshine like huge silver birds flying happily out towards the sea. The sound of many engines in the sky somehow always sends a thrill up my spine: the power and might of England and the Empire seem to sing in every turn of the engine.

Friday 25 July

Spent a busy morning doing varied jobs in the house as I do not want to have a lot to do when Meg is here. Finished my washing and ironing in the afternoon and now I am off for a walk with dear Domino after supper, he has not been for a walk for a long time now, he feels the heat very much and this week has been hot, glorious summer we are having now anyhow in spite of poor Dommie hating it so; spaniels seem to feel the sun very badly they have such heavy coats.

Received a wire from Tim to say they left Liverpool at three o'clock today and hope to get into Exeter at 11.15. Lexy is meeting them. So I rang up Lexy and she had also a wire and fixed it all up to fetch them in Tim's car, hoping he will drop her and drive on here himself but he is not at all accustomed to driving in the blackout so Lexy and I both quite expect them to prefer her to drive them down herself.

Saturday 26 July

Had a long letter from Henry which he wrote the day after getting mine, they both took over three months getting over. I was beginning to wonder if he had ever got mine as I had received no answer for so long.

Lexy brought Meg and Tim back. She caught the train from Exeter and did the drive down here in twenty minutes in the blackout. They arrived here at 12.30 after a very good journey yesterday night. Lexy and I giggled a bit.

Today we met Lexy after lunch and all went down to Sandy Bay for a bathe. The sea was cold when we first went in, but after a bit it felt warmer. The sun, however, was lovely and quickly warmed us through. We all enjoyed it tremendously. Lexy had to go early as she was going to a party but we stayed on later to bask in the sun on the beach.

I saw a conger eel lying dead on the sand, which reminds me of the terrific explosion I heard the other night. A mine went off at Dawlish by the Parson & Clerk, caused, it was supposed, by conger eels playing about in the rocks …

Sunday 27 July

Meg, Tim and I went along the cliffs with Domino to Sandy Bay where we had a glorious bathe. Dommie loved it as well and insisted on swimming out to me quite a long way out; he does not seem to be half as nervous now as he was when I first took him down for a bathe. It was such a lovely morning, sunny and blue with white clouds rolling round the sky, so the walk was delicious in the strong breeze.

Maimie and I went to tea with Miss Price and her sister to meet the daughter of the latter, such a charming girl. I thoroughly enjoyed my tea and fixed up a bathe at Ladram tomorrow, weather permitting.

In the evening Tim and I had a very interesting discussion on bee keeping which bored Maimie so much that she rushed off to bed in a huff! Rather awkward! I, however, learnt quite a lot and hope to remember it. All Tim said will be helpful when things have to be done in the hives later on. I wish Maimie was in a better state.

Monday 28 July

We had a bloody shopping morning, how I loathe all forms of shopping! Got all I wanted.

After lunch got into tennis things and went to the club where I met Lexy and at last some other people who we played two sets with before tea, we then came back to tea.

Lexy and I chatted and I showed her the hens and chicks. She loves coming round looking at things but it came on to rain at last quite hard. We have been expecting rain all day, it has been so cloudy and miserable all day but the rain is not now enough to do any real good. The ground has got so fearfully dry and caked like cinders.

Tuesday 29 July

Marjorie came over for the day and we all had tea on Woodbury Common but it was windy and trying to drizzle so not as beautiful as it might have been.

Wednesday 30 July

We all went to see Marjorie and her flat before having tea with Aunt Margaret, who is getting very old now. She did not seem very well and looked so sad and lonely.

Thursday 31 July

Maimie and I went to do some shopping after lunch while Tim and Meg went by ferry to see Mr and Mrs Fletcher in Dawlish. They were back for supper.

Maimie and I had a moderately good day at chores. They actually had a little food to sell in some of the shops. On the whole I was successful, thank goodness. To find no food is so disheartening.

Friday 1 August

We all went visiting in Topsham. The river was very lovely running down blue towards the sea between the marshes of the Exe valley, although the tide was low the mud was reflected blue from the sky.

First we called at Beach House on Miss Glanville and Miss Symons. They promptly asked us all to tea, they gave us such a delicious one too, cheese sandwiches – the cheeses coming from Canada. Miss Symons gave me some lovely carnation cuttings. They were both so sweet and friendly and their garden charming. I had forgotten how pretty the garden was in spite of me living next door and in those days I used to like walking in and out of their house and garden.

We then walked in to see Captain and Mrs Holman, who were pleased to see us and very nice. They are both looking a lot older than when we lived there.

Our last port of call was to see Lexy in her home in Sunhill Lane. She had her brother with her. He looked very thin and better looking. I am sorry for him as he has lost his father and mother very recently and will miss them terribly having always lived at home looking after them. Lexy gave us a huge box of silks and wools for embroidery …

Saturday 2 August

Meg and Tim bathed in the morning. It was a dull cloudy morning at first, but by eleven o'clock it had all cleared away and the sun came out gloriously. They said the sea was quite warm and they enjoyed themselves no end.

All the afternoon Tim tried to take photographs of Ming, Rusty and Domino. Domino was troublesome and in the end could not be taken. He danced all over the lawn, making faces and would not stand still for a moment, the sight of the camera seemed to excite him terrifically, and he went quite mad instead of doing his stuff by making a picture of himself. The poor little chicky family tried to pose but they were not considered to be worth a picture!

Olive has not come all this week so I fear that the evacuee has been too much for her and she will not be able to come again. It is such a pity, she was such a nice girl and so pretty. To hell with all the evacuees! They are sending down another 1,200, so heaven knows what the place will be like. The Exmouth drainage system will soon give up I should think! It will be unhealthy anyhow I should imagine with all these filthy people …

Sunday 3 August

We all, with Domino, went to Mamhead Park where we had tea, sitting on a bank under a huge oak tree overlooking the Powderham Park woods and the estuary of the Exe with Woodbury Common in the background. The view was really very lovely. All the ripe cornfields glowing among the trees over the down land towards Starcross and Dawlish, making the deep green forest trees stand out against them. In the far distance there was a blue haze over the landscape which added to the beauty of the scene, although the horizon was lost, especially over the channel when the pale blue sea was like a mist. Dear Dommie adored the game of ball I played down the hill into the park from where we sat, he got so hot and puffed hardly time to breathe, he was so thrilled.

Monday 4 August

Lexy came over for a bathe, it was a rotten day with low-lying clouds when we all started but by the time we had walked down Watery Lane it was raining and it rained all the way until we were pretty well soaked. At last we got to Sandy Bay along the beach and Tim bathed in the horrible rain, we then walked home along the top of the cliffs. Lexy loved the view and thoroughly enjoyed the walk in spite of its being wet. She had never walked over the cliffs before as she always went up the hill in the car. I must say, it was a deplorable day from my point of view as I loathe bathing picnics in the rain.

The little Queen's birthday today; she is forty-one – quite old!

Tuesday 5 August

I have been in a bad mood so far so I talked about all the things that might be likely to annoy Tim at lunch. Fortunately, Lexy rang up to ask Tim and Meg out for tea in the evening to amuse Reggie who is getting twenty-four hours leave. So I am left alone before I go mad with boredom and suppressed fury. What a life.

During the afternoon a gardener came up to tell me that the chickens were in Mansfield garden! They had been in the lane and run in front of a soldier all the way to Douglas Avenue, where this man had shoved them through the gate of Mansfield and came straight up to tell me. Madge, Maimie and I all walked (with Domino) down to Mansfield and the gardener there called to us that the chicks were scratching near him; there they all were! We drove them into a shed where Madge and the gardener caught them, putting them all into a sack, except the young cockerel that I carried. Off we went home and let them out in their run. Madge put a wire along the bottom of the door into the lane. I hope they will not get out again in a hurry as a dog might easily kill them or they may get completely lost and no one able to find them again.

Wednesday 6 August

We all motored up Haldon where we parked the car and walked with our tea to the obelisk. Tim really loved the view and seemed to blossom out a little more than usual. We all laughed at a very nice party who came to look at the glorious view, but they were so overdressed for the place which made us giggle. After our tea, Maimie walked back to the car to read her book while we all went hunting for bilberries in the woods. However, it was quite obvious that other people had had the idea first and picked the bushes almost clear. With much wandering about we found enough for a tart but it took us nearly two hours with all three working hard. Dear Domino loved the expedition and ran about in the woods, always coming back to me like an avalanche when he thought he had left me long enough. Meg loves him and is always saying what a darling dog he is but Tim hates him, I fancy. He is always pushing him away and puffing smoke at him from his pipe. Domino does not like him much either and never bothers much about him …

Thursday 7 August

Meg did some gardening in the morning. She tidied up the Virginia creeper outside the dining room window and made it all so nice.

Mrs Everett came in to tea and talked for quite a while. She was full of stories as usual and kept us all amused.

We ate our bilberry tart for supper and thoroughly enjoyed it because it really was most delicious. We got out a tin of Ideal Milk instead of pre-war Devon cream, and it was very good too.

After supper we all went up to Peak Hill. The view was superb; I had rather forgotten how beautiful it was. The evening was very clear and the cliffs all round West Bay stood out dark blue against the sky from Start Point, behind Berry Head, to far beyond the white cliffs of Beer. We could see the whole Dorset coast easily. Under the headland we stood on the sea was as calm as a pond, the little town of Sidmouth nestled between the steep hills far below. Away to the north looking over Woodbury Common the peaks and rugged tors of Dartmoor stood out clear and glorious.

Friday 8 August

Meg and Tim left early this morning. Lexy came to fetch them after breakfast and they caught the train in good time, after which Maimie and I rather collapsed owing to being so tired. We slept all the afternoon, going to bed soon after the evening news so we will be alright tomorrow.

Saturday 9 August

Frankie rang up to tell me to come to a party at Winslade House, where the marines are having their sports day. So I donned my best showery-weather clothes and off I set to meet Frankie, who was looking well and so nice in a navy blue get up.

After a chat in the car we set off for Winslade and after our passes had been well looked into by the guards we found ourselves in the sports field. The park was a lovely setting for the athletics.

Geoffrey and Johnny were there in full force, we hardly saw Johnny except in the distance when he dashed by doing his stuff. After the sports were over we made our way up to the mess where we drank copiously of iced cider cup, which was delicious.

When we had refreshed ourselves we walked down to see the concert, which was very good. I laughed like anything at some of the turns. Two of the marines had beautiful voices and sang grand songs; some of the funny ones were very funny!

After this we met Johnny, who told us to meet him later at the Blue Ball. This we did.

Monday 11 August

It is time for a gardening commentary. The mixed asters in the rose beds on the lawn are coming into bloom. The American pillar hedge is over now but has been a picture for several weeks. The bush roses are in bud ready for their autumn flowering.

I am busy planting out young seedlings, wallflowers, sweet Williams and Canterbury bells for next year.

Today I cleaned up the creepers on the house by the front door, nailed up the white jasmine and cut off the long trailers of Virginia creeper (which was overpowering the large pink clematis) and nailed up the yellow winter flowering jasmine on the side of the garage.

There is a lot of trimming to be done to the trees and hedges round the garden. I want to thin out a number of lower branches to let in more sunshine.

I'm getting more fruit trees later on: a dozen black currants and some American blackberries. Madge is going to increase the loganberry trellis and take out the three wild blackberries growing up. I am also going to get half a dozen sea kale plants to extend the row of rhubarb down the path. Madge is looking forward to cutting down the huge old macrocarpa hedge to be replaced by a rose trellis.

Tuesday 12 August

We put the chickens into their pen with the dog kennel for a house, they all walked in as good as gold at their tea time, unfortunately, however, they found a nice way out after finishing tea – how they actually got out I do not know, but the fact remained. How to recapture them was my question and to do it before dark. Mrs Llewellyn and Maimie came out to help me after supper – we chased the poor little family all over the lawn, Maimie waving a handkerchief when she thought something ought to be done to amuse them; Mrs Llewellyn rushed after the cleverer ones that thought they would make a quick get-a-way waving a large white blanket. I did slow movements in the hopes of taming the by now rather excitable birds. After much effort we drove three of them into the conservatory where I caught them with much ado. One odd young cockerel I caught quickly while he was trying to eat out of my hand, but the last bird was the bother; I could not get him into a corner in spite of trying every inspiration that came to me until at last I chased him into some undergrowth where he got caught up in the rubbish …

Wednesday 13 August

Mowed the lawn and the machine went well thanks to Tim; he spent a lot of time on it. Finished the whole lawn during the afternoon and evening, I'm glad I did as the sky looks full of rain.

After supper I bottled five jars of blue plums. It is now finished and sitting in the oven for the night looking very good.

On the news tonight it stated that the RAF raided ten towns in Germany during daylight yesterday and Berlin had a terrible plastering. While I was playing tennis yesterday afternoon with Barbara Guinness I saw three huge black bombers inland over Exmouth from the sea, am much wondering if they were Flying Fortresses which were being used in the bombing raids over Germany. Perhaps I shall hear one day what these enormous planes were. The RAF lost eleven bombers in these raids.

The Flying Ace with no legs is missing in the paper today; it seems such a shame after such a splendid record, to be finished.

NOTE --- The unfortunate legless man is a prisoner of war it appears, poor chap. I am sorry for him.

Thursday 14 August

I took both the Misses Thomas to see their cousins at Bradninch. I had been there before some years ago, but had forgotten how lovely the views all round were. While they visited the relations I sat on a gate going into a cornfield overlooking a gorgeous view of east Devon hills and woods. The village is a dear old place – very old-world and rural, built on a hill miles from anywhere, but quite near the main Bristol road.

Frankie rang up during the evening full of the joy of spring and her weekend here with me. She has fixed up a sailing expedition up the river for Sunday and insists on my buying her a chicken to take on the picnic on Saturday. I do hope the weather will be fine enough to have a supper party out of doors; it is _so_ unsettled now and rains quite a lot. Anyhow, we four will be able to amuse ourselves in one way or another. I am so looking forward to having Frankie, she is so amusing, always on top of the world. She is like a glass of bubbly and I laugh to think of her and all the fun we have had. She was the life of the office when I was in the ATS.

Saturday 16 August

Maimie's birthday, which was very quiet for her as all the fun was for me as I quite forgot it was her birthday when I fixed up things.

We both fetched Frankie at the station and did a bit more shopping before going home to tea after which we set to like mad to get the supper together before Geoffrey and John came over. We were both quite pleased with the result of our shopping and think our menu a good one for wartime – we had cold chicken, pork sausages, lettuce, mustard and cress sandwiches: finishing up with apples and plums.

Geoffrey and John turned up after a party (an official one) and we all went off to the golf course, Budleigh Salterton, parked the car and walked to a sheltered position under a hedge overlooking the sea, after eating until we could no longer munch, we decided to walk up the cliff path to see the view from the top. All the while the sunset was lovely but very stormy, black clouds and gold ones rushing across the sky. Ended the evening with a call at the Rosemullion which was very gay and full of marines from Dalditch Camp. Domino was very good all the time, he loved his new Uncle Geoffrey who took care of him.

Sunday 17 August

Frankie and I woke up full of the joy of spring, we got a huge lot of food together for the day's picnic, which took us quite a time to prepare. Our two charming marines arrived to the tick of twelve o'clock and changed into mufti. We walked round the docks, and decided to lunch in a new and beautifully clean-looking boat lying on the beach by the funny yacht club. We sat in the boat on the sand until it began raining then we made a hasty retreat to Clara, by this time it was after two o'clock so we went home and sank into comfortable armchairs where Frankie and Geoffrey slept peacefully while John, Maimie and I talked inconsequently and without cessation. After tea Colonel Cowel came in for a chat and was very nice as usual. Then we all went for a walk along the cliffs and back via the Royal Beacon where we drank beer until it was time to go home to supper. They took Frankie to the station at ten o'clock and departed having given me a very amusing weekend which I enjoyed no end and hope will soon be repeated …

Monday 18 August

Esme rang me up after breakfast, such a pleasant surprise. She wants to come to tea tomorrow and is staying with her aunt in Topsham. Betty Supple rang up last night to ask me for a drink on Wednesday and is coming in to tea tomorrow, she is on a week's leave from Scotland and took twenty-five hours getting down to Devon.

Betty came in to tea looking very well and wearing an awfully nice blue tweed coat and skirt. She seemed quite happy and told me quite a lot about her job as instructor to the ATS doing a course in clerical work. Betty instructs shorthand and typewriting which she learnt in Town before going up to Scotland on this particular job. She has fifty girls directly under her and the company is 500 full strength. She lives in a hostel with about 150 other ATS. It is a lovely hotel really and quite in the country. The country is <u>The Country</u> when you get north of Inverness, nothing but heather and moorland scenery, very beautiful if you are a good walker – poor old Betty is not a good walker, so she misses that form of sport or shall I call it amusement!?

Tuesday 19 August

Esme came in quite good time before tea, just missing torrential rain which poured down in absolute sheets soon after her arrival. She was looking very fit and young dressed in a pin-stripe grey coat and skirt (like mine) and grey hat and shoes with a spotted navy blouse, very smart and pretty. It was good to see her once more, I have not seen her since the war began when I stayed with her family at Lynton in the summer before war was declared. Now she is in the WVS and even goes far enough to wear uniform and a badge of honour. She drives round a mobile canteen to the troops four times a week: goes to the Post at all odd times and rings up the fire brigade whenever an alert is sounded, so she has her hands pretty full. As a sideline, Esme looks after other people's dogs. How she does it all is a mystery to me. Miss Harrison came to tea as well.

We persuaded Esme to stay and have a scrappy supper with us, which we had to rush through owing to having to catch a bus at 8.05 which Domino and I took Esme to catch, Dommie delighted with the walk.

Wednesday 20 August

Cut the hedge along by the front gate all the morning, fell asleep all the afternoon and after tea had to wake up and dress up to go to Betty's party. At last I arrived at the party and found the house full of people – great fun as I knew them all and had not seen them for ages so we had plenty to say to each other. Bunty was there; I had not seen her for years. Elizabeth looking <u>most</u> attractive in pale blue, she was charming. Also Phyllis and Betty Carter (who I liked much better than I used to in old days before she married), Madeline, Joan Hazel and her husband. Joan's husband, Pat, was on leave too and was a marvellous 'host', he really is a nice boy. The two Devon Regiment officers came in late and I thought them both dull looking and have forgotten their names. Joan and Pat's baby boy Michael was one year old today, so we all saw him and his beautiful toys.

I drank considerable quantities of 'White Lady', much to my own joy as it is <u>one</u> of my favourite drinks. Pat had 250 unopened boxes of cigarettes and a box was going round the room holding roughly fifty so I was a little envious, I must admit!

Thursday 21 August

In the morning Domino and I walked down the town to do some shopping. I interviewed the Agent for the Rolle Estate about cutting branches off the chestnut trees outside our hedge, whose overhanging branches are rather spoiling our kitchen garden.

After this was done I went along to see if Phyllis Comins could cut my hair and make me look a little more human, she said if I came back later I could have it done, so Domino and I filled in the time getting cigarettes, going to the dentist for an appointment and doing some general shopping. Dear Dommie had to visit his 'Pet Shop' for some horseflesh!

After supper I met Betty, who took me down in the car to the cinema, we saw *The Son of Monte Cristo* and both thoroughly enjoyed it too. It was a real thrill with plenty of blood and thunder, to say nothing of rapier fights and dungeons. It was the first cinema I have seen for simply ages so was a real treat. Betty also seldom gets the chance of going to shows as there is only one very antique picture house in Strathpeffer.

Friday 22 August

I caught the 1.30 train to Exeter and Esme got it at Topsham and we managed to get into the same carriage after some struggle as it was pretty full, as usual! On our way to the Plaza Picture house we did some shopping and I renewed my driving licence at the castle.

We got two very nice seats in the flick and the film *Spring Meeting* with Diana Churchill, our Prime Minister's daughter, starring. It was most amusing and the two Irish girls reminded me of Jill and her sisters, and the life I have pictured they live when they go home to Drumdoe on the West Coast. We both thoroughly loved it but we were rather disappointed in Diana Churchill. She seemed very stiff and not nearly as pretty as her mother, but then <u>Mr</u> Churchill is no beauty, is he? So I suppose one cannot expect too much, but I thought her rather forced and not at all natural.

We caught the express back at 6.15 and fixed up to meet on Tuesday morning, when I take the car to Mr Leigh to have its wing put right.

Saturday 23 August

It poured with rain all day. I put off my shopping in the morning in the hopes that it might clear up later, however the rain continued all day.

We met little Frankie at the station. She was quite cheery and bright, recovered from her fit of the blues of the middle of the week. After supper she insisted on washing my hair and setting it in a new style, she certainly has a gift for arranging hair and does her own very well, although it is quite simple it always looks smart and dressy for any occasion. Frankie is such an easy guest, perfectly happy just sitting doing nothing all day unless there is anything thrilling doing. She is not very well at the moment and the wet weather has brought back her cough, which is a pity.

I made her get some wonderful tonic stuff at Mr Derry's and hope it will do her good as it did me no end of good when I had flu last winter and Dr Murray made me take it.

It is funny how the life of the office in Exeter does seem to get you down and no mistake. I know when I was there I always found it terribly difficult to get rid of a cough or cold.

Sunday 24 August

Frankie, Maimie and I went to church. Unfortunately the vicar and Mr Heal were not there so the service was rather dull, which was a nuisance, but never mind. Afterwards we went to see Mrs Everett but found her in bed with bronchitis, so Maimie went up to her room while Frankie and I talked in the car, which we enjoyed. By the time we got home it was lunch time and after that we all slept on the lawn in the sun, which was gorgeous after food.

Frankie's cough better today but she is not feeling A1 I don't think. Next weekend Alexis is driving her home in Bertie, who is going like a new car and causes his Polish owner no end of delight and amusement.

After supper Maimie and I ran Frankie down to the town in Clara to catch her train back and we hope to see her soon again. She is a gay little thing and always makes me feel happy and lively like Mona does. Where is Mona by the way? She rang me up a little while ago and I have seen nothing of her at all, what an annoying thing! When I meant to see a lot of her while she was down in these parts!

Monday 25 August

I toddled up to the tennis and played a set before tea and again after tea. I played with Colonel Condon against Barbara Guinness and Mr Marshall. We played three sets and enjoyed them very much and the time went by like clockwork, it seemed no time when I discovered it was nearly seven o'clock and time to feed my poor little chicks and hens. I rang up John about playing some tennis sometime and he was very cheery. Getting up a game nowadays is a job of work as there are so few people about anywhere, at least people one knows. Everyone is new and a stranger.

Tuesday 26 August

Took Clara to be overhauled and have all scraped paint put right by Mr Leigh in Topsham. I saw Miss Knapton for a minute before taking Esme out for a walk round the town shopping. Got the train back to Exmouth. Met Miss Thomas in the town and she gave me a lift as far as the club which was a real joy as I was rather loaded with fowls food and cake.

Madge nearly finished cutting down the huge macrocarpa hedge between the lily pond and the KG. I finished clipping the privet hedge all along and put out some young wall flowers into their flowering quarters. I'm longing to cut out the turf for a new round flower bed on the right side of the lawn; it will be such an improvement and I have plenty of young stuff to go into it when it is done.

Wednesday 27 August

Biked down to see the dentist and on my way back I went into all sorts of funny food offices about registering for coke during the winter. It is such a job getting anything these days and it took me ages even doing this.

I started taking the turf away from the new flower bed to be outside the drawing room window. I only got a quarter of the turf up and am longing to finish it and get going with the planting out, but Madge will have to help me dig it up as it will have to have a real deep digging and the roots cut by a very strong arm!

During the evening Lady Evelyn brought Michael and Caroline in to see the goldfish again. Caroline has grown quickly.

Thursday 28 August

Finished taking the turf from the new round bed, got it all dug in and now it is only waiting to have the soil thoroughly broken up and the surface raked over. I'm longing to plant all my seedlings in it.

Saturday 30 August

Maimie, Mrs Llewellyn, Domino and I took Clara out to Peak Hill where we picked blackberries to bottle. I was lucky and found quite a few right down in the valley where the blackberries grow thickly in great clumps by the stream which runs along by the hedge at the bottom. Poor Domino lost me, and Maimie said he nearly went mad rushing about looking for me until he at last tore through the brambles and undergrowth arriving at my feet panting and very hot but happy having found me. We picked these annoying little fruits for three hours until I had filled my basket: then Mrs Llewellyn came to fetch us for tea, so we all walked up the winding path up the steep hillside covered with heather and ling, resting sometimes to look back at the glorious view over Lyme Bay and Woodbury Common with Hay Tor, Saddle Tor and Rippon Tor in the background.

After a particularly welcome tea we drove home, late but not <u>too</u> late to feed all my hungry fowls. It was a perfect afternoon and one I shall remember. The fruit has made five 2lb jars and are in the oven now so I hope with the help of more petrol and a certain amount of courage I shall be able to pick more.

Sunday 31 August

John rang up to say (his batman rang up to say) that he had been called away on business so could not come to tea after all. Poor John, it being <u>the</u> most perfect day you ever saw, I bet he cursed being on duty but he should not be the best officer in the unit and the adjutant and not expect to be overworked.

I spent the day at home, had a sudden thought that I would let out the old hens as well as the chicky family and let them loose on the lawn but, oh, what a nuisance they were!

I finished softening the earth in the new round bed I have made and planted it with Canterbury bells, wallflowers and sweet Williams. I'm longing for Madge to begin getting the turf off the bank – that will be such a thrill!

Mrs Everett and Mrs Dalrymple's cousin, Pat Blake, came in to talk about tennis, I fixed up to meet Pat tomorrow at the club and introduce her round to all the best players and we are to play on Thursday when I have got the rest of the girls together, but that will be the difficulty nowadays …

Monday 1 September

The hoover electric fitting on the landing went wrong so I had to go and ask for a man to come up and look at it when I was down in the town shopping. Got some cakes for tea, but could not get any food for the fowls other than the rationed meal. Poor little hens, they will be so hungry. I shall have to let them run on the lawn for a while every day to get food.

By noon it began to rain and became a wet day, so we got no tennis but Mrs Dalrymple and Pat came to tea and we all talked and the time soon went by until they thought they would walk home, only ten minutes after their leaving our house the thunder began and the rain came down very hard again – I hope they got back before they were very wet.

Tuesday 2 September

While I was at the dentist Madge started taking the turf off the bank. He is making it a foot wider than the grass bank and taking off the turf at the top and digging it into the middle and bottom of the bank so making it into a far gentler slope. The effect will be that the house will stand on the top of this slope instead of being built on a steep bank, a much prettier landscape in itself, to say nothing of the flowers growing on the slope instead of having it a weedy turf.

So far I have planted out the two camellias from tubs in the conservatory and also planted three large pots of agapanthus between, so I now have three pots for next year's tomatoes and two tubs to plant ornamental geraniums at the top or bottom of the steps in the middle of the new slope. Tomorrow I hope to plant an edging along the top as far as Madge has gone also the clumps of irises along the top; we are having roses along the bottom and have to wait until October before planting them. It is really very thrilling and I am longing to see the whole bank when it is finished next month.

Wednesday 3 September

Two years ago today Great Britain declared war on Germany. How well I remember it. Working like HELL in the office for my beloved ATS. Planes flying overhead. Everyone in a terrific rush, young men rushing off to enlist, girls too, and an incredible feeling of pride and love for dear England.

Thursday 4 September

Had some good sets of tennis with Mrs Dalrymple's cousin, Pat Blake, Joan Bowerbank and Barbara Guinness. It was great fun and the weather perfect. All went well except the boy mowed the courts all round the one we played on and the noise of the machine put me off badly; I cannot concentrate in a hideous row so rather mucked up my game, also the sawing rather tired my arm.

Mrs Everett and Violet Hatfield came up at tea time bringing with them a big tea for us and plenty to drink. We had it in the veranda of the clubhouse and were quite a good party. Maimie came up and joined in for a chat having had her tea; after tea Joan had another set to play and Barbara went back to her hotel so Pat and I played singles. I was beaten, but we had some lovely games: but having not played for over two years and Pat is a very good player (plays at Wimbledon) I did not do so badly. Singles are terrific and one really needs to be training for them. I loved it in spite of the effort as I used to like singles best and they are such wonderful practise. Pat is a nice girl and I hope to play her again one day!

Friday 5 September

George Anderson rang me up. He has been home on leave with a bad foot (he crushed it with a lorry).

I took Miss Thomas, Miss Macpherson and the nurse for a drive to Starcross to see the old home of the Thomases. It is being converted into a sort of rest home for weary fire fighters in the event of our being badly blitzed in the coming winter. A lovely spot, the house is big and standing in fields right back from the road, a huge garden. The walled one at the back full of fruit and vegetables but the front one quite derelict which is a shame but the house has been empty for eighteen years since the Thomases left it.

After lunch I gardened, planting some more irises along the new bank and drowning caterpillars on the cabbages.

Saturday 6 September

It began to rain quite early so no hope of playing any tennis. I rang up Pat and asked her to tea, she is a nice girl. Fetched Frankie from the station and we played rummy after tea.

Frankie told me a little about 'Alex', the Polish count who bought my car. He is now expecting to be promoted to Squadron Leader any day and I am dying to meet him; but he is such a remarkably brave man and is called upon to do such wonderfully dangerous exploits that I tremble in case he is killed before we meet.

Among many other things he has been a first-class spy and spent many days in enemy territory doing actual sabotage himself, dressed up and thoroughly disguised by beard, etc. Of course he does not tell anyone what he is doing now, but Frankie rather imagines that he is dropping spies at this moment from planes over enemy territory and collecting them again when their deed is done at an appointed place and at a given time. This work is carried out by special planes built for the purpose and their pilots are chosen. 'Alex' is the finest pilot in the squadron and evidently one of the best in the country.

Sunday 7 September

Another national day of prayer ordered by HM the King. The church packed and quite a scramble to get a seat in spite of arriving early. The vicar preached and the sermon was a good one. We gave Mrs Everett a lift back also Mrs Hatfield. Maimie went to tea with Mrs Dalrymple while Frankie and I had tea on our own at home on the terrace in the sun, afterwards fetching Maimie at her tea party.

I must admit that, the more I think of it, the more proud and glad I am that I sold my little car Bertie to a hero, while I might so easily have given him over to an ordinary silly man. He is so pleased with him too and being an expert mechanic has made the engine so perfect. 'Alex' took Frankie home for the weekend in Dorset and she said the car went gloriously, they just tore along at a tremendous speed, the miles flying before them.

Yesterday we had an air raid, the first one for months. Having the wireless on fairly loud, we did not hear the alert but heard the loud droning sound of a German plane overhead, then a lot of guns going off which made the doors rattle but we took no real notice when suddenly the 'all clear' went!

Monday 8 September

Had some very nice sets of tennis with Colonel Baker, Colonel Condon and Mr Marshall. We played four sets until it was beginning to get quite dark, the evenings are closing in now quickly but the light still holds until it about 6.30. While we played a variety of planes flew over us, chiefly the new fighters at the airport, they made a great noise, especially as it was one of those dull, still, heavy evenings.

I wrote to Gwen yesterday asking her to stay, I do so hope she will come; it is ages since I have seen her. Frankie says she is not at all well again. I wish she could get better and enjoy life more.

I'm busy waiting for my five bottles of big red plums to get heated through in the oven; they look nice and I hope will be successful. In the morning I trimmed up the Montana growing up the bower outside the drawing room door window. It looks much tidier now and will be pretty when the shoots all naturally fall in the way I have trained them.

I'm longing for Madge to get more of the bank done. He has got up to the steps already and so in another two weeks or so I suppose we shall just about finish the job except planting the roses.

Tuesday 9 September

Rawdon turned up for tea on a push bike. He had left Margaret in Exeter having her hair done and came on. He looked younger than ever and very happy. I had not seen him since before the war. He has been everywhere, even having his ship torpedoed when they crawled into Philadelphia or somewhere to repair themselves before coming home to England. He was in the Battle of Narvik and brought back a number of Nazi prisoners who were glad to come to England. He also brought back a number of Poles who they rescued from a ship when it was sunk near Norway and said he liked them enormously.

Rawdon made me laugh; he was as amusing as ever. He said he did not approve of divorce because he was 'a bloody Papist, you see'. However, he had to go back before supper as the last ferry goes at 7.15. It is good to see old friends sometimes.

In the morning Mr Fisher came over to put a bee escape on the super which I am to see tomorrow. On our way back from Budleigh we called at Snow's Nurseries and bought five lovely miniature trees, all different sorts. In the afternoon I mowed the lawn with the big mower ready to tidy up by hand.

Wednesday 10 September

I took the super over to Mr Fisher and we extracted 10lbs of finest eating honey and 4lbs of unsealed honey useful for cooking. So, my hive, which I have only had for ten weeks (June 25), has given me 14lbs of honey in their first summer! I'm longing for next year when I can have another hive full when they swarm. (Must order a hive from Burgess.) The Fishers' view from the windows and garden is lovely – the sea so blue and the white cliffs of Dorset glistening across the bay and the cornfields on the hills by the cliffs gold in the sun.

Friday 12 September

Rawdon rang up to ask us over to Dawlish, so we went over and had tea with his people, then went across to see Anne and all the delightful clothes R. bought in Canada for his family, such pretty things.

Saturday 13 September

A delightful day for blackberrying! After lunch I took Maimie, Mrs Llewellyn and Domino to the hills behind Budleigh Salterton. We went along the little lane by the railway bridge, then across the bridge across the Otter. Here we drove along a tiny track by the river under beech trees until we decided to stop the car, get out and start picking. We followed a bramble hedge running up the hill, the berries were hardly ripe yet, although abundant and a good size. At the top I went down another hedge going along the top of the hill and found quantities of lovely berries. Here Domino and I stayed for a long time as I had to pick both sides. The views from here glorious: on one side the woods and moorland of Woodbury and on the other the white cliffs of Beer going down the Dorset coast.

On the top of this hill the RAF keep their funny balloon target things that they trail behind. I saw about half a dozen planes come swooping down to let off the target which blew down into the field I was picking in, it was fascinating to see them let the balloons swoop down to the ground. It was late when Dom and I got back to the car for tea.

Sunday 14 September

Gwen came over for the day. She looked terribly tired but happier than I have seen her. She had an interview with Miss Acland lately and in consequence is hoping to get her discharge. Peggy and Barbara are getting commissions, which is good news. Colonel Cowel came in to tea and was very nice and cheery. Gwen made me laugh; she told me this rather amusing incident which happened recently. One of the hostels caught fire and Patience Thesiger rushed down to see about it from her lunch in the officers' mess. The police arrived and began taking notes etc. One of them went up to Patience and asked 'Miss Thesiger?' She replied 'Yes, I am Miss Thesiger, the Commandant and daughter of Judge Thesiger'. To which the constable remarked 'Never 'eard of 'im'! Paul has gone overseas; Gwen has not heard yet what he is doing. She loved my new garden arrangements and thinks the bank is a vast improvement to what it was.

Last night the RAF raided Brest again, bombing some enemy warships there; I heard the fighters going over our house when I was going to bed.

Monday 15 September

Lexy rang me up and I fixed up for her to come to tea after playing tennis at the club. Nobody was up there before tea except Mrs Elliot, who talked as usual!

After tea Colonel Condon rang up Mr Marshall, who came up and we played a few sets which was great fun and kept us on the run until seven o'clock. My poor hens were so hungry, poor things, when I fed them on my return home. Lexy told me one or two interesting things, one about the electric works at Box and how a German had said to a British Army officer before the war that they would never be able to harm it in any way: the Englishman had never heard of Box or the electric works but pretended to the Nazi that he knew what he was referring to. Does it not show how much those bloody Germans know about England!?

I am making tomato sauce from a receipt of Mrs Fisher's and 8lbs of tomatoes was nothing out of my beautiful crop, so I feel very bucked with myself.

Friday 19 September

Yesterday evening Maimie and I went to a rummy party at Mrs Dalrymple's, we had great fun. Mrs D. and I lost the game as usual!

I have been very busy in the garden all week, been digging all the flower beds in the front of the house by the drive, they will do now until February or March. My asters are lovely this year, so gay and pretty but I must improve the Michaelmas daisy display next year. Madge has done digging the bank and now has the steps to make up the middle and a path one side. He has done the job well but really finds it a bit hard at his age. I got half a dozen sea-kale pots for practically nothing at a sale up the road so am awfully pleased with myself; must order some nice plants from the nurseryman soon …

Sunday 21 September

I'm feeding my little bees with sugar syrup. They love it!

The day seems to drag on like a nightmare. We heard today that Rupert was killed flying. The poor parents had a wire on Friday to say that he had died from injuries received during operations. I cannot believe that I shall never hear his cheerful voice over the garden hedge again. He is the second of three friends who I have a funny feeling I shall never see again. The first was Jimmy, who was killed while flying over

Belgium in the Fleet Air Arm; now Rupert, a fighter pilot in the RAF. The third is an old friend in the army – I only pray that he will be spared, but my funny feelings are usually correct; I wish that they were not. What will poor 'Roly' Marshall do without his beloved brother Rupert, they are devoted to one another and I cannot imagine one without the other. Why are all the finest and best men taken? It is true indeed that 'those whom the Gods love, die young'. It is so awful and final. I have lost several friends in this war already, what is going to happen when our army goes into battle against the Nazis I dread to think even for a moment …

Tuesday 23 September

Today I began digging and weeding among the violets and shallots, a rather monotonous days work but it looks nice when done. I have finished pricking over all the flower beds in the front, except the one under the house with the fuchsias; have also hoed the drive and path round by the back door. The latest thing is grubbing up all the rough grass by the beehive. I am going to plant it with herbs, lavender, rosemary and balm: next year I hope to have another hive which will stand beside the other.

As the soil is bone dry, owing to lack of rain, I cannot plant out any of the many flowers waiting, but after a few wet days I shall get busy with moving plants round the garden. Madge has today made the path at the other end of the terrace. He has taken the dreadful steps away and next week I hope he will be able to start building the centre steps, which are going to be really nice ones, at the moment Madge is getting going with digging up the potatoes, this will take him two days, after that the steps, then rooting out the macrocarpa trees which he has cut down. I am going to plant the edging along the second half of the terrace when the weather breaks, but let's hope it will keep fine!

Thursday 25 September

We packed up a few sandwiches and apples in the lunch basket, jumped into the car at noon and drove off to the downs behind Budleigh Salterton, where the blackberries grew. It was lovely there, in spite of their being a thick mist blowing up from the sea which hung on the hills like great grey billows. Towards evening these blew further away into the far distance, leaving the views towards Woodbury lying underneath a huge blanket hanging over it. The blackberries were much riper than last week when we were there. Altogether we picked 11½lbs of large juicy berries.

Dear Domino accompanied me all the way, never leaving me for a minute, he lay about a few feet away from me while I crawled about in the hedges.

Being so misty, the planes were not practising on their targets as last time, with the result that it was beautifully quiet, except for the cows and the rooks cawing and a few wood pigeons flying noisily in and out of the beech and chestnut trees.

I picked about 6lbs in three hours which I thought quite quick picking and if the basket had been bigger I could have got many more. Dommie and I got ourselves back to the car by 4.45 for tea …

Friday 26 September

Domino and I went for such a lovely walk after tea, we took the little lane at the end of Douglas Avenue, keeping down the hill over the brook at the bottom, here Dommie paddled about joyously, getting covered in red mud. We then walked up Bony Lane, the bank on either side thick with brambles and the berries hanging down in black profusion: at the top of the incline the view of the sea glorious, the colour a deep, vivid blue with black thunder clouds covering the distance. When we got to the crossroad we turned down to Littleham village, where we crossed the bridge, walked past the church and turned along the tiny lane to Green Farm. Along here we sauntered through meadows with cows grazing and calves lying in the grass. Domino loves these fields; he always trots along the little footpath barking and growling with pleasure to himself, but this evening he was too puffed to give tongue so he just grinned at me.

Saturday 27 September

I had a morning at the house, which was a good thing done. After lunch Frankie rang up to say she was coming by a train at 4.15 as Alex could not bring her with Bertie as he was off in the air at a moment's notice, fighting or something! Domino and I trotted down the town to meet her. On our way we ran into our tobacconist and he put me on his books, so now I can have quite a lot of cigs: three cheers! – I must admit I do find I need them badly, especially lately when they have been so impossible to buy anywhere. We got down to the station just as the train came in. Frankie only brought a tiny little case so we took it in turns to carry it on the way home. We walked up by the Beacon but the fog was coming in thick and fast over the sea, so we could see nothing. Frankie told me all about her boyfriends, the company and above all the RAF Poles, who she adores. She says Gwen is bad again. Frankie went to a marvellous dance at Bampton given by a friend where she met a whole load of old boy friends and was in her element of course …

Sunday 28 September

Quite a social day. Frankie and I sat in the garden all the morning. The sun was shining brilliantly after a night of rain and thunder. How happy the garden looks; it had not had a spot of rain all the month.

After lunch Colonel Cowel called for a large bunch of flowers I had picked for Gwen, who is doing CB for her health, ordered by the new ATS doctor – an extraordinary state of affairs, so we all think! Frankie so worried, she told us about it yesterday. We rang up Colonel Cowel, who is going in to see her today. Rawdon and Margaret came to see us by the ferry. R. was back from his visit to 'the loony bin' and has another month's leave before getting a ship. It was great fun seeing them again. They are always so amusing and full of chat and fun. Rawdon told us some coarse stories – much to all our amusements he told them to Maimie! She did not understand them all, but when she did she was <u>not</u> amused!

Frankie had to catch an early train, so R. and I walked halfway to the station with her bag and herself, and R. and M. had to catch their ferry an hour later. I did enjoy seeing them all again it is fun to have one's friends round one …

Tuesday 30 September

In the morning I gave Mr Marshall a lift to his dentist where he was having three teeth out with gas. He is looking so aged and ghostly white since Rupert was killed, poor man – Mrs M. came in to see us off and she promised me some blackberries to plant up the fence behind the delphinium border.

I gardened all day, planting the bank now it has rained and the soil is moist. I have planted big clumps of mixed irises near the top with young plants of wallflowers, Canterbury bells and sweet William between and the edging is mixed, all kinds of things all along. The path by the conservatory up the bank is camellias and the one outside the dining room window is lavender on both sides. The steps in the middle are tiny trees but Madge has still to cement the bricks and make the steps before it is finished and I can plant pinks and thyme on either side.

Rawdon told me that a brother Naval Officer once said to him, 'A man has fun when he is fond of a woman but when a woman is fond of a man, it is HELL.' Oh, how true! I must say, I think it very clever and amazingly good …

Saturday 4 October

I finished my outdoor painting today. Altogether I have thoroughly creosoting the garage – which took one gallon of creosote – the hen house, dog kennel and one garden seat. Have had fine weather for it and the job has been done well and will last for two years now. I now have to Solignum all the deck and garden chairs; when it is wet I can do them in the conservatory to occupy my time.

Next week I hope to machine the lawns again and Madge will finish the steps so the garden is really coming on apace and I hope will be a real success next spring. I must bike over to one of the farms to get hold of some farmyard manure before the winter.

Sunday 5 October

A lovely surprise: Mona came and spent the afternoon with us. She was over here bringing an officer over to see his wife, who is staying next door with Lady Evelyn – they were supposed to be using the petrol for official use! It was grand seeing her again after so long, she looked so smart and pretty in khaki. I gave (sold) her some of my khaki shirts and stockings also Frankie's grey shoes which are too big and hurt me. We chatted about everyone we knew, all the old friends.

Mona's fiancé has tried to escape but was captured again and first sent to Stalag XXID then to a <u>terrible</u> prison in north Germany where they had no water to drink even. But now he is back in an oflag again and Mona is half afraid he is going to try and escape once more. He sent his photograph recently and looked well and happy.

Mona is a FANY and stationed at Tavistock at the moment. She is thoroughly happy, having fun driving all kinds of vehicles and people all over the place. But tomorrow is taking on a special job of driving only for a colonel and is expecting to do about 1,000 miles a week. She says it means stripes and may mean office work later, which she hates the thought of ...

Friday 10 October

Ambrose came in for supper and we talked for ages. It was so nice to see him again after so long. He is very busy at Aldershot; just been through a course and now is hoping to be made an instructor there. He looked very well and happy, quite enjoying being in the army. I think he will do well and be efficient as well as popular. He is so reliable.

Madge having finished the steps up the bank and put down the paving at the bottom, I spent the morning planting thyme on the steps and masses of dianthus up the sides, it really is attractive. Behind the dianthus which trails down are the little miniature trees and behind them again are three big bushes of hydrangea. I am longing to put the bush roses in among the polyanthus that I have already planted in clumps.

Today too I put in three more climbing roses in the L beds, which makes up five in each. When they have their posts to climb up it will look quite lovely with the old sundial standing in the middle. I also took out a yellow jasmine and forsythia and put them up the wall and think it a great improvement already ...

Saturday 11 October

Finished bedding up the bees for the winter. They seem very gay still and rushing into the hive heavy with honey. I have put three pieces of carpet and six newspapers on the top of the glass quilt under the lid of the hive. Today I also fitted in their front door the winter side up.

Started hacking away at the hedge at the bottom of the lawn, trying to arrange it so one can be private and not viewed by all who walk in the lane outside.

Sunday 12 October

Frankie rang up after breakfast asking if she could come out and spend the day with me. I was very glad as Maimie is in bed with a cold and I had planned to rest all day, so with Frankie to talk to, the day went very quickly lying in a deck chair. Unfortunately, it was dull and cold not brilliantly sunny as it was yesterday afternoon. I was thankful to hear that Gwen has transferred into Anne Fletcher's old job of recruiting ATS. She is billeted outside a hostel entirely on her own, and the hours are from nine o'clock until five o'clock, so she will not be so tired and nerve-wracked without the extra worry of hostel life at night time. Peggy and Barbara are off for the OCTU training on Tuesday, which will be delightful for them although the course is a very stiff one.

Frankie herself is going on eight days leave on Tuesday and is spending three days in London. It will be lovely for her to beat up Town again after her hard work as Staff Sergeant. She told me a list of promotions in the company which will make some of the girls' hair turn green!

How everything is changing since I was there; if I went back now I would not know it for the old company.

Tuesday 14 October

Maimie in bed as her cold is rather nasty still. I spent the afternoon and evening cutting the hedge and laying the young saplings along the top of the bank in a hope that it will form a sort of fence to keep out the gaze of any curious passer-by in the lane.

There is now a Roman Catholic school for slum children from Bristol in Douglas Avenue and they run up and down the lane all day, which brings the lane much more into the public eye and ear.

Wednesday 15 October

The whole house turned into bedlam with the uproar caused by Mrs Llewellyn refusing to keep the kitchen clean. I lost my temper and told her a few home truths so she said I was silly. In the end I told her to go at once, and I went upstairs to tell Maimie that I had sent her away.

Had an early lunch and took my bike across the ferry to Starcross where we turned along the road past Powderham and so to Veitch's, who have their nursery gardens outside Exminster. Spent an hour choosing various fruit trees and roses until I was tempted so bought one azalea and one rhododendron also a gentiana sino-ornata which the manager said would do well anywhere. Had plenty of time as it only took me about twenty minutes biking from the ferry and I was very hungry, so went into the village of Exminster where a very kind shopman allowed me to buy a cake from him as he had bought several today.

The cake was eventually downed sitting on the park wall at Powderham looking at the deer playing. Got to the ferry in tons of time. The evening was cold but the views very pretty with rolling black clouds blowing all over the sky …

Thursday 16 October

Got up early to light the fires and do as much as I can before breakfast. Dirt everywhere. I scrubbed the kitchen floor all the afternoon and took up the lino. Maimie is getting me a lovely new one from Walton's, very expensive but worth it, as I am going to do the cooking in future and I shall keep the lino clean instead of getting it filthy like maids do. I was up until twelve o'clock at night washing the kitchen. I washed the walls down with lux in the water so now the room itself is getting on but there remain all the cupboards to tidy and scrub also <u>all</u> the pans and china to wash. The frying pans are in such an awful state that I have had to take one down to the ironmonger for him to try and clean. To think that my lovely house ever had such a filthy kitchen and scullery makes me feel quite sick. It is a shame for these beastly people to take money for ruining everything they can get hold of. Anyhow, I shall not have another 'living in' maid while the war is on. Daily women are much nicer and do their work far better in my opinion.

Friday 17 October

Still cleaning like mad. Mrs Llewellyn came to collect her clothes in the afternoon. I wondered if she noticed the lino up on the kitchen floor and the paintwork clean at last, but she treads dirt so I expect she never looked at the difference! She insisted on shaking hands before she finally went complete with all her goods and chattels. Her room – well, it would fill up another page to describe it!

Sunday 19 October

I got time for a turn out in Mrs Llewellyn's room this morning, after clearing out huge piles of all the vast accumulation of rubbish collected in large cardboard boxes, the room itself did not take long, it was thick in dust but clean underneath.

Friday 24 October

The man came to put down the lino, it took him some time to lay but now it is finished the room looks lovely, so spotless and the fawn lino goes well with the stone-coloured paintwork: I have put some nice blue oilcloth along the top of the dresser and on the table; it goes awfully well with the blue-and-white china, so now I feel a queen in my new kitchen and quite enjoy the cooking. Have never seriously done any cooking but find it very easy. So far I have made no terrible mistakes. Last night I made a blackberry tart, an open tart and two tiny jam tartlets, did up some meat with vegetables and flavoured lightly with herbs from the garden – it was delicious though I say it myself. Now the pans are all clean the food tastes so much better and the knowledge that everything is clean is more appetising somehow.

When we get a char to help in the house life will be much easier. At the moment things are a bit hectic I must admit but it is my war work after all and no hardship.

Saturday 25 October

Cousin Cally had tea with us; it was so nice to see her. She is staying for a few days with Miss Dickson. She looked fairly well though rather weak and draggled. If it had not been for my awful toothache I should have thoroughly enjoyed seeing her, but my face is in an awful state, even my nose hurts like mad and my whole face aches incessantly, so tiring. Have got the kitchen clean at last and now are waiting for a char to come and help me keep it so. There is a lot for me to do, especially with this damned toothache all day long.

Sunday 26 October

My toothache very bad and I feel rotten with a swollen face and red eyes. Do wish I could get rid of the pain.

Saturday 1 November

I took Domino for a walk and on our way we met Mrs Carroll so we had a nice little walk together. She is also maidless and going to have daily help like we have decided on. It is quite hopeless trying to have a maid while the war is on; all the best girls are naturally doing war work and the ones left behind one is better without. We both agreed that the food goes twice as far since we have done the cooking ourselves.

Sunday 2 November

I made a terrible discovery on going down into to the cellar to look at the things packed away from air raids, I found to my dismay that everything was not only damp but soaking wet and rotting as they lay there packed in newspaper. First our most beautiful old inkstand, a family relic of great value and price. It was covered with mould and mildew and had come completely unstuck, all the tortoiseshell inlay had come off and the whole thing an utter wreck. We did all we could for it and shall have to take it to Brufords to put right, they are really fine jewellers and will make a good job of it, I think. Maimie and I both nearly had hysteria when we saw our glorious old heirloom rotting away. I then fetched out all the china and put the huge cases it was packed in out in the sun to dry. Got out a box of silver and my own jewel box, everything getting spoilt quickly and I am thankful I did not wait any longer before looking at the frightful chaos. So much for doing one's bit in the way of removing valuable stuff to a comparatively safe place; it is better where it was all over the house risking being bombed, anyhow. At the end of the war there would have been nothing left …

Tuesday 4 November

Maimie decided on our day's shopping in the city of Exeter, so off we went in Clara, leaving Ming and Rusty at home with Madge to take care of them. First we took the poor inkstand to Bruford to ask his advice. He could do nothing himself until after the war as he has no men now, but said we could do it ourselves with glue and a lot of patience and time spent piecing the inlay together.

We then had lunch at Colson's where I had booked a table. After eating well and long, I bought a charming fur felt hat, an American one with a brim all round and two pretty blouses to wear under woollies to keep my neck warm as I feel the cold so much after wearing ATS shirts and ties for two years. Then on to Woodley's for shoes; Maimie got a lovely pair of lined (fleecy) suede, low heeled, with crepe rubber soles in dark brown while I got a heavenly pair I had seen in the window some time ago, a London tan suede seamless with built up crepe soles – a perfect fit and I feel as if

I am walking on air. Then I got a pretty house coat for housework but it took seven coupons, so I had to be content with one. Maimie got a pair of charming dull pink vegetable dishes; they will go with our set as they are so different!

Wednesday 5 November

A white frost this morning, oh, isn't it cold! Simply perishing, but a glorious day of brilliant sunshine all the time. After lunch Domino and I did some gardening. We tidied up the three-cornered rose bed, hoed the path and cut some grass edges. The leaves are terribly untidy and the whole garden chaos until we can get rid of them. The chrysanthemums are all out now, but not very good as I did not take new cuttings early last spring; the old plants are never very good. We ordered a load of Phurnoid for the kitchen boiler fire and it came today, so I am hoping to keep the fire in all night. It will save so much time in the morning and also the house will not get so fearfully cold in the night.

Thursday 6 November

Colonel Cowel took me to see a very good film, *The Prime Minister* with John Gielgud as Disraeli and Diana Wynyard as Mrs Disraeli, Owen Nares as Lord Derby and Fay Compton as Queen Victoria; a really fine production which I thoroughly enjoyed and was glad to see. It was very interesting and some of the ideals of Disraeli are only now beginning to be realized. I wish he could come and see England and the Empire today.

The colonel came back to tea with me, and Maimie and he talked business for more than an hour! He is such a kind man to say nothing of good looking!

In the morning Maimie bought Domino a huge and beautiful basket for a Christmas present. He loves it and I take it round wherever I am sitting. He so hates nowhere to sit and now he always has his own basket to curl up in anywhere.

It is wonderful how full the shops are still, in spite of the war going on for over two years. One can get anything one wants, if not exactly <u>the</u> thing, something equally good. I do think we are lucky people so far.

I often wonder when our turn for hell is coming. It may come soon or it may never come. I think <u>we</u> are up to <u>something</u> in the spring. Who knows really!

Friday 7 November

Autonovisk, the Polish Night Fighter squadron leader, I met some time ago with Eugene, was killed last week. How sad that he will never see his family or estates again in Poland.

Saturday 8 November

A Mrs Hunt came to help me with the house. She seems very nice, quick and cheerful, so now I feel much more at ease with the house and capable of keeping things nice, both the house itself and the cooking. Did half an hour's gardening after lunch and fed the fowls early before going to tea with the Misses Clay, who live in a sweet little house with a charming garden. I took them an astilbe plant in exchange for two beautiful plants that they gave us. Miss Clay had promised me a few sea kale roots in the spring which will indeed be lovely as I have the pots but as yet no plants. So now I have only to get a dozen asparagus to fill in the gaps in the bed. By the time I am middle aged the garden will really be a luxurious one, full of the best of everything! Both the little Misses Clay were most amusing and delightful. Their blue china in the glass cupboard in the drawing room very pretty; I love beautiful china, it makes a room look so perfect somehow. No room is right without china somewhere (drawing room I mean). Their garden too seemed so neat and tidy; ours is in a dreadful state with all the leaves and weeds coming up everywhere. I must try and tidy it up.

Sunday 9 November

Being a sunny day, although very windy, we phoned up Mrs Everett to come for a drive on Woodbury with us. She had Mrs Dalrymple having lunch with her, so she came as well. We were quite a party. Domino came because I promised him a walk on the common. He sat on Mrs Everett's lap and she sat in front with me while Mrs D. and Maimie sat in the back. We chose the road over Black Hill which leads one to Yettington, it was unrecognisable now that the Marine Camp has sprung up all over the common there, all along the road. They have chosen the most beautiful view of any part of Woodbury but the army huts are not in keeping with the exquisite surroundings. When Domino and I went for our walk we chose the path along the back of Yettington which comes out right on the top of the castle hill, but we branched off making a round back to the car before going up to the castle. The autumn tints are lovely, the soft yellow of the oaks and orange of the huge beeches grouped amongst the firs with their rich, dark, silvery green made the landscape very beautiful, the brown bracken too, and soft brown of the heather smelling of peat made our walk a memorable one.

Monday 10 November

I had my bloody tooth out, the one that has given me such hell lately. It is aching now; I knew the brute would let me know when it came out! I must admit toothache just finishes me off. I have had too much of it and now it makes me furious.

Thursday 13 November

A very pleasant surprise: the phone rang and I heard Nolly's voice the other end. He is on his way to spend the evening with us on his way back from a week's leave.

He arrived late as he got out of the bus the wrong end of the avenue, also missed the train in Exeter but it did not matter at all, the dinner was not spoilt by waiting. I had not seen him since before the war. He looked frightfully well and very good looking. The army life seems to suit him well. He has just transferred to the RA and has asked to be sent overseas, so I suppose he will be off soon in all probability. Poor Mr and Mrs Rowland, all the adored boys will be overseas soon. Jappy is doing very well indeed. He is just twenty-one and a captain and having quite an amusing time in Gib, always going for joy trips with the navy in the Mediterranean which he loves of course. He nearly went into the navy when he was a child. Ruth is a WAAF and stationed near Oxford, she loves the life and looks topping in her uniform. She is the only one of the family not in the army! Paul is sixteen and growing fast. I suppose I should not know him if I saw him; he was a small child when I was last at Egloshayle.

Friday 14 November

I spent the day planting the roses which arrived from Veitch, with Madge's help. He planted the fruit trees first and they look so nice in their places. (We did this yesterday, by the way.) Now the bank is quite full, irises on the top near the path with clumps of annuals between, dwarf fir trees, hydrangea and carnations by the steps and roses all along the bank, polyanthus and tea roses in clumps. I am longing for next year to see the result; the whole garden is quite different now and has really become a pretty one at last. Today I spent the morning paying bills with Domino in the town and in the afternoon we cut away all the horrid brambles on the hedge by the fir tree, it has opened us up a little but looks so much nicer now. There is a honeysuckle and wild rose, also several bushes of sloes on the top of the bank and so I hope they will grow now the brambles are finished with, and shut out the view of our garden from the curious eye. I am going to have a seat there and will be able to sit and look at all the roses – it will be so nice in the summer – and now I am to cut the whole hedge down so it can shoot out again.

Saturday 15 November

HMS *Ark Royal*, the 22,000-ton aircraft carrier and the most famous ship in the navy was sunk yesterday, after having been torpedoed the day before, in the Western Mediterranean. She was in tow after being hit. The casualties are light, believed to be only a few men who were hit in the explosion. The aircraft on board were flown off. The wireless has this moment announced that only one man lost his life when HMS *Ark Royal* was torpedoed. The crews discipline was magnificent and for this reason they were all saved safely …

Sunday 16 November

I wrote to Meg at last – have been meaning to write for a long time now but somehow I have not had the time before. Frankie rang up asking if she could come to

1 Extensive bomb damage in the area of Chapel Street after three high-explosive bombs exploded at 1 a.m. on 18 January 1941. The remains of the well-known local grocer, Wilson's, is on the right-hand side of the photograph.

2 Searching for survivors among the rubble in the aftermath of the air raid.

3 Damaged houses at the back of Market Street. 'Every house in Market Street ruined;' commented Esther Rowley in her diary.

4 The Parade in the late 1930s. On 1 March 1941, five bombs fell in the area, demolishing shops to the right of Woolworths. The owners of the drapery store (signed on the right of the photograph), Mr and Mrs Wills, survived but two people died in Milican's meat shop (on the extreme right) and two in the nearby Strand Gardens. Woolworths had closed for the night.

5 Bicton Place. On 12 February 1942 a bomb exploded in the area just after 8 a.m., killing five elderly women and injuring seven other people. Other bombs fell along the Beacon. Esther heard one of the attacking planes shot down.

6 Extensive damage to the south side of Exeter Cathedral from a direct hit in the 'Baedeker Blitz' of 4 May 1942. Esther reported that 'the cathedral had not got one window left' when she visited it later in the month.

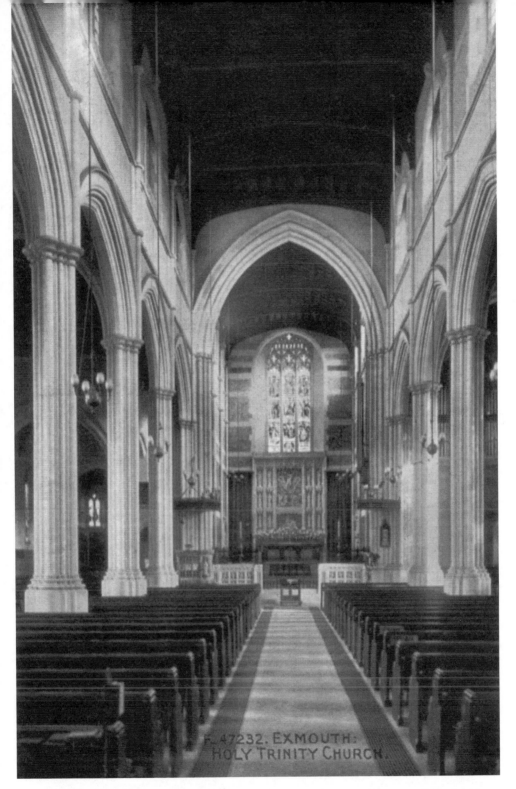

7 The nave of Exmouth's principal church, Holy Trinity, where on 2 May 1943, Esther heard the Archbishop of Canterbury, Dr Temple, preaching to a packed church. 'A man with a very tremendous faith,' she concluded. It was the first time the Archbishop had visited Exmouth. The church had been damaged the year before in a raid on 12 February 1942.

8 The Strand in the early 1930s. In the Exmouth blitz of 1943 eighteen people died when they left a bus standing on the right-hand side of the road, after hearing the siren and crossed to the shops on the left-hand side. From the jeweller's, Boyce (behind the second car in the centre of the postcard), a row of shops collapsed, when hit by a bomb, killing the bus passengers.

9 Exmouth harbour in 1954. Ten years earlier Esther had witnessed thirteen landing craft in the harbour, where they had been constructed prior to D Day, in June 1944.

1	2	3	4	5	6
Exmouth	50° 37′ N	15 m	250 m W	Nr. 36	**A 32**
	3° 25′ W				

Entfernungen:

Bill of Portland 68 km   Start Point 47 km   Cap de la Hague 143 km

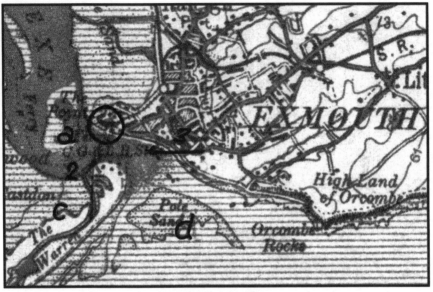

1:100.000

0   1   2   3km.

10 Target Exmouth. A pre-war aerial map of Exmouth issued to German air crew in 1943 with target areas and other features overprinted (in red on the original). The area circled is the docks and the number 3 to the right of this is over the Strand area, confirming that Exmouth was not randomly bombed by 'tip and run' raiders en route to another larger place, but was regarded as a strategic bombing target.

The Focke Wulf 190 German fighter bomber, used in the air raid of 1943, was one of a number of enemy attack aircraft which could be adapted for aerial reconnaissance photography.

A translation of the German instructions for the pilots:

Exmouth lies at the east side of the River Exe estuary, which stretches 8km from inwards, leading to a 2km wide bay with mud flats.
For the town are indicated:
a) The small dock harbour at the west point is marked.
b) The 40 metre high wedge shape, red soil prominent landmark of Straight Point.
c) The Warren, a 2km long spit of land on the west bank of the Exmouth estuary.
d) The dry sandbank, Pole Sand, lies in front of the river mouth estuary.

11 The new German strike aircraft the Focke Wulf 190, which attacked Exmouth in February 1943 – a fighter bomber which was armed with two machine guns and four cannon. It carried a 550lb bomb.

12 The RAF Hawker Typhoon, the successor to the Battle of Britain Hurricane, which had four cannon or twelve machine guns. Superior to the FW 190s in both speed and armament, it shot many of them down, including two of the eight which bombed Exmouth on 26 February 1943.

lunch, however the weather got so bad and it rained so hard that she rang up later to say that she could not come after all. We had a bit of a chat though on the phone. She is thrilled to bits because she has had a wonderful chance of a new job. It is all dead secret for the present but if it comes off it will be marvellous. I must say, I am quite glad I am not in my old company now, all my friends have left and the new promotions are awful, but I wish I had been able to transfer myself to another company instead of being discharged. How I miss my beloved khaki but I still love my home if only it was peace time, and not a time like this, when every soul in England ought to be in the services doing some work for the country. I have a feeling from reading the papers, listening to the politicians broadcasting, and seeing what is going on now that next spring will see our army in the thick of the fight. The war is obviously working up for a climax for us too but not for a little while longer, but then Heaven only knows what will come, but it will be big when it comes …

Thursday 20 November

We both walked up to the club to the lecture; it was very interesting and amusing. The man who gave it was once a Political Secretary in India and made all the arrangements for King George V's and Queen Mary's safe arrival and departure in India when they went to the Durbar in 1911. It gave away the private undercurrent going on among all the men in the government and therefore was quite different to anything one usually reads in papers or books.

Sunday 23 November

We caught up Mrs Marshall and took her to church with us. Mr Marshall joined her presently and we took them both home after the service. Mr Marshall has lost a stone and looks like a walking skeleton. He has never looked himself since Rupert was killed. They are now fearfully worried by Jim being in this tremendous tank battle in Libya. I do hope he will be alright … Colonel Cowel came to tea and witnessed Maimie's signature in her will as did Mrs Marshall who kindly came in to do it …

I was interested to hear yesterday that the woman spy caught in one of the hotels on the Beacon was shot without a trial. She was a German wife of an English soldier and was the third spy shot in the county of Devon since the outbreak of war …

The siren went in the middle of supper. I heard the heavy old Jerry overhead long before the warning was given; they dropped bombs near enough to shake the windows but I do not know the exact spot, some say Teignmouth … Had an interesting talk with Colonel Cowel about the economic situation and he knew all the exciting things that Captain von Muller did in the Einden in the last war. He said he was a gentleman all through, I was glad to hear it as my family are related to him!

Thursday 27 November

I took a day off from my work at sweeping up leaves to drive Miss Thomas to Exeter to her meeting, while I took the opportunity of doing some shopping. I got a nice 'heatproof' pie dish and little round dish and a beautiful pair of shears for cutting the grass (as I broke our old pair recently when I was cutting down the brambles in the hedge). As I was walking up High Street I met Mrs Rait, who has left the ATS and got a man's job in some office and, further up, Mrs Ratcliffe who is very het up because her two maids have been called up and she cannot live in that big house all alone, so, hating the idea, she says she is afraid she will have to live with her daughter and have the house confiscated, poor thing. These are very worrying days for old ladies living by themselves. It must be very hard to leave one's home indefinitely but many are having to do so now.

In the afternoon Domino and I biked down to Louisa Terrace to wash and polish the little car, she was dirty but her engine going very well this morning.

They are taking quite a bit of garden off the thatched house on the corner in Exton, I suppose with the idea of widening the road for the army lorries rushing up and down.

Friday 28 November

A new bill is to be passed by Parliament making every man and woman liable for military service. This is the first time in history that conscription has been applied to women in Britain. There will be a new comb-out of reserved occupations …

Sunday 30 November

Mrs Carroll brought Maimie some khaki wool for knitting for Indian troops' comforts. Maimie rang up Lexy to ask after Reggie, who seems to be really ill. Poor Lexy is very anxious about him and is afraid he is having a nervous breakdown. It does seem a pity. Mrs Everett rang up. She said Pat had a fearfully septic throat and is looking pale and ill.

I spent the whole day doing my stamp collection …

Saturday 6 December

Last Tuesday a German bomber flew over Exmouth after supper in our hearing, and afterwards made a perfect landing at the airport thinking it was in France. It was very foggy …

Monday 8 December

America and Great Britain are at war with Japan. Now the whole world is at war, East and West, white, black, brown and yellow. This will lengthen the war considerably by several years. Mr Churchill spoke to us tonight. He said we were ready for them out East but we must work much harder here and it would be a very long war. So here we are!

The dirty Japanese have already been busy bombing Islands in the Pacific, they are now trying a landing in Malaya but we are meeting them there. They killed 2,000 service men of America in these bombing attacks last night <u>before</u> they had officially declared war. General mobilisation was ordered in Hong Kong yesterday. The whole of Honolulu was awakened by the roar of anti-aircraft guns and the crash of bombs on Sunday when the Japanese made an attack on Oahu Island.

Thursday 11 December

Today Maimie and I went to a lecture by Major Reilly, the subject was Russia and very interesting it was too. He had been out there quite a bit and I only wished he could have talked much longer. I must admit that I now feel quite sure that, had it not been for the Lenin regime, the Nazi hordes would by now have annihilated the Russian Army.

All boys between fourteen and seventeen are to join the Home Guard. All reserved occupations are to be called up except those with key jobs already employed in the war effort.

Friday 12 December

Conscription in full swing in America, all men from the age of nineteen to forty-five are to be called up for military service and all men between the ages of eighteen and sixty-five are to register …

Thursday 18 December

Today Maimie and I went to see Scottie, who gave us a delicious tea, then Miss Glanville and Miss Symms, after them Captain Holman. Scottie was charming and full of talk, she seemed quite happy and looked better than I had expected after her dreadful illness in the summer. Her brother is doing very well in the army of course. Topsham the same as usual: not at all attractive to look at, I do not like the place in the least except the beautiful view across the river.

Thursday 25 December

Hong Kong has fallen to the Japanese – what terrible news for Christmas Day.

It was impossible for the RAF to support them and the Japanese were landing in increasing numbers: the water supply was cut off, so they were ordered to cease fire … HM the King spoke to all his people this afternoon. He was splendid. He told us that we must be neighbourly to one another, trust in God and fight on until we win. He spoke too of the heroism being shown by the men in his forces. It was a speech to remember – earnest and fine. It is fortunate that we have in our

King a man with such ideals and high sense of honour. It is always a pleasure to listen to him ...

Maimie and I had tea with Mrs Dalrymple, Mrs Everett and General and Mrs Nicholson, it was great fun, we were all in good form. I was well topped up with my own brew of sloe gin, so the world was rosy!

Saturday 27 December

I drove Maimie, Mrs Dalrymple and Mrs Everett to a meet at Woodbury Castle, the hounds looked very thin and there were only a dozen couples, not like the old pack. It was a lovely morning, although very cold, delightful to smell horses and see a pack of hounds once more. A number of the people there were evacuees ...

1942

Maimie's Crisis, Exeter Blitz, Singapore Death

Sunday 4 January

Yesterday Frankie and Baby Davidson came to tea; they were very gay and made me laugh a lot. The Company Commander is away with an appendicitis, so the orderly room is quiet! My old company is going strong it seems, growing every day. I miss my adored khaki.

Today Domino and I took ourselves for a grand walk along Bony Lane and across the fields to the cliffs along Sandy Bay. We just got home before it began raining, although the turf was wet, it was sunny.

Monday 5 January

Had a letter from Jill this morning, she has got her commission in the ATS and is on a course at Aldershot. She told me some exciting news, her baby brother Miles has won the MC in Libya, he got it at his ack-ack.

Margaret Fletcher rang up this morning and told me that Bernard has won the DSO in Abyssinia. This is grand news too. Two friends in one day, what a good day for me! Bernard won an MC in the Great War.

Maimie was so thrilled by hearing about Bernard that we decided to run over to see his mother in Dawlish and tell her how very thrilled we are. After lunch we started off, Clara went well all the way. Poor old Mr Fletcher is very unwell, he seems to be completely collapsed – brain and body – poor dear old man, it is very sad to see him now, especially when I can remember him when he was strong and full of life. After tea we went across to Rawdon and Margaret's house where we tried out several drinks. Rawdon's sloe gin was particularly delicious; he only made it the other day. By the way, he was looking very well and is hoping to get a ship soon after he has seen his medical board. He does not want a shore job so I hope will go to sea, but it will be trying for poor Margaret; he has already been through so many dangers at sea. They are both coming for a night or two next Thursday. It will be fun to have them. I am thinking of the menu, it will be nice to have someone to cook for and I shall make some dishes on Wednesday ready.

Tuesday 6 January

I met Mrs McCrea today, she told me all about Kenneth. He was captured by the Italians in Libya, but after a fortnight he escaped! Well done Ken! We saw in the paper that Mr Falkner, headmaster of St Peter's Boys School (prep) has died. I thought he looked very unwell when he read the lessons in church on the Sunday before Christmas but had no idea the poor man was ill. Peter is in Libya fighting.

Wednesday 7 January

Maimie, having a slight cold, stayed in bed all day after some persuasion from me, I think that it is much the best remedy to take care of it at the beginning before it develops. She does not want to be really bad when Rawdon and Margaret are with us and they are coming tomorrow, so a day's real rest will do Maimie a lot of good. I filled in my day by cooking various dishes in readiness, so I shall not have to spend half my time in the kitchen when I should be amusing my guests. I got a whole lot of bones boiled down for soup and put a lot of fresh artichokes through a sieve and into the stock. I also made a vegetable pie, a blackberry tart, two sweets, half a dozen rabbit pates and a casserole of liver and thick gravy and some cheese straws. I put some cooked salsify through a masher, then mixed it with rich white sauce and served it up with the liver on toast, rather delicious like this. I only wish that I had more experience in cooking and could make all sorts of dainties, but I am just playing with cooking at present but I think am beginning to learn a little about the science of it now.

Poor Domino hated his granny being in bed; it is funny how animals always loathe to have a member of the family upstairs. They so dislike the routine being upset in any little way, it does not matter if visitors come to stay, but if the family go away or are ill dogs are so annoyed and disgruntled.

Thursday 8 January

Rawdon and Margaret came for two nights. They were in fairly good form but rather washed out by the Dawlish atmospheric conditions. It is quite time they had a change away, if even for a day or two. M. looks very tired and worried; Mrs F. has evidently been wearing her down as is the custom with relatives!

After laying for a bit by the warm fire, we decided to exercise our limbs by a stiff little walk along the cliffs as the sun was lovely, though the air bitterly cold. Mrs Cardwell came in to see Maimie on her way back from Mr Falkner's funeral. She is heartbroken about Howard, who is missing in the Fleet Air Arm. It is terrible for her, especially the suspense of uncertainty. When we arrived back from our stroll, Mrs Cardwell had gone home unable to wait any longer for her tea; we <u>were</u> horrified at going out! However, Mrs Everett came to tea instead and Margaret likes her so very much, so we had some fun talking and so on. Margaret remembered seeing her before once upon a time in the dim ages! Margaret was smartly dressed as usual in a very nice coat and skirt. She has a beautiful figure and shows off a suit to its best advantage.

I do like a good figure above all else; it is so becoming for clothes and a poor one does not show them off a bit: of course M. always has expensive and beautifully cut suits made of the best tweeds. Very nice!

Friday 9 January

We three walked round to the Beacon before lunch and consumed several heavenly pink gins, much to my joy on a cold winter's morn! They ran down the frozen throat like nectar to change the inside into a glowing ember, much better! After lunch we sat round sleeping, talking and generally lazing until it was time for tea – wasn't it awful to do nothing! I must admit, it was glorious to be inert after going to bed at 1 in the morning! Rawdon and Margaret went out before supper to find the RC Church. They found it, but it was locked, however R. felt better for knowing the position of the 'Hot bed of Papistry' as he called it! He is still a bit nervy about his religion, but he always has been. They took Domino with them; he loves his new uncle and goes with him everywhere. Dear Dommie, he does so love a lovely walk with any friend who cares to be kind enough to take him out for a run, as long as he does not leave his mother for too long! After supper Margaret told Maimie's hand, her character and so on. Unfortunately, I slept through it, otherwise I should have been interested to hear what she said; I think lines in the palm of the hand do show a general outline of the character very often. I know Margaret is very good on the subject; she has told my character before now and been quite good at hitting the nail on the head with accuracy.

Again, we crawled upstairs after midnight!

Saturday 10 January

Had a quick pink gin at the Beacon before lunch. Rawdon and Margaret went off on their bikes in the afternoon to catch the ferry back to the train at Starcross but they thought they might bike all the way back to Dawlish. We are hoping they will come again on Wednesday for the weekend, but one never quite knows what they will do until they have done it!

Domino went off with Rawdon on his bike and was quite happy, he rather loves his new uncle and follows him quite happily anywhere, but he was very pleased when I joined the party in the Royal Beacon this morning, full of tail wags and licks.

Bitterly cold today, we are obviously in for a cold spell of winter frosts – sure to get it at this time of year but I must admit that I feel the cold less than ever before, it must be all the early morning rushing about and the cooking, I have no time really to be cold this winter. Maimie is in a continual state of perished ice all over, it really is trying for her, all the old people here are feeling it now, it is a pity in a way to live on the south coast because one grows into a hothouse plant and withers in the cold frosty east winds. In the spring, summer and autumn it is so lovely and the sun never really loses a warmth and brilliance quite unlike northern counties.

Sunday 11 January

As Maimie still has a bit if a cold and the morning being a particularly cold one owing to a severe frost, we did not venture to church; it is a bit cold there nowadays as the coal shortage means smaller stoves, so less heating. However, I was not sorry in a way, as I woke up very late and had a lot to do tidying up. In the afternoon I took Domino for a walk along the Littleham lanes where we ran into Dolly and her spaniel Shandy, so we joined forces. We are going to repeat the walk on Sunday week.

Monday 12 January

A bitterly cold day so Domino and I decided to take the car down the town to do the shopping, to prevent the car freezing up. She went well and on our return I dressed her up in five rugs, we stuck up all likely cracks in the garage which might let in the cold winds and frost. By late afternoon the air seemed much warmer and the wind changed; I'm now wondering if it is working up for snow.

I'm busy thinking out a menu for the week and I am getting on well with my ideas. Got some curry powder today from Mr Perriam, must think out how to use it, there are so many different ways in peacetime but now meat stuffs are very difficult.

Sunday 1 February

Yesterday the two loads of manure arrived from Farmer Kemp. The carter was such a dear and the horse a beauty. Madge is using it all in the kitchen garden, but I do think I might steal a barrow full for the old roses in the three-cornered rose bed, they have had none for ages and I am sure they would be better for a bit.

Thursday 5 February

Bitterly cold again with showers of snow between sunshine, ice on all the water and a strong wind blowing but it was bearable in the car so we set off to Cheriton Fitzpaine stopping in Exeter on the way to buy some penny buns and a bag of oatmeal from Snow. We arrived at the exact moment and found Mr and Mrs Leach looking very well and quite cheerful, except for one frightful moment when a wire arrived in the middle of lunch, we all thought it was something dreadful about David but it was only from Joan, <u>what</u> a relief. Poor Mr and Mrs Leach, they <u>were</u> in a state. David is still at Singapore and is now a flight lieutenant and doing so well. He is only twenty-two.

It was fun seeing them both again. It was so peaceful all the way there, one could hardly imagine a war was raging, the country lanes so empty and so far from the noise and uproar of war, but a bomb dropped a few nights ago two miles from Cheriton Fitzpaine and shook the house, breaking one window in the church and thirty windows in a farm in the parish. Mrs L. saw the German bomber overhead a minute before. A very nice parson called to see Mr L. and stayed to tea he came from Exeter and was very interesting I thought. Tony, the cat, came in to lunch and tea. He is such a beautiful cat and as fine a hunter as ever, in spite of being so old now. I can remember him years ago when Mr Leach was rector of Rackenford, he was then a young cat and has been to Woolacombe and now Cheriton Fitzpaine.

Sunday 8 February

Joan rang up last evening to say she could not come until Monday evening as she has to see her doctor. She does not seem to be at all well. I do hope a little change will do her good but am afraid she will find it cold here, as our house is much bigger than hers and the weather at the moment is awful.

Maimie and I went to tea with Mrs Dalrymple and had a nice chat. She is very cheery and amusing.

Many villages in Yorkshire are completely buried in snow; it is deeper than for years. This is the fourth severe winter running in England. We do appear to be having much colder weather of late. They have had snow in London. I heard from Jill lately, she is awfully happy and doing so well, already had a good appointment given her, I am so glad she is so pleased with life as she only joined the ATS because I was in it, and she joined my company a month after war was declared. She is getting on famously as I always knew she would, she has the personality and the brains to carry her job through.

Mrs Dalrymple's dog is a darling, <u>so</u> good and has a wonderful little face. He is a miniature poodle.

Monday 9 February

I took the car down to meet Joan at the ferry. I had not seen her for years, in fact not since she was seventeen and now she is twenty-two, so I expected a bit of a change. However, I managed to recognise her but she is very different, got a thin long face now instead of a round one and she is a 'woman of the world' from the word go! Appears much older and more experienced than I am! She looks very smart in soft brownish corduroy trousers, yellow polo jumper, coat and socks, the effect very snappy. She is slim and trousers look nice on her. She is obviously terribly nervy and thinks of nothing but her health. She is engaged to a married man and expects him to divorce his wife; it seems to me that he will probably find it difficult to find her out to be the guilty party! Still, let us hope the man will be sent overseas, then Joan will find someone else no doubt! She really is a fool to get mixed up with married men, especially at her age, when there are so many unmarried men to be found in the large and populous world. No wonder her mother is horrified by the whole thing.

Tuesday 10 February

Joan and I sat up till morning talking over old times it was fun to chat about all the people I used to know in the olden days when I was young and full of beans. The result was that Joan slept until 12.45 today and I then forcibly woke her up for lunch, but she looks all the better for her long sleep, although she is pretending to think sleep a bad thing! By the time we had finished our lunch it was too late to do anything, so we muddled in the house all the afternoon. She told me several things of interest – one thing about a huge man I can remember who has been caught and sent to jail (I hope shot). Anyway, he used to throw small time bombs into the holds of the fishing boats in Brixham harbour. He blew several of these boats up but when he was caught, he had mis-timed the bomb and it went off at the quayside and he was the only man who had been on the boat that day except for the crew. I thought it was interesting. The Brixham trawlers are not being used very much but they are fishing with the Belgian boats and these are the ones to have suffered. Can you beat it! He is an Englishman Joan says. I wonder how many people are lurking round the country.

It seems that they are getting fairly particular in Torquay; I only hope they are, that's all. I wish they would lock up all filthy foreigners; some are alright, but the tenth man or woman out of ten may be a spy and so in my opinion they ought to be all under lock and key. There have been several spies found out round Torbay …

Wednesday 11 February

Domino and I went shopping in the town, we biked and paid several bills before rushing back to get the lunch. He is a wonderful dog and the shops simply love him; they all welcome him whenever we go down. I find the shops are awfully pleasant to me here – they know me now. When I came home after my two years service in the ATS none of them knew me but now they are all smiling when I go in. What a queer life it is.

83,000-ton *Normandie* is on fire in New York harbour. The Americans captured her recently and are turning her into a troop ship.

Thursday 12 February

At about eight o'clock when I was dusting the kitchen I suddenly heard bombs dropping and the air-raid siren screamed out. I went out in the garden to listen, the A-A guns at the airport were in action and I heard a heavy thud followed by a queer sort of crackling sound, one of the three attacking Dorniers was down anyway. Cheers!

Then the bombs were much nearer. In the town. Then one terrific crash. I ran in to call up to tell Joan and Maimie to come downstairs at once. Exmouth was having another blitz! A lot of machine-gun fire began along the seafront. Then silence.

After breakfast Madge came in to see if I was alright and when Mrs Hunt came she told me some of the damage. They dropped ten bombs along the Beacon, some unexploded, about half a dozen people found dead so far and many injured. The hotels along the Beacon ruined, some of them had direct hits. The German bombers were trying to get the Royal Marines doing their invasion practise in barges in the docks. Fortunately the men had not arrived at the time …

Sunday 15 February

Singapore has fallen! Damnation! The Prime Minister spoke on the BBC tonight and broke the news to the Empire. When the decision to surrender was reached on Sunday, the water supply for the 100,000 people had been badly damaged by enemy action and it was impossible to carry on the defence any longer because of heavy losses from enemy action; and the shortage of water, petrol, food and ammunition. Our men put up a magnificent fight, but the odds against them were too great.

Monday 16 February

The RAF were evacuated from Singapore a few days before the town fell – they arrived at Batavia (I hope dear David is among them safe). Tim's cousin, Ian Stuart, Colonel of the Argyle and Sutherland Highlanders, was sent to Batavia with a few other officers, I rather fancy he must have been wounded, as only the <u>wounded</u> soldiers were evacuated from Singapore.

Thursday 19 February

I received an infuriated letter from Meg this morning which I answered, one from Esme inquiring about the Exmouth bombing and one from cousin Tom, who has definitely decided not to come to a hotel here after all.

Dear old Madge says the news is very bad and England has never been so low before. He loves England and is looking quite an old man, thinking about it. He told me that we brought down two German bombers the day they raided us here and only the bomber which released its cargo on us got away.

It is freezing hard, has been for days now. The ground is hard on the top but Madge did a lot of gardening today in spite of it. He dug in the manure on the long new bed for potatoes, he heaped up the manure ready for digging in on the right side of the KG and dug and limed the new onion bed to be.

He told me that Ming had spent the afternoon trying to catch the wagtails and sparrows as they hopped about on the newly dug soil, but he was too slow! Rusty stayed indoors; he likes the fire this weather, the lazy little kitten.

Saturday 21 February

I had a hot chocolate with Mrs Carroll and Joan. It was the first time I had seen Joan since the war. She had not altered one bit and is very happy at Tidworth in the ATS. She loves the life and says it is a wonderful life and she would not be out of it for anything. Lady Evelyn Anstey joined us for a chat. She is a cheery soul, full of beans. It was such fun seeing them all, especially Joan, after so long.

After lunch I went up to see Miss Dickson; she rang me up to ask me if I could drive her out in her car sometimes. It is a beautiful car, a deluxe grey Wolsey, and she only bought it in July 1939.

Friday 27 February

After breakfast I took Miss Dickson to Exeter. We first called for Mrs Dudley (who has lost most of her income in Malaya) and arrived in the city in good time for a morning's shopping. The beautiful car went like a bird and looked lovely as well as behaving perfectly. It was a wonderful winter morning; a white frost and clear blue sky with no wind. This is the first white frost for some time as we have had a long spell of black ones. Everything outside has been frozen for weeks now, the ground getting hard, but in spite of this, Madge dug up a big piece of kitchen garden yesterday for the frost to get into nicely and so kill all insects.

After breakfast I fed the wild birds every day with a few bits and some nuts and fresh water; they flocked to eat it almost before I had finished scattering it. We have a lot of blackbirds this year, some thrushes, heaps of starlings, sparrows and blue tits with a good smattering of chaffinches, bullfinches, greenfinches and goldfinches and some wee tiny wrens. Of course the plovers run about on the lawn all day but are too shy to feed at the table on the terrace. Robins are rather scarce. I've only seen one or two flying about.

In Salop they have 6ft of snow now, not yet melted or cleared from the roads. It has certainly been a very hard winter all over Europe. Russia is having the severest winter for 100 years, so no wonder we are frozen up here in the south of England.

Saturday 28 February

I am so tired of war and ugliness, so am redoing the spare room; have made up valences for the two single beds out of our old drawing room chintz, which has red roses exactly toning with the red curtains. Also am not cutting up one chair cover, so we can put the chair, complete with its old cover, when washed, into the room to match the valances. It will really look very pretty I think. I'm still wondering if I will buy some new material for the little single room over the kitchen. I must, some day, embroider a whole lot more cushion covers, but that can wait of course as there is no hurry for them, but I want some nice cushions on the oak bench in the hall, it would brighten things up a lot out there.

They are quite seriously talking of probable German invasion of this country in the near future, so one cannot help wondering if it is wise to spend anything extra on the house at the moment; of course if I wait much longer it will be impossible to get any material.

Wednesday 4 March

The first three weeks of February this year were the coldest since 1895. Temperatures were ten or eleven degrees below the average for the month. Canals, ponds and even rivers were frozen over for weeks in some districts.

Thursday 5 March

Sir James Grigg, the new Minister of War, has ordered a purge of inefficient and over-age army officers at home and abroad. A report has been called for on all officers up to the rank of lieutenant colonel who are forty-five years old and over. Sir James Grigg was born here in Exmouth in 1891. His grandfather lived at 4 Bicton Place. Sir James was educated at a council school, winning scholarships, eventually getting into St John's College, Cambridge.

Tuesday 10 March

It was too wet to take Miss Dickson down to the town to do her shopping so I took the opportunity of polishing as much of the brass as I could get done in two hours. Maimie spent the day putting a border round the spare room quilts to match the valances; it does really look sweet now it is finished and the chair in the window matching. Yesterday we bought a couple of bedspreads on our way for a drive round to warm up the car, which has not been out for ages now. Maimie fell down again the other day and sprained her ankle, which is still swollen and painful. She so often falls now a days, it is a really serious thing for her.

Madge spent the day cutting up the dead eucalyptus tree, which he and another man cut down last week. It came down easily although the trunk was big, in spite of the tree being dead since the first year of the war, the wood is still harder than the live oak tree. Madge says it will be lovely fire wood for next winter; it burns well and smells delicious.

I finished embroidering Meg's cushion cover today and have just ironed it ready for making up. Then the bother will be how to send it to Belfast?!

Domino was sick and kept me awake for three hours last night, so I have definitely decided to make him sleep elsewhere in future. I cannot stand anyone in my room at night. It always thoroughly disturbs me and gets me mad with temper and sleeplessness …

Sunday 15 March

We did not go to church today but I took Maimie, Domino and Sammy to see the white poodle which is staying at the farm with Mr Norrington. He is a wonderful-looking dog, snow white with the longest and thickest coat I have ever seen. Domino did not altogether like him, but I think he was a little jealous! I hope I shall be able to have him.

We went to tea with Mrs Everett to see Constance Everett, who has come down to stay owing to Mrs Dalrymple being so ill. She has pneumonia and is bad, being so delicate before. Her sister is worried to death about her. I took Sammy with me and she rather liked him I think, but she thought he was too much for Mrs Dalrymple to look after.

We had not been home long when an awfully nice couple came in to ask me if I would take the white poodle. They say his owner is ill but does not know how ill she is and she hopes to be able to have the poodle, 'John', back again. Her brother, however, says he does not expect her to be well enough ever and will I take him for nothing. He is a thoroughbred and Mr Norrington told me worth quite fifteen guineas. I am really very thrilled by the whole thing …

Saturday 21 March

The annoyance of the day was that the beautiful John arrived, looking like a lovely white woolly rug with a good-tempered grin in his face and his tail wagging all the time, but Domino lost his temper and barked furiously and became so formidable that we all decided that John would have to go back again. I was very disappointed and annoyed with Dommie he was so stupid and rude and beastly, while John was so sweet and good tempered. However, he seems to be very fond of Mr Aberington so will be quite alright with him, but I am sad that he cannot come to me. By the way, John is a beautiful specimen of a large white poodle, just the dog I have been looking for, so much so that I have often tried to get one, but they are scarce. I wrote to the PDSA and even they had not got a puppy white poodle. It is sickening to have to give up a real gift like this merely because of Domino's nasty temper, he is always so sweet to all dogs he meets and now he suddenly turns on a lovely sweet dog for no reason at all. Never mind. I will have a white poodle yet but somehow John is such a darling dog. I suppose Domino will only put up with a pup. He adores Sammy and they are the greatest friends but John is the same age as Dommie; he is about three years old and should get on so well you would think.

Sunday 22 March

We went to St Saviour's Church this morning, a tiny little church in the middle of the bombed area of Exmouth town. Mr Heal preached a very interesting sermon as usual. We gave Lady Lewis and Mrs Everett a lift back. Mrs Dalrymple is better and now living on champagne at £1 18s 6d!? a bottle. I hope she will not want Sammy back yet; he is such a darling pup and gets on so wonderfully well with Domino, who has taken him in completely. In the afternoon I met Dolly and Shandy for a walk, we chose the cliffs as the weather was perfect for the sea.

The sea was absolutely glorious, as blue as the sky above it, with great white foaming surf roaring up on the beach. However, at the bottom, where in normal times there is a wooden ladder, the way was barred by barbed wire. The dogs did not care about wire; before we could stop them they had scrambled through and jumped down onto the beach but they could not get up again so they jumped, barked and howled up at us! Well, there was nothing else to do but for Dolly and me to get through the barbed wire entanglement and join the dogs on the beach. We got through safely except for mud, got down to the dogs who were overjoyed. They all went mad and ran round on the sand in circles. Half way along the beach we passed a smashed aeroplane, but I could not make out if it was British or German …

Monday 23 March

Mr and Mrs Leach came to lunch, arriving very punctually for them! Poor dears had an awful job to find the house; they had forgotten where it was. It was his birthday and he chose to spend it with us, which pleased Maimie and me so much. I gave him a birthday kiss, and to his joy and Combo's amusement, I left his cheek well plastered with lipstick! They both seemed to enjoy their lunch, the meat was poor but they liked the salsify very much, then they loved the queens pudding and cheese straws, so I was quite satisfied with my efforts in the kitchen. They had a cable from David on Saturday, he said he was well but of course they have no idea where he is. Isn't it grand to think that he is alright, evidently escaped from Singapore. I should love to know where he is. In a letter recently David said the state of affairs in Singapore was deplorable. The residents and garrison having no 'total war' ideas at all, simply fooling about amusing themselves (this is of course confidential to my diary).

Mr Leach is quite in love with Rusty and is going to have one of his tiny brothers when they are born. I am to choose the kitten and take it over myself. It was awful how their glorious Tony was drowned in a horrible well just behind the house on the grass bank. They had no idea that this well was there at all. Poor darling Tony, he was sixteen years old and the biggest cat I have ever seen, a huge long-haired tabby and such a perfect creature all round …

Tuesday 24 March

Today I gave the lawn its first mow, thanks to Rawdon, who so kindly mended the bottom blade for me. It worked beautifully and cut well though I had it set moderately high being the first cut of the year. A rather funny coincidence: Margaret wrote, the letter arriving while I was mowing, to say that Rawdon has got a new appointment at Scapa Flow and she is not allowed there so is staying at a Convent in London now, to be near Anne.

We have actually had no air-raid siren today which has made a perfect spring day even more spring like and peaceful. All the fruit trees are in large buds; the plums and pears are going to be a mass of blossom. I am going to sit some eggs soon, I hope, as I can manage this year to find them, and by next year I think foodstuffs will in all probability be practically impossible to get.

The siren has now gone!!

I am longing to prick over all the flower beds and hoe all the paths, the lawn edges want cutting too and then the garden will be lovely, it is full of bulbs, Maimie picked a bunch of daffodils today, they look lovely. Yes, winter has gone away again and the summer is ahead, they say it will be a hot one owing to the unusually cold winter. It was snowing up the country a fortnight ago and in Salop it was piled up several feet on the road sides to let traffic pass up and down …

Wednesday 25 March

Another glorious day, cloudless from sunrise to sunset, the wind coldish but very little of it. I hoovered the upstairs thoroughly and soon after eleven o'clock got into my beloved garden where I hoed the terrace and raked all the gravel along to the rockery. After lunch I began digging the new rose bank, the roses are looking grand after my rather early pruning, a mass of healthy shoots and beginning to grow already. After tea Domino and Sammy played all over the lawn, they ran after each other round and round the silver fir on the lawn by the tennis court. Sammy got round the circle being small but Domino could not keep the circle and kept on running wide giving tongue all the while. Eventually he got hold of Sammy and rolled him over and over onto the tennis court, they were a funny little pair of dogs!

Rusty caught a mouse in the wood pile after tea; he came prancing along the terrace with it in his mouth to show me. It is the first I have <u>known</u> him to have killed, as Ming was lying in a sunny corner in the conservatory. It was so hot so we had tea in the conservatory, just like old summer days – such a joy to see the sun brilliant once more. Miss Thornhill called to see us. She did not look at all well and is grieved at having to put her car up when they stop our petrol allowance next June. I must admit the outlook is pretty grim for old people who cannot walk to bus stops or stations …

Thursday 26 March

I drove the two Misses Thomas to Exeter in the morning. We also took their brother, Dr Thomas, who tried to buy a chicken for his son, who is coming home for the weekend, but he could not find a chicken or even an old hen in the city! I had better luck with my shopping but I only wanted cakes and found some lovely ones for myself and Miss Thomas at Palmer and Edwards. They still have a shop full of delicious confectionary. I must say that the local cake shops are extraordinarily rich in supply. Another cloudless day and the cathedral and ancient close looking superb in the brilliant sunshine, but a very cold wind has risen up today from the east.

After lunch Mrs Dalrymple's personal maid, Clark, came to see us and Domino's beloved little 'nephew' Sammy. He knew her in a minute and was delighted to see her. Clark was awfully pleased with Sammy and said she had never seen him look so well or pretty. His coat, she said, was in lovely condition and he was obviously so happy with us. Poor Mrs Dalrymple is getting much worse and is having a very serious relapse now. They are worried to death about her. The doctor cannot find out the cause of her temperature keeping up for such a long time.

Before tea I biked up to take Miss Dickson out to Woodbury for a picnic. On my way I took two bunches of violets up to Mrs Dalrymple and had a talk with the cook-housekeeper. We had our tea up under the firs on the Castle Hill, looking over the common and out to the Channel over the huge Royal Marine camp spreading for miles below us on the opposite hill …

Sunday 29 March

We went to church at St Andrew's this morning. The vicar took the service and preached a short and particularly magnificent sermon before the special prayers of intercession ordered for today by HM the King. The congregation was a big one, but the church is big enough for many people. Outside we chatted to Colonel and Mrs Clayton, Major Fines and Miss Swinton, all very pleasant. After the service I talked to the Carrolls and Miss Thomas. The vicar preached about the Lord's Prayer and every word he said could not have been more splendid. He certainly is a wonderful man for giving one inspiration, and I do not agree with Mrs Everett, who dislikes him so much. He must be a fine man to have the spiritual thoughts he expresses so fluently in his sermons.

During the afternoon, while I was gardening, who should walk in but little Frankie. It was nice to see her and looking so well and young. She had her hair done differently. She says she has come to life again now the sun has come again and feels like coming to see us often again like last year, but the cold winter has cramped her style considerably this winter. She had bronchitis several times, so usually stayed in Exeter weekends by the fire in her digs. She is rather like me; feels quite thrilled by the sunshine. I already feel ten years younger with the thought of summer coming and the awful winter over! Frankie loved my blue coat and skirt also the American hat I got to tone with it and a new pair of shoes.

Monday 30 March

St Lazaire, strategically important German-held port on the French coast, has been smashed, and the huge dry dock is blocked by the explosion with twisted remains of the gallant destroyer *Campbeltown* and the shattered dock gates. The most daring and in many ways the most important of combined operational attacks so far undertaken has met with splendid success, but the cost has not been light. Many of the commando troops who forced home the attack fought on until they were either casualties or taken prisoner, but they completed their task. Long after the main force had been withdrawn, units which were cut off – the Germans put their number at 100, fought on until they were overwhelmed. The attack took the Germans completely by surprise but Lieutenant Colonel A.C. Newman, who led the commandos, is missing.

Tuesday 31 March

Harry and Pat with Mrs Everett came to tea today. They were all very cheery and amusing. Harry and Pat looking very well and none the worse for their ice-bound winter in Salop (where they still have snow piled up by the roadside).

Thursday 2 April

I spent the whole day in the garden. In the morning, while the lunch was cooking in the oven, I dug the little flower bed behind the rose hedge by the apples which grow across the three-cornered plots. The white azalea is out, also masses of wanda primula and violets; it is perfectly sweet all along there. After lunch I hoed the path, took the tools across the lawn to the new big round border which is in front of the drawing-room window. I managed to get the bed finished before tea. All the mixed hyacinths planted all round last autumn are just coming into bloom, some lovely colours among them. After tea I, and the dogs, began digging the delphinium bed in the other part of the garden on the other lawn by the lily pond. I am longing to get on with all the flower borders, they all want digging over badly now but most of them are not weedy, only cracked and hard on the surface. The daffodils are beginning to be glorious now all over the garden, they seem to be springing up in every corner and under all the trees, even among the vegetables in the kitchen garden. Madge is digging like mad now and planting a big onion bed, it is planted with 100 young onions and the rest seeds. Four long rows of broad beans are coming up. One long row of peas, also one of sweet peas, the whole bit along the privet hedge is planted with early potatoes and some are already coming up.

Friday 3 April

Maimie and I fetched Miss Dickson and went to the first part of the Three Hour service at St Andrew's, the vicar of Sidmouth took the service. We got home by 1.30 and had a substantial cheese luncheon after which the dogs and I went out gardening. The cats stayed in the house today, I think they thought it was going to rain! Maimie 'listened in' to *The Dream of Gerontius* all the afternoon, while I dug the delphinium bed – it was needing it very badly, the soil hard and caked and full of weeds, but now it looks lovely, the clumps of blue hyacinths all out and the delphiniums at the back shooting up nearly a foot, so my digging has greatly improved the border. When that was finished I pricked over all the four iris beds round the lily pond; they also wanted a spring clean very badly. After tea the rain came on hard for the evening so I had to postpone cutting the grass round the edges of all these beds, but when that is done the garden will really be rather beautiful and so thrilling …

Sunday 5 April

We went to church in the morning and sat between Lady Lewis and Major Fines in the front seat where Maimie could hear well. We chose St Saviours, where they had Matins and Mr Heal preached a beautiful sermon, the subject being that there is no death for people who believe in God which was proved to us when Christ left the sepulchre on Easter Day. He also explained something a few Sundays ago which interested me very much. He said the prayer where we say we pass through the shadow of death (it's in one of the Lessons) points out that the thing we call death is only a shadow we pass through and out into another life on the other side. I thought this a wonderful explanation of words which I have often pondered over. Mrs Dalrymple is still very ill and they all think it is really serious.

After lunch I dried the car and made her beautiful, then the sun came out so the dogs and I decided on some gardening, so we got up the grass verge by the camellias, and filled in two places with it where I had dug up and moved two shrubs in the autumn. I then put a stone edging along under the camellias and planted a row of seedling candytuft. Then moved a gorse bush to the bank opposite the apples and after tea planted out all my chrysanthemum cuttings under the west wall under the two plums. Tomorrow I must weed the borders on either side of the entrance drive ...

Thursday 9 April

Poor Ming's leg so bad this morning. I rang up his charming vet, who arrived almost at once. He says that the leg is in a very bad state, the bone being dead and it may have to be scraped, poor little cat. He was so angry at being done and fought like a mad thing while the leg was dressed.

In the afternoon I took Sammy to tea with Mrs Carroll, who loved him. Both the other guests liked him too.

Mr James, one of the curates, was one of the other guests and a Wren stationed here, a very nice girl who I hope to get some tennis with later on if she is still here, but they move from one port to another all the time.

Poor Domino was so annoyed about being left behind that he had a fight with the fox terrier Jim (from up the lane) and behaved very stupidly altogether, poor thing. He does so hate being left alone and not being in the limelight himself. It pretty well rained all day so I got no gardening done today, except I did tie up my pillar roses to the posts that Madge put in last Tuesday. All the roses are so far doing very well and shooting well, much better already in this new position.

Saturday 11 April

Bammy paid us a surprise visit; he is having five days leave between two courses. He is now a sergeant and if he passes his next exam he will be a staff-sergeant, so he is coming up and well he deserves to. I am so glad. When he was last on leave he was hoping to get two stripes! I always thought he would get three as he knows his job so thoroughly. He is to be an instructor, as far as he knows, unless he goes overseas. Bammy is very grim about the war and has aged a lot, he is so serious and rather sad looking now.

Sunday 12 April

A very nice day; a warm wind but sunny. The dogs and I decided to garden, so after making our first rhubarb suet pudding and putting it on to cook we went out in the garden and nearly finished pricking over the big herbaceous bed up the drive by the lawn and pond. After lunch we got it done and mowed the lawn and cut the edges so it really looks lovely now with the masses of daffodils and hyacinths. The anemonies in the iris beds are a blaze of colour also my ever glorious pasque flower by the edge of the lily pond. The dogs and cats loved the day in the garden, they played together all the time, running after one another round and round the beds, when they ran too fast to get round them, they jumped over. They brought me their ball to throw and found various funny toys on their own.

After tea Mrs Everett and Colonel Cowell came in for a chat. They were full of talk and were very interesting. Poor Mrs Everett is having an awful time with her cross old maid who hates her cat.

Tuesday 14 April

Sir Kingsley Wood, Chancellor of the Exchequer, in his Budget has doubled purchase tax. Income Tax remains at 10s in the pound. 2d a pint more on beer. Whisky is 22s 2d per bottle. Empire wines are 2s more a bottle. Cigarettes and tobacco gone up a lot. Damn! Tax is doubled on entertainments.

Wednesday 15 April

I spent the entire day in the most attractive and inviting garden. Began by mowing the lawn by the shrubbery; that took me an hour to do. I then forked up all the ground round the shrubs and trees, cutting round each one as I dug it, this took me till tea time with an interval for lunch. It really looks quite lovely. There is going to be masses of blossom when they come out. Uncle Richard's cherry is blooming. Unfortunately my glorious red rhododendron is not too good as it got so smashed when the dead tree was felled some time ago, but I hope in another two years it will improve.

The daffodils and narcissus are flowering better than I have ever seen them. The whole place is a blaze of golden beauty, the hyacinths are heavenly also, the pale blue ones especially lovely in the new big round bed by the drawing room window.

Friday 17 April

Just got back from taking Miss Dickson out shopping and was sitting with Maimie eating our rather meagre lunch when, Crash! Bang!, a plane tore over the house and was gone. No siren. No guns. No fighters. How I should like to see some retaliation from our side, I must say. This time they got St Andrew's Church and the back of Morton Crescent. Certainly the hotels here are having a bad time. One of the hotels was recently converted into the RN Officers Mess. I should be glad to know how the information of any importance here gets across, but it does. There is no doubt about it now. In the winter when they bombed round the docks one night, it was the night when some mines happened to be waiting to be laid, and had arrived, were dumped on the quay for the night. Various things of this sort keep on occurring; it cannot be chance every time! There must be fifth column going on here under our very noses. Seven Nazi bombers came here and another several visited Budleigh, where they bombed the High Street and the church, only damaging the north aisle. Why can't we all have ack-ack guns all along the coast to give them something for their money? Yesterday, during supper, they bombed a train at Starcross and machine-gunned it. It made quite a row across the water. I do not know if it was a troop train or anything of any especial interest. They used to bomb the line when the troops were on the move for Libya in 1940.

Monday 20 April

After breakfast I went down to the post office to send off a box of my nursing uniform to Doreen. Domino came with me; he loved the run. While in the post office who should come up to me but Mrs Bogle, so charming and full of talk, she invited me to a coffee so we could talk. Margaret is a sergeant now in charge of one of the hostels. When she was up on a course at Lichfield the chief asked her why she was not an officer? I cannot imagine why Patience has not put her up for a commission months ago. It is a very great mistake on her part anyway. Mrs Bogle said that Dunny was still in the War Office but looking fearfully ill. Poor Mrs B. is so worried about him.

This morning I received an airgraph from Henry. I was delighted to hear from him. He says that he was posted for overseas but was taken ill by the heat, so had to remain behind. I am thankful, otherwise he would probably have been a prisoner at Singapore or something awful.

Mrs Everett came in after tea for a chat. She says Mrs Dalrymple is very bad, getting no better and they have not been able to find out the germ so there is not much hope now. On Saturday she had a blood transfusion. It certainly looks as if Sam will be my dog before long. I would love to have him as he is a darling and Domino loves him so much and would hate parting after so many weeks …

Wednesday 22 April

Our two minimaxes were fixed up, one in the hall and the other on the landing. Had a day of odd jobs – got a bed dug and planted with chives, planted some radish seed in one of the frames, potted up sixteen of my own seedling tomatoes and repotted all the ferns. Yesterday I planted four cakes of mushroom spawn in the tennis lawn and all the gladioli bulbs in groups by the bank near the beehive. Have nearly all the flower garden dug now, only a few odd places left. Then the hoe will carry on for the summer. Madge has finished planting the potatoes, onions, peas and beans, artichokes, some carrots and lettuce. The asparagus bed is looking nice, with a dozen new plants all staked and a load of manure on top. The new rhubarb bed is also looking nice. The plum on the wall by the kitchen is a wonderful sight and the gooseberries are coming into fruit. The only bad thing in the garden at the moment are the paths, they are very weedy round the back. I have hoed the terrace but the rest is looking awful!

The flowers all over the garden are too lovely for words, the daffodils a blaze, primroses a mass of soft creamy yellow, anemonies blowing, forsythia brilliant, both bush and wall variety, white and red camellia covered in blossom. Mauve, pink, purple and white aubretia brilliant, also polyanthus and forget-me-nots. Hyacinths over also violets …

Monday 27 April

German bombers made a terror 'reprisal' raid on Bath on Saturday night. The bombers flew over Exmouth, as they have done nearly every night this week! Working-class homes suffered the most. Residential areas, churches and buildings were also bombed.

Poor Exeter had a real blitz on Friday; they got Paris Street <u>very</u> badly, the Close, where one of Canon Langhornes's daughters and three maids were killed. St Thomas, Alphington. Porthouse laundry. <u>Many</u> casualties. Margaret, now a sergeant, with other ATS spent the night helping to put out incendiary bombs, while the Exmouth garrison was rushed to the city to help dig out the dead bodies under the debris.

Tuesday 28 April

Heard today from Mrs Leach that David is missing. Isn't it awful. Bloody. I always knew that he could never come back. All the nice ones are killed, always, and the rotten miseries are left behind to propagate the earth. Oh, how sick it makes me. The same happened in the last war and is happening fast in this. How many of my friends are gone. David has been missing since 5 April.

I was in the garden talking to Madge when who should walk in but Mona. She was lunching here, so came and had it with us while the Intelligence Officer she was driving had lunch at the mess down the road. Mona was prettier than ever and her khaki suits her so well, she looked very well and cheerful. She had seen Exeter on her way here and said it was a mess. She is stationed at HQ at the moment in Tavistock and says the people there are very catty and bad tempered. It was lovely seeing her again, I did enjoy it awfully. It is so seldom that we meet nowadays and I always seeing Mona, she is so nice. Her stepfather is now loathing the moor and wants to move out! He is better from his dreadful accident, I gather. Mona spent forty-eight hours with them last week and three bombs whistled over the house during one night, a Nazi making a quick getaway from the RAF…

Friday 1 May

Betty came in last night to see me and tell me she has passed out with a commission. I am so glad, after just on three years service she well deserves one. She is on leave for a bit and we are hoping to meet on Saturday which is the first day of the club day for tennis. I am looking forward to a game very much; it will be fun.

Maimie is ill again. She woke up at midnight feeling terribly sick and at 2.30 rang her bell for me, but of course I heard nothing until she had rung several times. I went in and found her very weak and feeble so I rang up Dr Murray, who was so nice and told me to give her two tablespoons of brandy. Being so hot, it would probably stop her sickness, or sick feeling I should say, as she was not really sick. She immediately lay down and went to sleep. In the morning she was very feeble and completely off her food. Domino and I biked down to the town to try and get some Horlicks, but there was none anywhere. Mr Derry, however, gave me a tin of Allenbury's Diet, the only tin he had! Maimie liked it. Dr Murray turned up during the morning. He gave me a reassuring account of her state. She is to be very quiet and do less – one day a week in bed – and she is alright, but has no resistance at all, so when she gets down, it is very difficult for her to pull up again. He told me also that her illness is mental upsetness as much as physical, she is not exactly temperamental but I know what he means.

Saturday 2 May

Maimie says she feels so very ill, I rang up for the doctor to come. He came after tea and told me she must have had a stroke in the past twenty-four hours. She cannot talk properly and is so indistinct that I cannot understand half she says. I went to get some pills from Derry and looked in on Mrs Everett on my way home. She was so kind. She agreed with me to send a wire to Meg and she also insisted on coming down to spend the night with me. It was sweet of her, especially as she hates sleeping out of her own bed. Towards night Maimie began talking complete nonsense. She was quite sensible up to a point and then went off into some quite peculiar thing. She has begun to look so funny, her expression so strange and far away. It is funny how awful things seem to happen so often in the spring. So lovely when the sun is shining but so cruel. I am wondering if I will write to Amamy, she is such a perfectly sweet person and said I was to let her know if Maimie was ill at any time. She is at present staying with friends and I think would be able to come, but she likes luxury and servants and of course we have none of that now, it is not comfortable enough I am afraid, so I am rather nervous of asking her to come down to stay. Then if Meg comes now, I do not know if she will be able to come later on in the summer.

Sunday 3 May

A terrible day for me; can never remember a more awful day. Maimie much worse and Dr Murray not at all pleased. He wired for Meg to come and while he was here Meg rang up from her home so I asked the kind doc to talk to her himself, which he did. She will be here on Tuesday about tea time and is in a fearful state I am afraid, it is so dreadful for her, poor Meg. The day dragged on and after tea Mrs Everett and Colonel Cowel came in and talked to me, it was so nice seeing them, especially after being alone so long. At 6.30 I took the car down to meet the nurse, Sister Hayward. She is a dear and I liked her immediately, such a blessing. Some of them are a bit alarming but she is not like that at all. She is already a real joy and I feel I can lie back and breathe, for a little anyway. Nurse is going to take care of her at night for the present: she washes her morning and evening and gives me full instructions what to do during the day, so much easier for me. I was given a large sleeping tablet and went off quite soon after retiring only to be woken up at about two in the morning by a blitz going on, guns roaring and German planes bombing over the roof top, so I got up and went in to see Maimie. She was half asleep but seemed to quite like holding my hand while the raid was bad. Poor Exeter again getting it I am afraid …

Monday 4 May

Maimie really seems a little better. Doctor Murray quite pleased when he came down from seeing her. God is answering my prayers after all – perhaps. We must not be too pleased but she does seem better, and not too quickly either. But I am so thankful. I cannot say how thankful. If it will only last. I was terrified yesterday and the change is wonderful.

I am debating as to the menu and feel I ought to do some cooking tomorrow. Today I am having a lazy day as I feel so tired. Dear Mrs Everett is coming in this evening to look me up; she is such a dear and so kind and thoughtful. She made me some lovely barley water for Maimie yesterday and took so much trouble over it. She went in to see Maimie and drew down her curtains and things to make the room cooler in the evening while I was fetching Nurse.

Today is another heavenly day, sunshine all the time and a cloudless sky. The flowers are all so beautiful. The tulips are in flower and the white clematis over the Bower is so pretty and fragrant now. I cannot think of anything nicer than our little garden at this time, with the trees just out in their fresh green and everything glorious. I heard the cuckoo yesterday, but only once. The big lawn is awfully long and badly wants cutting but I am afraid the motor mower would upset Maimie, she <u>must</u> be so dead quiet at present.

Tuesday 5 May

I love the sweet little nurse; she is so quiet and understanding. I am wonderfully lucky, they are not all half as sweet as she is, it is a pleasure to have her in the house and such a comforting person.

Meg arrived while we were having supper. She had a very good journey across and the train was well in time, so she got here quite early – sometimes the trains are so frightfully late nowadays. She is looking well and flourishing. I was so thankful to be able to give her good news of Maimie and so wished I could have let her know in the morning that Maimie is really better, still, in spite of waiting all day when the good news came she was overjoyed anyway.

I had a perfectly wonderful letter from darling old Uncle Snuffy and another from sweet old Aunt Margaret – they are both so nice. I wrote to Amamy, but she has not replied yet …

Monday 11 May

Last week the King and Queen visited Devon. They toured bombed areas of Exeter. Plymouth and Dartmouth were other towns visited. They also heard a first-hand account of the St Nazaire raid by officers and men who took part.

Friday 15 May

Forgot to go down to the dentist until it was time to be there, however I did not take long getting there on my bike which goes like the wind, when rushed. Did a few little shopping jobs in the town which took me some time although not very long.

In the afternoon Meg and I had tea with Mrs Everett, who was very delightful and cheerful as usual. She looked tired, I thought, and is worried about Mrs Dalrymple who is still just waiting to die. We walked up through the club grounds and up by the allotments, it is very pleasant up there and so country. Dear Domino loves running up the little path under the hedge, he is a funny dog and enjoys life tremendously. He is making Sam more lively too; when I first had Sam he was such a serious poodle, like a queer little monkey, but now he is thoroughly boisterous and gay, running here, there and everywhere as fast as he can, grinning all over with pride and fun. He spends hours every day rushing round the lawn with Domino, making him run after him and chase him. They play all the time from the time they get up to the time they go to bed.

I received a delightful letter from Uncle Snuffy. He is such a darling old man, a real uncle. I do miss all my uncles who are dead, so much.

Saturday 16 May

Awful day in fowls world. Amber has squashed all her chicks so that is the end of that. The little pullet is still sitting on hers but has squashed two chicks, so I shall simply have to buy some more chicks from Mrs Lee if I can. It is a maddening state of affairs, I must say. It makes me see red absolutely and to think that all those eggs had chicks in them is what makes me so mad. All my time and trouble and in the end no chicks because the mothers are such fools. Amber killed them all as they came out of their shells in the most beastly way. I'm rather wondering if the reason was want of grit in her feed as this wartime meal is rotten stuff with no nourishment in it at all. In future I shall add a little cod-liver oil in the broody hen's feed to make her more contented. I blame myself a bit for not thinking it all out before, but it is too late now. I think she must have been wrongly fed to make her such a fool. Last year Amber was a very bad mother but not quite as bad as this.

I am going to have most of my old hens and the young cock killed soon so as to have all young birds for laying, am wondering if I shall buy chicks, pullets or another sitting. I really think chick pullets would be the best at this time of year as I do like my chicks much earlier than this but the hens would not go broody before the end of April this year.

Sunday 17 May

Another pouring wet Sunday, it will still do a lot of good; although I do love the sunshine the garden is looking so much better for all the rain of the last fortnight. The weeds are growing unfortunately, but they grow all the time anyway. The flowers in blossom now are: Apple trees, crab apple, azalea, laburnum, horse chestnut, irises, thrift, pink and white clematis up the house, tulips, forget-me-nots, silver-leaved daisy, pink campion, bluebells, wallflowers and candytuft, viola and pansy, aubretia, gentiana acailis, alyssum. The garden is looking rather lovely, the lawns cut and I have finished cutting the middle bank so now only the grass bank at the bottom of the lawn will want doing. The three tons of gravel has arrived for Madge to lay all down the broad path by the roses, so it will be nice for some time to come. The roses are in bud and growing like anything, also the new red-brick steps up the rose bank are charming, edged with carnations and pinks falling down the sides with the miniature fir trees behind them on either side. I am really delighted with my pretty garden and am only longing to see it in yet another year when the hedge has grown up a bit, and got thick enough to entirely keep out the gaze of any neighbour! Then it will be as I want it, but all these things take time to do and the bushes and trees take a few years to reshape after a cutting.

Monday 18 May

Domino and I saw Meg off after an early breakfast; she has to go up to Town, then on up to Scotland, where she gets the Belfast boat. It was a dull morning but dry which was something. I am sorry she could not stay longer as I hardly had time to appreciate her visit. At the beginning I was in a sort of daze and towards the end I felt so tired out, I suppose it was the awful strain I had been through. Never mind. Meg is coming over again sometime before Christmas if she can. Maimie fairly cheerful in spite of Meg's departure and Mrs Everett came in to see her after tea to brighten her up a little with all the local news and bits of gossip (if there is any).

The garden a picture, all my irises at the top of the rose bank beginning to flower, they are going to be a beautiful sight. The new roses are in bud too. Meg's bit of mimulus from Ireland is the most wonderful colour I have ever seen, it is brilliant orange-flame and doing so well, which is splendid as it was only sent in a box last autumn.

Mauve lilac is over now but the white one by the front door is a picture, so will the weigela be in another week, it is a mass of buds. The new yellow azalea is beautiful and the scent heavenly, but of course the corner where that is planted is not finished yet so it does not look perfect until its setting is complete.

Poor Ming's leg bad again; broken out afresh after a fortnight.

Tuesday 19 May

Had a great home day. First of all I have ordered a pure Light Sussex broody hen with sitting of Light Sussex and Brown Leghorn eggs from Mrs Lee at West Hill. She was most pleasant and so sorry I had had bad luck.

I then rang up Mr Fisher about beehive supers (as my order at Burgess has been bombed) and in the afternoon I rang up Mrs Everett to ask her to come to Budleigh with me. So off we went, and I got a super and brood chamber with sections which are nearly worn out, but never mind, as I was able to order 2lbs of foundation from Harris of Totnes, so shall be able to mend them up before adding them to my hive.

Then in the evening I discovered that Honey Bun's sister has gone broody, so I hastily put the young cock in with the hens and hope in a week or so to sit some more eggs of my own. Altogether life is coming on once more at the moment anyway, and I am feeling all in a thrill again after all the disappointments of my sitting hens and the new beehive being demolished.

Mr Fisher gave me one or two very useful hints about hives and things, and I hope to be able to go on for ages now with one hive and dozens of supers instead of another hive, of course one trusts to luck that the bees will not swarm. I think I will write and tell Uncle Snuffy about everything, he may be able to help me.

Friday 22 May

Had a thrilling day in the home again. The brood foundation I ordered from Harris of Totnes arrived before lunch, so after the meal was over and washed up I took the parcel and the empty frames in the garden in the sun, and there we (I and the dogs) started redoing all the frames with new wire and a new sheet of foundation in each frame until we had finished all the ten for the brood chamber. We had the job done by tea time, so now we wait in patience for a sunny warm day when I smoke the bees and give them this second brood chamber on the top of their old one. I do hope they will be thrilled; they are a bit overcrowded now I think as they are a big colony for one hive and I cannot get another owing to Burgess being bombed out.

After an early supper Domino and I went along the fields to Littleham and along the little lane with wild bluebells and pink campion growing on either side, to West Hill Farm, where we met Mrs Lee who got me a sitting of eggs (she gave me some extra as I had such bad luck last week). We then had a look at her baby goslings and chicks, eventually arriving at the hen house where I was given a choice of Light Sussex broody hens. I chose one and put her into the sack we had brought and back we came. The hen weighs quite a bit I discovered before I got her home. She sat at once!

Sunday 24 May

Maimie getting up for tea today, isn't that lovely. Meg rang me up this morning and we had a little chat. Betty rang up to ask me round for a talk before lunch, she loves her new work as an officer at Crownhill, and finds it very interesting as well as amusing. The other officers are delightful and life is rosy for her. I am glad she is so happy; she has worked hard for three years now in the ATS and deserves to enjoy it.

The Light Sussex hen is sitting very tight on her fifteen eggs; she is obviously a splendid sitter, which is more than I can say for my own hens!

When I got home from seeing Betty I found kind Nurse busy in the kitchen making the salad. She is so kind in so many little ways and we are more than lucky to have her here; some nurses are not half so nice from all accounts. The poor little dogs hated me going out his morning without them. Much to my horror Mrs Everett informed me that Mrs Dalrymple has decided to give Sam to a cousin of hers. I am sick about it!

The little dog simply adores Domino and is as happy as the day is long with me. Why should he be given away to someone else all of a sudden? It is annoying!

Wednesday 27 May

I went into Exeter in the morning to find out where Burgess had put himself since the blitz, when Guinea Street was completely bombed and burnt out. I found him occupying a wood storage by the canal in Bonhay Road. Webber is letting him have a tiny office and big store room. The girl secretary told me that old Mr Burgess, who is eighty-two, took the blitz splendidly and said straight away that he was going to carry on in spite of losing everything he had in the Guinea Street shops. But a week after, one day he was walking along the High Street and suddenly collapsed from the shock. However, he is alright again now. They hope to let me have a new beehive quite soon in spite of everything!

I then walked round what used to be beautiful and peaceful Exeter, it was an awful sight. First, on reaching the traffic lights at the top of North Street, I saw straight in front of me the remains of South Street. On the left side looking down, there was nothing left, only heaps of rubble; on the right side at the corner, where South Street joins High Street, the whole corner was down to the ground. The glorious fourteenth-century Chevalier Inn was absolutely gone, not a stone left. On looking further down Fore Street I saw nothing but rubble and stones, right down to the bottom, not a shop left on either side. I then sadly walked up High Street as far as the ancient Guildhall, which mercifully is still standing. Then, I turned into the Close. There was the lovely old cathedral, standing solemn and glorious, but on getting near it I realised that it had not got one window left and I found myself looking right through the nave. Some of the tracery had gone but not much. There were men working inside at the east end where a time bomb landed in the lady chapel behind the high altar. I could not get much of an idea of the damage but I believe it is considerable at that part where the bomb hit the building. I walked along by the Canons houses to Southernhay, but saw with horror that the backs of all the lovely old houses were simply <u>not</u> there; their gardens were heaps of plaster and stones, pitiable and terrible to see. Southernhay towards the Arcade was no more. I then walked back past the Close into Luxury Lane and looked up High Street! I could not believe my eyes at first. From Lyons right up into St Sidwell Street it was flat. No shops, no church, nothing at all. Bobby's shop and Lloyds Bank were empty shells, beyond that it was flat as far as I could see. Now, these were some of the buildings that used to stand on the left side looking towards St Sidwell's. Wheaton's and Commins and Eland (bookshops), Charles and Charles and Woodley (shoes), Evins (suitcases), Church, Bruford (jeweller), Wippell and Row (ironmonger), Devon and Somerset Stores (grocer) and various small modes shops. The other side: Bobby, Colson, Randall, Singers, Rowlands, Tighe Wynne & Son, General Post Office, Arcade, Joan Cresswell, Co-operative. Then coming along in the bus, we drove along streets running out of St Sidwell's and into Heavitree, which had <u>no</u> houses, buildings, shops or walls of any kind on either side. I never saw such a sight, row upon row of houses knocked down like a pack of cards. Going up Heavitree past various large houses occupied by doctors etc (one by Dr Mabel Gates), were shells, completely gutted by fire all up past St Leonard's Church and School, which also are gutted out. A nightmare city. To think that it was once so peaceful and seemed so far from wars or anything of the kind! A strange state of affairs and a pathetic one ...

Thursday 4 June

Mrs Dalrymple died at six o'clock this morning. I am anxiously waiting for news about Sam; he is to be offered to one of her cousins who I hope will refuse to have him, but one does not really know until she writes about it.

Another glorious summer day, I wore a cotton frock for the first time this year and no stockings which is a lovely free feeling and I hope not to wear either again until October, especially nowadays when they are rationed and very difficult to get at all. I paid 7s 6d for an artificial silk pair last week which I consider ridiculous.

Spent the day in the garden, that's to say the afternoon. I washed my hair and went out in the full sun to dry it and clipped all the edges round the lawn, rose beds and fruit trees. The garden is looking very pretty, the irises at the top of the rose bank a real show and the roses are beginning to come into bud and one or two are in flower. My pillar roses which I moved last year, a picture of good health and shooting well. There are quite a few pears formed also apples, the standard plum has no fruit, but the bigger one outside the kitchen window up the wall is a mass of fruit. So our trees are starting to bear, which is a great thing after spending so much money and time on them. The yellow azalea smells like heaven. I really am thinking of getting another one in the autumn.

Friday 5 June

On the anniversary of the evacuation of Dunkirk the commandos raided the French coast between Boulogne and Le Touquet. German troops, defending, fired point-blank at their own men in their confusion. Our troops badly rattled the Germans: wading waist deep, they advanced over the dunes, some going a good distance inland after cutting through barbed-wire defences. A pill-box at the edge of the dunes put up a stiff resistance until the commandos concentrated Bren-gun and anti-tank gun-fire. Then, in a matter of minutes, it was silenced. While the special service were doing their job, the Royal Navy sank an enemy patrol vessel and they also engaged two enemy patrol ships while the troops were ashore.

I was woken up in the middle of the night by a big explosion from the channel, so now I know it was evidently the combined efforts of the navy and commandos.

Sunday 7 June

Betty rang up to ask me out for a bathe and tea at Orcombe Point, she is home on forty-eight-hours leave. So off I went when she came to fetch me with little Michael, who has grown like anything. He is such a pet and full of fun. We took him out in the sea quite a long way until it got too cold for him. Betty and I then went in properly, it was very cold at first but one soon got used to it and then it was lovely. We all ate a huge tea and then played or went to sleep. Finished with ices from the funny old Italian man at the end of the promenade, why he is still loose in England in times like this beats me!

Last night I gardened until 11.30. I took out the old forget-me-nots in the two front drive beds and put in their place some of my seedling asters, which ought to be lovely when they flower. I also began cutting the end bank at the bottom of the tennis court, it is dreadfully long and all the grass is in flower. I also started cutting and tidying up in the wild bed under the wild rose hedge. It is terribly untidy at the moment, owing to a number of docks coming up recently and a good deal of goose grass but now I have begun, it will very soon look better. The next thing will be to cut the bank all along the lower end of the tennis court; it is a boring job but very necessary I must say.

Monday 8 June

I did a bit of clearing up and got the spare room looking nice for Combo. It was a cold day but dry, the wind pretty awful. I took the dogs up the lane to look out for Combo's bus from Exeter, but she wasn't on the one I met, so we began tea when she came having come by the next one. She was really looking wonderfully well, especially as she has been very unwell lately as she is so terribly upset about David being posted as missing and they are so vague about it all and say so little of the circumstances. It is a tragic thing. Fearful.

The flowers were looking lovely, Sister had done them all over the house and it looked gay enough for any party, flowers in every room and on every table, all beautifully done and so carefully chosen.

Combo a perfect guest and so kind and helpful in the house. She is a dear thing and so good looking. I can't help looking at her; she has a lovely profile. She is very pleased with Maimie's appearance and says that Maimie is looking better than she has done for years. Last time they came over they both agreed that Maimie looked awfully ill. Of course she has obviously been working up for this illness for ages now, and now after the complete rest, she will be better I am hoping. She does look a much better colour in my humble opinion: more colour and not so deadly looking. The summer will do her good.

Tuesday 9 June

In the morning Combo and I went down the town with the two dogs, shopping. She wanted a dressing gown. So we went to Thomas Tucker and they showed us a lot of lovely ones. We eventually chose a very nice silk light navy with light pink stripes house coat, long with flared skirt and neck which could be high or lowish. Very attractive and it suited her dignity very well. I loved the rustling silk when she walked. I hope Mr Leach will like it. He is a connoisseur on dressing gowns! Combo adores shopping. I found it difficult to drag her out of the shops; she would be there now if I had not been with her.

After lunch we all saw Nurse off at the station, it will be funny without her. She has been here so long now and done so much for Maimie and me. She is a dear and so helpful and kind in a maidless house. She is going on her holiday on Friday after a day or two in Exeter to do a few jobs she wanted to do. She is going to stay with her cousins on the farm in Somerset on the border. It is really on Exmoor but under the moor itself. I love the sound of the place. She loves it all too and is longing to go there I think and get out of uniform and run wild for a week or two. Combo took charge of Maimie when Nurse departed and so we are all settled again for this week so far …

Thursday 11 June

After lunch Mr Leach rang up from Exeter on his way home form London; we asked him to come and join Combo here until Saturday, which he quite eagerly did. It was such fun having them both. We took Maimie in the car to meet him at the station here and he at once suggested going up on Woodbury Common for tea. It was very lovely up there, the trees still a beautiful fresh green and the flowers in the hedges in bloom, of course we passed various places where they have cut down the trees and left skeleton woods, which is always sad. Lord Clinton has cut down a large number of woods on Woodbury and is still felling trees up there, but it is the same all over the country in wartime. We had a delicious tea in the café right over on the Exeter side of the common, home-made scones and cakes, all beautifully served with China tea. So we were all very happy. Maimie found a special little comfy chair to sit in and she thoroughly enjoyed the afternoon. After tea we drove right over Woodbury past the castle and home. The views over the estuary of the Exe and on over Haldon with Dartmoor in the background too heavenly – really, summer in Devon is a dream! It is the same everywhere I suppose when the distant views are slightly hazy in a soft blue mist and the foreground is woods and fields with the blue sky above. Lovely.

Friday 12 June

A thoroughly wet and awful day, so dark and chilly with the rain coming down in a steady downpour but we all decided to walk down and do some shopping before meeting for a coffee in the Sunlit. Actually, we kept wonderfully dry, considering the distance we are from the town and we walked all the way round by the road to try to keep our feet moderately dry. I left Domino and Sam at home, thinking they would only get really saturated.

We met Mrs Everett in the Sunlit and she came over for a chat with us, we then all ran for a bus which did not wait after all! But the one behind did, so we were alright, in spite of the first fright.

We slept all the afternoon (having talked late the night before) and after supper Mowbray Garden came in for a chat. He was with David in Singapore, and he told us some awful things, thrilling but I feel more utterly ashamed of English <u>civilians</u> than ever before. He was evidently in David's squadron. He is the only man known to be alive now of the squadron. He is a flight lieutenant like David, and was wearing his uniform tonight; he looked very nice in it too. I have not seen him for years. He went out East five years ago. He told me all about the loss of the *Prince of Wales* and was the first pilot to be sent out to 'stand by' while the ship sank after the frightful battle, and he said that had Admiral Philips taken an escort (air) it could <u>never</u> have done anything against the overpowering numbers of bombers sent by the Japanese to sink her.

Saturday 13 June

Very sadly Sam and I took the Leaches down to the town to catch their bus and train, they both had returns so used them up, Combo was to catch the Crediton train in Exeter and meet Mr Leach there. Mr L. took all the luggage in the train. We first got some fish to take back with them. They seldom can get fresh fish at Cheriton Fitzpaine so it is a real treat to them both.

Mr L. looked very pinched this morning. I think he was upset by what Mowbray Garden said and I think he has quite given up all hope of ever seeing David again. From all accounts it sounds absolutely hopeless. He came down in the sea and there were sharks galore in the water as well as the Japanese, who shoot every live man on these occasions. Poor little David. He was such an attractive boy, or I should say man, but I have known him since he was five years old. He was exceptionally good to look at too, which is always a pleasure, as well as being so nice and beautiful clothes – a son to be frightfully proud of. Poor Mr Leach is simply completely upset by it. He is hating being alive now, in fact all his own ambition has gone now David is missing. It has just knocked the stuffing right out of his father. Combo is extraordinarily brave about it, but she too is miserable. Utterly miserable – oh, how hateful this bloody war has begun to be!

Sunday 14 June

A lovely fine morning but very cold, unfortunately by the afternoon thunder rolled up, the sun went in but Dolly came with Shandy for the walk. As it was so unsettled and the sky so black we decided on a quick walk in the fields towards Littleham, the dogs loved it and rushed about everywhere, they got specially excited when Shandy went swimming in the brook and they dared not go in deeper than their tummies. Domino barked furiously and Sam tore round like a lunatic, he did venture into deeper water than Domino did but was not really a brave pup for all his efforts to chase Shandy wherever she went. By the time they got home they were all pretty wet in spite of everything. As the clouds got blacker and the lightning became more constant with the rolling thunder we turned for home at Greene Farm and got in ten minutes before the rain began, so we considered ourselves wise. The 'goings on' in the drawing room became so low and coarse that my two dogs had to be sent to bed much to Shandy's delight. She was shocked with them both and looked very grateful when they departed. She rolled up in front of the fire and slept while she dried herself, such a sweet dog. She made one mistake when she woke Rusty up from a sound sleep on the sofa. He was mad as he had not noticed the visitor until she woke him up suddenly!

Thursday 18 June

I went up to the party which Dolly asked me to go to at the club. It was given by the ARP for comforts for the soldiers – to buy wool to knit etc. It was quite fun in a way. I met Betty Moore which was nice; she is such a delightful girl I always think. She is working in the War Office in Oxford and digs in Keble College, for her sins! She says the cold of the college passageways in the winter time is frightful! She has two eiderdowns and umpteen blankets and still shivers at night. The colleges were built for men, not unfortunate girls! Betty said she loved being at Oxford because it was terrifically gay, parties given every night, wonderful shows from Town at the theatre and cinemas galore. So far it has not been bombed once. Oh, how I hope the dear Germans will not get there with their bombs and muck. It would be maddening if they ruined our glorious universities, but I am sure they are just itching to do so. Had my fortune told by Mrs Seymour who said everything was happy but there was not much to say. I was glad it was so good as I am rather chary of having it done since a woman in Paignton told me so much and it has all come true. She told me of the war and everything, and it was about five or six years ago. So now I do not often go as I think it much wiser to leave it alone in case of anything nasty and I would hate that, if it came true!!

Friday 19 June

The dogs and I did the usual shopping round in the morning and got various very necessary things, including dog meat which the dogs always get on Fridays. In the afternoon I mowed the lawn by the lily pond before Molly Murray came as she kindly arranged to look at my bees. Yes, they have swarmed alright! Isn't it a blow. She is coming again next Wednesday to have another look for the queen as we failed to spot her among them and in case there is not a queen there. I am to carefully look once more. I am now going to try another swarm if I can find one anywhere. What a job! Just when my bees were going to be so successful and give me so much honey. Damn! Never mind. I shall understand more about them by next year I hope and if I have trouble I shall see it and be able to take the swarm myself, I hope! What a party!

After tea Mrs Everett came in for a chat with Maimie and talked about the fuss going on with Mrs Dalrymple's belongings which go to relations she has never even seen. It seems rather sad to think of all her little personal things just going away to be never heard of again, so to speak. One begins to wonder why one takes so much care of one's things when they end like that when one dies!

Saturday 20 June

Phoned up Mr Fisher to ask him the name of a certain lady who gave me a swarm of bees last year. He told me that Mrs Foster had a number of hives for sale as her daughter is in the ATS and cannot look after them now. In the afternoon I took Maimie and Mrs Everett to see Mrs Foster at Tidwell house, it is a beautiful old red-brick Georgian house between East Budleigh and Knole and I knew it well from the road. We met Mrs Foster, who showed me three good Perfection WBC hives, all in fine condition; they are the old pattern and have no supers in them but everything complete except the queen excluder. I promptly chose one and put it in the car to bring home in triumph and I'm hoping to be able to afford another one when I know the price. It is such a splendid opportunity for getting hives as they are very scarce just now owing to shortage of wood etc. I am in a thrill and <u>must</u> get some bees to go in it if I possibly can. I shall have to be quick as the summer will soon be over, but I have one consolation. They tell me it is a very bad summer for bees! After supper I rang up Mrs Adamson, who said she has no swarm now but if she gets one she will let me know at once. On Monday I am going to ring up someone else Mrs Foster told me of …

Tuesday 23 June

Yesterday I spent the morning at Miss Clay's beautiful garden, it was a really lovely sight, every inch was colour and so artistically arranged in great groups. They have such a variety of different plants and shrubs. The rockery was a marvellous display of dianthus, thyme, saxafraga, campanula, candytuft and masses of other things besides, including the lilies in the tiny pond in the middle. I am to go up there in the autumn to have lots of bits given me by Miss Clay. I am thrilled to bits by it all and am going to start tidying our rockery soon, as it has recently got very wild looking. I made out a list of flower seeds for Sutton tonight and will send it off tomorrow, hoping they will send them soon for me to get into the soil well before the autumn. I worked in the garden all the evening and after supper finished staking out the outdoor tomatoes and the carnations so now I shall be alright for some time except for a bit of hoeing. I was too busy last night to go to bed until 11.30! Our own roses are a wonderful display. The bank is a picture; all the new ones are doing so awfully well.

Thursday 25 June

Domino, Sam and I walked down to the ferry to meet Marjorie. It was a heavenly morning and we took the path through the golf links, past the lifeboat house and so along the seafront, until we arrived at the jetty to see the old ferry boat steaming down river towards us. Marjorie looked very attractive and extremely well. She adored Sammy on sight and said directly she saw him from the boat she hoped he was my dog because he looked such a pet. She had no idea that I had two dogs now. We walked home via the town as Marjorie wanted some cigarettes, so we called on

Mr Griffiths. It was a really pleasant day – old friends certainly seeing the best somehow, there is so much to talk about and so many jokes to laugh over. We had a sherry, which Marjorie said made her see double! Then we ate Amber (the two year old buffsock who killed her chickens), she was very good and we had our first new potatoes, beauties! After lunch we sat sleepily talking until tea when we had strawberries and cream (for making cream I could be fined severely). I began to feel the war must be a long way off by the end of tea!

It was fun having Marjorie after such a long time. We had not seen her for nearly a year. She is beginning her new job at Boots as one of the librarians, she will be very good at this work and is doing it to relieve a younger woman for war work …

Friday 26 June

More than 700,000 Polish Jews have been slaughtered by the Germans in the greatest massacre in the world's history. In addition, a system of starvation is being carried out, in which the number of deaths, on the admission of the Germans themselves, bids fair to be almost as large. The most gruesome details of mass killing by poison gas has been reported. In a 1940 New Year message Gauleiter Greiser said the only use to be made of the Poles was as slaves for Germans and for the Jews there was no future. Men and boys between fourteen and sixty have been driven together into one place, and there killed, either by knifing, machine-guns, or grenades. They had to dig their own graves beforehand. Children in orphanages, pensioners in almshouses and sick in hospitals have been shot. Women have been killed in the streets. In November slaughter of the Jews by gas in the Polish territory incorporated in the Reich began. A special van fitted as a gas chamber was used into which they crowded ninety victims at a time. The bodies were buried in special graves in Lubardski Forest. On average, 1,000 Jews were gassed daily.

Sunday 28 June

Had a noisy night again. No sooner had several of our flights of bombers gone over to raid Bremen than the Luftwaffe flew over our house by the dozen; they appeared to be fairly low as they made a terrific roar which continued for some time. I slept again long before the 'all-clear' went. They broadcast that some coastal towns on the south and south-west had been raided.

Had some good games of tennis with Betty Earle and some other Wrens and Royal Marines. I played disgustingly but next time I hope to be in better form, with luck. Somehow I just stand looking at the ball and do nothing about it! My feet seem stuck to the ground!

By pictures in the papers, Canterbury has been having a very bad blitzing, the glorious cathedral is badly damaged and the adjoining library, fortunately some of the more ancient books had been removed. The old High Street and the oldest street of all, the Deanery, and most of the dear old houses in the Close have disappeared altogether apparently.

I am beginning to fear that we shall lose all our priceless old cathedrals and the wonderful old towns built round them, the dear Nazis are doing their damnedest to destroy our beauties.

Tuesday 30 June

Had a big day in the garden, after breakfast Madge set the motor-mower for me so it cut much lower, and off I went with the great devil and completed the top lawn and tennis lawn by 12.30 in time to have a bath before lunch. It looks so nice after all the effort but it is a hell of a job, the machine went so badly. I really must get a mechanic to look at it before I use it again. In the afternoon Maimie sat on the lawn looking after the chickens while I cut off the long grass ends and began the lower bank under the trees which is in a terrible state. After tea we had to go up to the garage to get our one gallon of petrol, so we called on Lady Lewis, who was out, however I met her afterwards in the road, so we had a chat with her also Miss Thornhill, who was going down to see her. Lady Lewis looked charming but very tired. After all this chat, we then called on Miss Price, who was at home and glad to see us and so pleased to see Maimie looking so bobbish. She said her dog was terrified by the planes roaring over-head on Saturday and Sunday night when the siren went, he goes through hell every time there is a raid. I do feel sorry for all the poor little animals, they get so frightened by the noise and do not understand.

Thursday 2 July

Too dull for a bathe so Dolly came round with Shandy for a walk. We went along the fields towards Littleham where the dogs had a glorious time in the pond at Green Farm. Shandy swam right through, followed by Domino, then funny Sam thought he would like to go in and join them, so in he plunged and found himself out of his depth in no time, so he trod the water as hard as he could and scrambled back again, but he was quite pleased with himself and felt so cool and nice after it. We then walked past the church and up to the lane towards Budleigh. When we came to the pine wood we took the path along by the side just inside the wood. The path here was very overgrown but the wild roses and irises, ragged robin and many other wild flowers were blossoming in profusion, the dogs loved running in and out of the undergrowth, especially the spaniels, they nosed out every thicket with their tails wagging frantically. Domino and Shandy make a pretty pair when they are out together playing about. The baby Sam is rather easily put off by brambles and thorns; he is more of a town dog at present but I think we will break him into roughing it in the fields. We walked home the same way as the lanes and fields are so much better for the dogs than the main road back to Exmouth where they would have had to be kept to heel all the way home …

Friday 3 July

I took Maimie out to tea with the Misses Clay. This was the first time she has been to a 'tea party' since her illness and she stood it very well I think. Lady Lewis was there and of course very charming. It was delightful seeing her and she was so full of chat and laughter as usual. The little Misses Clay are so nice and their house very pretty, their tea delicious and their garden still better! After tea we went out and looked all round the garden. It was not quite so perfect as when I went a week or two ago, some of the flowers had gone over, but it was still an absolute picture. Miss Clay gave me several cuttings, some of a glorious white shrub with a flower between an orange blossom and Californian poppy, some of a sweet strawberry-pink shrub growing near the garage and one of a tall growing thymus, and then nine lovely cuttings of allwoodei dianthus which thrilled me to the marrow: the plants they came off were a glorious deepish strawberry pink, perfectly lovely. I do hope they will grow, it will be exciting if they do. I really am hoping to make this garden look beautiful by next summer with a few more improvements. I am planting delphinium, viola and dianthus seeds tomorrow in boxes for flowering next summer which I think ought to be alright. I want to introduce some blue in the rose bank.

Sunday 5 July

Today, being a lovely fine one again, I spent the morning hoeing the rose bank, which is looking quite a picture, the polyantha roses one mass of bloom and the ordinary ones all in bud for a second flowering. After lunch I looked at my bees to see how the young queen is doing, I missed seeing her but there were quite a lot of grubs and young bees just hatching, also a fair amount of honey in the brood chamber. Started cutting round and hoeing the fruit trees on the lawn but did not get much done before tea, the chickens enjoyed being out loose most of the day.

Tuesday 7 July

We had a nice little tea with Mrs Everett, where we met General and Mrs Nicholson. I had not seen either of them for some time. It is sad that they are leaving Exmouth for Guildford. I rather envy them; Guildford is such a beautiful part of the country and so near London.

The General was full of fun and jokes; he is a very delightful man. Mrs of course is most attractive in manner and appearance.

Friday 10 July

Maimie and I suddenly decided to go to a flick as it was wet (had been raining all day). The film was the much talked of *The Next of Kin*. Very good and I hope it will do some good and not just go over people's heads like water off a duck's back. It showed up the intense necessity of keeping one's tongue quiet and not blab to even one's friends. There is often a spy listening round the corner! We had an unpleasant interlude from an old bitch (a friend of Miss Dickson's incidentally), she was most rude to Maimie, so I ticked her off. She was very angry because Maimie explained that she is an invalid and simply cannot stand in a queue, so she moved nearer the top where nobody said anything except this old bitch and a bloody female with her. I was furious. It will probably be the last film Maimie will ever go to, petrol being so short and her health being what it is, and then to have these two filthy women going for her made me mad. When we got inside, the people behind us yelled 'get out of the way' to some miserable people groping about waiting to be shown to their seats. I began to think that the manners of Exmouth left much to be desired and I hope some of the bad-tempered old devils will go to HELL for their rottenness! Anyway, we both thoroughly enjoyed the film and were glad we had gone to see it. The news was quite interesting as well, although I have seen better.

Friday 24 July

I met both the Leaches in Exeter where we lunched at the British Restaurant at St Luke's; it is one of the new schemes to relieve bombed out people in blitzed areas. The food was good and tons of it and we quite enjoyed the meal. Mr Leach was very much annoyed recently by the disgusting way in which the waiters treated him in the Clarence where he lunched. They threw the food at him! He supposes it is because the hotel staff try to show their personal disgust at the type of people who patronise them now that all hotel meals are a fixed price. All the same, they should look and see who the people are before they start being rude!

I was so thrilled because Combo gave me a box with two dozen beautiful young strawberry plants in it; they will fruit next year and make me a lovely new bed which will go near the rhubarb. They received a wonderfully inspiring letter from one of David's crew, telling them what a grand officer David was. This man was his observer (has since got a commission) and he also said that he always hoped that his own baby son would grow up to be something like 'Micky', which was David's nickname in the RAF. He said he would rather be observer in a plane piloted by David than any other man in the RAF and that he was certain that he would have had a great future. He was far above the average: a brilliant pilot. Damn. Damn!

Tuesday 28 July

Received airgraph from Henry dated 22.6.42.

Thursday 30 July

Maimie and I had an early lunch before starting for Exeter to meet the Salisbury train bringing Uncle Snuffy and Aunt Fancy. It was the first time Maimie had seen the city since it was blitzed. We took the Clyst St Mary road, arriving at the Heavitree end of Exeter and I pointed out St Luke's school minus its glass and roof, and all the big brick houses opposite, where the doctors used to live; some of them are gone and others are shells, completely burnt out. We then took the bus route up to St Sidwell's Street; all the houses on either side were gone, with nothing left but rubble. Then down St Sidwell's and the High Street; St Sidwell's has no shops left either side until approaching the first traffic lights where a few blocks are still standing until you get to the corner by the theatre and the Arcade. Here there is complete devastation, nothing remains of the Arcade at all, the post office and all the beautiful shops near it are down to the ground as far as Bedford Circus, which is demolished including Deller's, the popular café, and on the opposite side, Bruford, Devon and Somerset Stores, Wippell and Row, Woodley, Charles, a bank and many other shops are entirely destroyed. Maimie had a wonderful view of all the destruction; it is interesting although sad to see one's own home towns in dire distress. It is remarkable how easily one can get lost in the much bombed areas when all the landmarks are gone. We met the train at the Central Station and Uncle S. and Aunt F. were in good fettle in spite of a rather tiring journey in a very full train.

Friday 31 July

Yesterday, after dumping Aunt Fancy at the Devoncourt Hotel, we arrived home and got out one of the new hives to put the bees into. Uncle S. brought me a magnificent stock and they quite settled into their new home. They are beautiful, strong, big bees and seem very good tempered after their tiring journey, poor little tiny things. I do hope they will like our garden to fly about in and find all the nectar they want in the neighbourhood.

After tea Aunt Fancy came up to unpack Uncle Snuffy and look round. She loved the garden and the house and said everything looked so well kept. I am glad she thought it all nice after my efforts in cutting lawns and everything.

Miss Brooke is coming to keep Aunt Fancy company in the hotel from Monday till Thursday when they are all going home. I hope Aunt F. will not find it very lonely until she comes. Today we went shopping in the morning. Aunt F. quite struck with Exmouth and says she hopes to come and stay here again. She had no idea that it was such a residential place.

Uncle S. very upset by the thought of a tea party. He hates most 'two legged things, and only makes companions of four legged things', so he says! He is still as humorous as ever and quite as pessimistic. He never says anything is very lively.

Saturday 1 August

Today we devoted to the bloody tea party! I tore down to the town, after a hurried breakfast, on my bike without dear Domino, much to his rage – he hates me to go shopping without him. Anyway, I got down pretty early and to my horror most of Clapp's cakes had already been bought. After a visit to every café and confectioner in the town I returned with my baskets laden with a remarkably good selection for war-time. It is extraordinary how good the buns and plain cakes are here, in some places I believe they have considerable difficulty to buy anything for tea, in any case the meal is only a mere luxury in my opinion. Uncle Snuffy horror-struck at the thought of the tea party. We only asked a few people in, but he is very upset by it and has made us promise never to do such a thing again when he is staying with us! Our guests included Miss Swinton, Mrs Everett, Colonel Cowel, General and Mrs Nicholson and Lady Lewis. The last named is an old boyhood friend of Uncle Snuffy. I really think he liked her quite a lot! They were all very friendly. Mrs Nicholson wore her pale mauve to please Maimie, so sweet of her to especially dress for her hostess. She charmed Aunt Fancy, who also was very smart and made up like a girl. Anyway the thing was quite a success I think, that is the main thing!

Thursday 6 August

We got the opportunity of using the car. The first was taking Uncle Snuffy and Aunt Fancy to Exeter to catch their train back to Andover. The second, to buy a new bee-hive from Burgess and the third, to have lunch with the Leaches for the last time owing to petrol.

After much crushing of suitcases into the car, including the empty bee travelling box, half full of plants, we went down to the Devoncourt to collect Aunt Fancy who was ready with her suitcases which fitted into the car quite well. As we passed through the city, we stopped in the Close and went into the cathedral, where the crowd is now allowed to see the bomb damage. It was very sad to see the ruined organ, the windows in fragments and the north side chapels rubble.

Then we dropped the luggage at the Central Station before going to Burgess in the hopes of buying a beehive, but they had none, so I got one skep and four feeders. We then went back to the station and said goodbye to Uncle Snuffy and Aunt Fancy. We shall miss dear old Uncle S. very much, he is a real darling.

We then took the car along through Crediton and so on to Cheriton Fitzpaine, where we had a wonderful welcome from Combo and Mr Leach. They were both looking very pathetic. They had received another letter from one of David's squadron officers, this time a senior officer, who mentioned his sorrow at their loss, so they have no hope at all ...

Sunday 9 August

Last week I had a long, delightful letter from Henry. I am so pleased, he has got on well. He is a captain and mess secretary at the Royal Signals HQ in New Delhi. He is such a pet and wrote such a pet of a letter. Most affectionate for him! And as usual as true as steel, he says how much he dislikes the Indians lack of truth and deceitfulness. Of course Henry is dead straight. That is why I admire him so much. I was indeed glad to get a letter from him. I love getting the airgraphs but they are not so chatty as a long letter. He seems so well and efficient. I do wish the climate was not upsetting him so much, in the airgraph, written after the letter, he seems to be ill. I feel awfully anxious about him and hope they will get him fit again before it is too late.

We walked to tea with Mrs Horsbrugh and met Miss Swinton there. Mrs Horsbrugh's drawing room attracted us both very much; the covers were soft plum colour with blue cushions and the curtains blue and mauve shot, so unusual and pretty – our hostess is known to be a very artistic woman it appears. When we got home who should be patiently sitting in the garden but Harry and his mother, we were so sorry they had waited so long but it was delightful to see them both. Harry looked a picture of health and was very cheery and full of beans as usual. He is always a great joke and so amusing.

Monday 10 August

Mr Bramwell arrived complete with queen bee, which we introduced into the hive, we gave her one of Uncle Snuffy's brood for the bees to work on and put her into the hive in her cage, which she will get out of in three days. We found one of the worker bees has been laying down drone eggs, so hope they will take to the queen when they get her.

Thursday 13 August

I went up to 'Fredonia' and had a coffee with Mrs Davis, where I met her daughter-in-law, Joan, a nice girl. We went all round the garden, which is full of fruit of every sort, but too big for these days of no gardeners.

After lunch Marjorie and Dolly came up to fetch Domino, Sam and me for a walk along the cliffs. It was a dull, damp day but alright for walking the dogs. Domino enjoyed his day very much; he has gone wild with excitement over the girls and Shandy, who is so good to my two dogs.

After tea time Bammy rang up from his home while on leave. He came to supper. He's now a staff-sergeant and just become engaged to a girl in the north. He showed us the ring, which really is lovely. Before supper Combo arrived in style in a taxi – she was looking very fit and well dressed. It was delightful to see her again. She has come down for Maimie's birthday and next week Mr Leach is coming for the week. I do hope the weather will be nice and warm instead of the cold windy days we are having now.

We sat up till midnight talking, as usual. It is awful how we all sit around talking when the Leaches come to stay. Somehow we get wound up like clocks and never get run down even when it gets to twelve o'clock at night. Last time they came to stay we talked till midnight every night.

Sunday 16 August

Maimie had some nice presents which she loved receiving before her breakfast. Meg sent her a very nice big square of thick 'utility' material in red, to wear as a rug or a wrap and a box of powder. Combo gave her a lovely little wooden butter dish and knife, and a bottle of tonic wine. I gave her a green and mauve wool wrap, a pyrex dish and a bottle of scent. Maimie got up early and we all went to church, not a good congregation but the vicar preached a good sermon. Had lunch, Maimie having a glass of her wine first, which she very much enjoyed. Mrs Everett came to tea bringing her pretty gifts of a mauve georgette handkerchief and a lavender sachet. For tea we had the lovely chocolate birthday cake Combo made for Maimie. It was absolutely delicious to eat and Combo had decorated it so prettily with some sweets I got especially. We finished up with sloe-gin for supper. I really think Maimie enjoyed her tea very much – in fact the whole day pleased her and she did not seem to be too tired after supper, but of course she will have to rest a bit tomorrow.

Summer has come again after a month of cold, showery weather. I wore my new blue coat and skirt for church but changed later on in case I spoilt it by the domestic jobs one has to attend to during the day. Sunday is rather a busy day nowadays with no maid to help or anything.

Thursday 20 August

Commando troops returned from a raid on Dieppe last night. It was the greatest raid the combined operations have yet carried out. During the operations our forces destroyed a six-gun battery, ammunition dump, radio location station, and flak battery. Brought down eighty-two enemy aircraft for certain and probably destroyed 100 more, for the loss to ourselves of ninety-five aircraft, twenty-one fighter pilots being safe. There were heavy casualties on both sides. The Germans claim to have taken 1,500 prisoners, sixty of them officers and to have sunk three destroyers, four transports and three motor torpedo-boats. Tanks were landed for the first time in a commando raid, and the fighting was exceptionally bitter and prolonged. This was the first operation on European soil in which United States troops have taken part in this war, and the first in which Fighting Frenchmen have fought in their own country since Petain capitulated.

Wednesday 26 August

HRH the Duke of Kent has been killed in an air crash. It does seem terrible. I do so hate to think of any of our princes being killed. It seems to make such an awful blank and the King now only has one brother to help.

Thursday 27 August

The body of the Duke of Kent, who, with thirteen others, was killed when a Sunderland flying-boat crashed on Tuesday on a 1,000ft hill in the north of Scotland, was yesterday taken to the nearest railway station, to be brought to London. It has been found that there is one survivor, the rear-gunner. He is recovering from concussion, shock and burns in hospital.

It was only a day or two ago that it was finally decided that the Duke of Kent should undertake the journey to Iceland.

Saturday 29 August

HRH the Duke of Kent was buried today at St George's Chapel, Windsor. It was a simple funeral and only members of his family and close friends were there. He was buried as any other officer in the Royal Air Force might have been. The coffin was carried by NCOs of the RAF, all from picked fighter squadrons. The pall-bearers were all vice-marshals. Heading the mourners was the King, in RAF uniform; the Duke of Gloucester, in khaki; and Admiral Sir Lionel Halsey, representing the Duke of Windsor.

Friday 4 September

The siren again, we have it several times a week now. Lately they bombed Torquay rather badly; Bristol, setting fire to several buses in the main street; and on Wednesday they bombed Teignmouth, several people killed. Recently they saw eighteen E-boats off Seaton and our Royal Marines and all the Exmouth Home Guard were called out, and although they were in easy reach of firing on the E-boats, the permission took so long coming through from London that the boats all went away unhurt. Today four enemy bombers came over while I was digging in the garden, several bombs were dropped and the RAF brought down one of the bombers.

Thursday 24 September

The day being quite a nice one, although very cold, we took the car to Snow's nurseries to see if he had any plants I <u>must</u> have. I bought a double cherry-almond Italian Cyprus, stocks, Siberian wallflowers, ceanothus, two brooms, a 'King George' Michaelmas daisy and 'Perfection' – all the other things I wanted he said he had not got. I must bike over to see Veitch about more fruit trees soon.

All last week I was digging the new flower bed down by the hedge. It will be really lovely when I have done it. There is a honeysuckle up a post by the little gate into the lane. Then a fuchsia and five rhododendrons. Then a big pillar with Paul Scarlet up it, and near a laburnum and all round them is to be flowers. I have nearly finished the edging of violas, dianthus, creeping veronica, primroses and various other things besides, but I am longing to get on with planting the back of the bed, the flowers will look so beautiful with a background of rose and honeysuckle hedge. The whole garden will look quite different when I have finished this new bed; it was so dull, just rough grass and weeds. The new trees are to go along the wire netting by the tennis court to make it look pretty and help block out the netting. I am trying to think out a plan in my head for the new arrangement there. But it is a rather difficult bit of garden to try and make <u>perfect</u> and it must be perfect if it kills me!

Saturday 26 September

Today a glorious sunny one, cold but bracing. I took the dogs down shopping with me in the morning and we walked back over the golf links by the sea. It was very lovely and we all three thoroughly enjoyed ourselves to the full. The little dogs tore round on the turf and gambolled together until they felt quite tired. By the time we got home it was only 11.30, so we went out in the garden and finished planting the basket of precious tiny rock plants that were given to me yesterday by Miss Clay. I have decided to have the huge bay tree down; it is spoiling the rockery and always is untidy, the leaves forever dropping all over the drive by the front door. It is all so exciting. I am longing to see the spot after the tree is down, it will have to be altered a good deal and improved which will be such awful fun; I am already arranging in my mind what I shall do. The flower bed by the hedge today took most of my attention. It is looking pretty already. Maimie and I also measured out and taped down the scale of the new beds on the lawn by the wire for the hens along the tennis court bank. We are having a narrow border all along under the wire with two V-shaped beds with a rounded one in the middle in which will stand the Italian Cyprus, with the cherry and almond in the Vs on either side. I'm going to plant bulbs and shrubs all along in the narrow straight bits between the other longer shaped beds; fruit trees, roses, clematis, honeysuckle and other climbers are going up the wire.

Monday 28 September

Having watched the Foster bees for some time yesterday, I felt so dissatisfied that today I opened up the hive and to my horror I found hardly any bees left. I rang up Mr Bramwell who came up during the afternoon to look at them. We found that the bees in the hive were all robbers and the stock had <u>all</u> disappeared entirely! Can you imagine my dismay? Nine guineas for nothing! Mr Bramwell said it was quite obvious that they had all been suffocated on the day of their arrival, when I followed Mr Foster's instructions to leave them in their hive all day until dark, they died, poor things and robbers took possession of the hive and so ends the Foster stock I paid so highly for and was so pleased with. Bee keeping is no party unless you are an old hand at it. I have spent about £30 on the bees this year and now this awful disappointment on the top of everything.

The Misses Clay came in to tea and it was nice to see them, to take my mind off the dreadful tragedy of the bees. They are quite thrilled at our idea of getting rid of the huge bay tree at the rockery and say the improvement will be tremendous. They also liked the new flower bed and think the creepers up the wire and the trees in front will be another big improvement and that the tennis lawn wired off will be much prettier than it was before. I am longing to get on with the job I must say, and am hoping Madge may begin getting up turf tomorrow.

Tuesday 29 September

All shops, theatres and cinemas are to close early all the winter and people are to stay at home, only allowed to go long distance journeys on special permit, so my visit to Town will be knocked on the head!

Friday 2 October

Domino, Sam and I walked down to buy some Kurmange for the dogs because they are both covered in a very tickly skin complaint which is making them both scratch all day. Being a really heavenly morning, we walked home across the golf links and down by the seafront. The roses in the public gardens were simply lovely and the sea silver and blue like the sky above it. We called on Dolly on our way back and fixed up for an expedition to pick blackberries near Budleigh one day next week. Directly we got home, I put poor Domino into a bath of the wonder packet from Boots. He hated it much but nor more than little Sam when his turn came. They both ran round on the lawn until lunch, but they remained wet! After lunch I decided to take both the dogs for a walk on the cliffs in the sun, to warm them up and dry their thick coats in case they catch cold. We took a basket for blackberries and when we got to a particular field we picked up the whole hedge and by the time I had got from one end to the other I had picked about 5lbs of fruit and the basket felt quite heavy, also the sun was getting quite low, which meant that it was time to go home, the fowls would be hungry to say nothing of Maimie.

On our way home, the views were glorious looking across the estuary to Haldon moor and Powderham woods with Exmouth church on this side of the river, a herd of Shorthorn cattle with a magnificent bull in their midst made a very beautiful foreground to the picture.

Sunday 4 October

We went to church in the morning and gave Mrs Everett a lift home. We went in and saw her for half an hour; she was full of chat as usual and is coming in to have tea with Maimie while I am out with Betty. Mrs Everett has several lovely young sumach trees and will give us one when I fetch it one morning. It will be lovely to have a redleafed tree somewhere on the lawn as we are very green in the late summer with no vivid leaves to relieve the colouring.

In the afternoon I had tea with Joan and Betty, great fun seeing them. Betty is very keen to have her leave when Meg comes home so we could go up to Town together. It would be fun if we could fix it up and we might stay with Jill if she has room for both. I am longing to hear from Meg and get some idea of when she will be coming over then I can get things going a bit. Joan has redone the drawing room curtains and covers; they are now a pretty green instead of blue. I thought the room looked charming. The little boy, Micky, sweet and so gay, always laughing, clapping his hands with sure delight of his funny little self. Betty looked very well, but I think she has put on weight a bit!

Yesterday Frankie turned up for tea and stayed for supper, she had her hair done in the new three-inch cut style and I am to have mine done the same on Thursday and see Frankie's new flat that she is sharing with Mary Langhorne in the Close, it will be such fun.

Tuesday 6 October

Had a great day bathing the two dogs for this awful mange that Domino has caught. Mr Harrington came in yesterday and diagnosed the complaint at once. He says Domino must have picked it up somewhere and he must have three baths in special stuff he will bring. Sam must also have one bath as a preventative. Poor Domino is perfectly miserable – always scratching himself and has a nasty smell, poor pet. I do so hope we shall get him well as soon as possible. I spent the entire day washing all their blankets, baskets, collars, brushes and combs; so now I trust things will be better regarding them and their surroundings! The type of mange he has is scoptic mange (whatever that means!).

During the morning I finished painting on the undercoat to the two beehives still waiting to be put away. I shall now have four hives repainted and ready for use, so I am getting on in my bee world. Mr Bramwell rang up this morning to tell me that he had heard from Mrs Foster about my bees and Mrs Foster was horrified at what had happened and told him to fix up some fair plan with me, so Mr Bramwell has arranged that she should refund half the cost to me. Poor Mrs Foster I do feel sorry about it, but it was the silly message that was given me that killed the bees, otherwise I should have let them out straight away. Anyway I have a good hive and two brooders full of comb and honey.

Saturday 10 October

I saw Mrs Crea the last time I went down shopping. Kenneth is very happy and now in the 10th Hussars; he was in the 11th. Some time ago he volunteered for driving up reinforcements for the 10th and after two months at it, they asked him if he would transfer to the 10th altogether. He has his own tank now and says the new Grant tanks, made in America, are wonderful and in a Grant tank he feels ready to meet any amount of the enemy. Our British tanks were altogether not a match for the Germans. It seems awful to think that our army was not properly equipped when we first met the German army in Libya.

Thursday 29 October

The Germans have been driven across the city boundary in the south of Stalingrad, and north-west of the city; their 'resistance has been broken in many sectors'. In six days fighting 4,000 Germans and Rumanians (some say 7,000) have been killed and the enemy has lost 160 tanks.

Friday 30 October

A rather amusing incident which made Mrs Everett and I both laugh. It happened when we were walking home from the town. I was leading my bicycle which was loaded with heavy bags so Mrs Everett very kindly suggested taking Sammy, who was on the lead. We both had already been badly let down by Domino, who ate Mrs

E.'s cake, taking it out of her basket while we were drinking cups of chocolate in the Sunlit Café! However, as I have said, we were walking up the hill when Mrs E. was stopped by a very well-dressed, smart elderly woman. She said in an awestruck whisper, 'Your little dog wants to make himself comfortable. Do stop for him.'

'Oh', Mrs E. replied, 'I did not know'.

'Yes', said the lady, 'he has got into position several times …'!

Friday 6 November

General Montgomery, commanding the Eighth Army, said today that the Battle of El Alamein had ended in 'complete and absolute victory' for the Allies. Strong British tank forces he added, were now operating in the enemy's rear. 'We have no intention of letting him recover', he said. 'We intend to hit him for six right out of Africa'.

Saturday 7 November

Waking up in London was a thrill. It is a wonderful place. Coming over Westminster Bridge yesterday on our way from Waterloo seemed so exciting. Big Ben standing up so strong and firm, the Houses of Parliament just the same. After over three years I felt as if the years had been a dream and I had never left London for so long and there had never been a war at all and certainly the war couldn't be on <u>now</u>!

Yesterday after dumping our luggage at our Service Club we went to Harrods and saw a cousin of Betty, who had tea with us. She had very kindly got us tickets for three shows. After tea we went to the Saville Theatre where we saw a very amusing variety with Leslie Henson, Stanley Holloway and Douglas Byng – Lesley Henson as a Home Guard and as a white hen, very funny. Jill met us outside and took us to dinner at the Berkely Buttery, such fun seeing her again. She was full of life and thrilled about her crowns. She is to be Commandant overseas and start the Women Military Police in Egypt, it is a wonderfully interesting job of course and should be awful fun as well as everything else. Before splitting up the party and going our various ways, we went round some of Jill's police posts in the West End to see the girls and generally have a look around ourselves! Quite amusing. I was rather struck (and so was Betty) with the amount of WAAF police in comparison with ATS. I met Frankie in Piccadilly, while Betty went shopping. We lunched at Gunters, great fun as her father now owns it, we were made into pets of course and Alex's charming sister lunched with us. She looked fearfully tired but delightful. The food a dream. I did enjoy it.

Said goodbye to Frankie till this evening, rushed off to meet Betty at the Coliseum to see *The Belle of New York*. Evelyn Laye really wonderful, she still looks twenty years old and is exceedingly fascinating as well as pretty. Enid Stamp Taylor was exactly like me, so Betty said. We both loved the music and the whole show. When it was over we rushed off to see *Blithe Spirit* at the Duchess. We liked it and found it awfully funny, but it is too far fetched to amuse everybody.

Sunday 8 November

Betty and I got up late after dining with Jill and Frankie after the show last night. We got to the Savoy in time to find Joan and Pat waiting for us. Pat insisted on us lunching there with them. I have never in peace time had a better lunch! It was magnificent, after much food and plenty of drink we all decided to go to see Noel Coward's latest film at the Gaumont in Haymarket – *In Which We Serve*. I thought it wonderfully good, though very sad. The story of the life inside a destroyer during this war and it was so true to life. Noel Coward took the part of the ship's captain and I liked him in it. Some people I suppose might find the picture of blitz life a bit too true when on holiday; people are so fond of being amused without stopping nowadays.

Betty went to see an aunt after tea and I stayed at The Club and talked to Miss Makins, who was very interesting and amusing.

Monday 9 November

I rang up Combo after breakfast and fixed up to meet her at the Regent Palace at eleven o'clock to go with them to see the Lord Mayor's Show, took Betty with me. She was in a vile temper because she said she wanted to go home and Joan arranging to travel tomorrow had spoilt her entire weekend! Poor old Betty. She got better after meeting the Leaches, who liked her. But by this time I was feeling cross myself! The show was poor but Mr Leach arranged for us to have a window in the café overlooking the whole parade, so we saw it in comfort. After this we all separated and Mr Leach and I decided to spend the afternoon going round St Paul's etc. We began with St Paul's, as wonderful as ever. We went all round it and up to the Stone Gallery, where we stood looking down at the greatest city in the world. We walked all round the Whispering Gallery as well. We then walked to the Temple. The bomb devastation there is very bad, the church just an empty shell and the courtyards all tumbled to pieces. Our next port of call was the Old Bailey, where we were shown all over No. 1 Court where all the murder cases are tried. We went down in the cells and sat on the criminal's chair in the dock. The atmosphere in there was indescribably foreboding and seemed like a mighty weight about to fall on one's head. In the evening Betty and Combo met us and we saw the Ballet at the New Theatre with Robert Helpmann in *Comus*. Very lovely and I think we all enjoyed it more than anything we had seen yet …

Tuesday 10 November

Saw Betty off at Waterloo in the morning, on my way to Oxford Street to buy Maimie some wool for a three piece. Then at 12.30 I found my way to the Regent Palace to meet Aunt Beeloo and Muriel. Found no difficulty in recognising them. Aunt Beeloo looked a bit older than when I saw her but otherwise the same. They were both so nice and I thoroughly enjoyed my afternoon. After lunch we went to a news film and then had tea together at Lyons Corner House where the foreign waiter (all the waiters are foreigners) was very nice and fixed us up with a table between us three. We then caught an Underground, they went back to Hounslow and I got out at Sloane Square to dress up for the evening. I wore my mauve frock and coat with fox fur and met Bob and Doreen at the Regent Palace once more. There we dined on duck and green peas. Bob as chatty and amusing as ever. We had a very nice evening sitting in the lounge smoking and drinking, watching the people go by, quite a good spot after blackout! They saw me to my train to Sloane Square and were awfully jolly and I was glad I had run into Bob outside a pub near St Paul's yesterday. When I got back to my Club I found they had put a WAAF into Betty's bed in my room! She was very nice and I did not mind her much. A fog is beginning tonight, quite thick in places but I hope it will pass by tomorrow. I dread fog they give me a bad chest usually ...

Friday 25 December

Maimie and I spent a very pleasant Christmas. I put the two cockerels into the oven, with pudding and vegetables boiling above while we went to church. There we met Mrs Everett, who we brought back with us. Ate a large lunch, washed it up and then sank into armchairs for the afternoon. Listened to the King's speech, I thought his best and he spoke so fluently. Then had tea, my wartime Xmas cake quite a success, so were the almond biscuits. Mrs Everett complimented me on my cooking, by the way! For decorations in the house, we had bowls of Christmas roses, violets, yellow jasmine and a couple of roses. The Christmas roses the best we have ever had here.

Saturday 26 December

I managed to do some gardening. First, we (the dogs, cats and I) painted the new railings that Madge has put up for the blackberries, green: it looks so nice. Then we cleared up all the leaves and old cabbage stumps off the lawn inside the fowls run, a good job done. The funny hens were so amusing while I raked up the rubbish. They got awfully in the way playing about.

Sunday 27 December

Dolly and Shandy came for a walk, so Domino, Sam and I went off with them to Littleham, up to West Down Farm and down to the cliffs through the fields. I had to keep Domino on a lead in case he ran after the sheep. Last time we went there he ran after the whole flock, and at this time, it is a bad thing.

I have spent some time this evening writing letters to friends. An awful bore and I hate it but it must be done. Letter writing is not in my line, I am afraid!

Wednesday 30 December

This morning the Luftwaffe bombed Exeter again. Six bombers flew over the city dropping bombs in South Street. Up to now there are five fatal casualties but they are still digging under the debris. I watched one of the bombers flying very low over

Exmouth with smoke from our ack–ack guns circling round it, but unfortunately they did not bring it down while I was watching. However, they shot down one of the six, three of which flew over here; I only heard the growling engines of the other two. Almost directly the German planes had disappeared, we sent three squadrons out over the sea, they flew over our house on their way.

1943

Terror from the Sky, Goats, Leaving Plans

Sunday 10 January

Frankie told me more about the raid on Holloway Street, Exeter, last Wednesday week. The antique shop, 'The man in Armour', got a direct hit, which being next to the ATS stores, completely wrecked the building, very badly injuring the ATS personnel working there. Sergeant Major Tolley was terribly cut and on the danger list. Poor little Davidson was in hospital, fearfully cut. Frankie's desk has not yet been found, so Frankie would have been killed had she not been in the reception station with dysentery at the time. The raiders machine-gunned the army huts in Belmont Park, where I used to work, and injured about thirty ATS personnel there. They also dropped a bomb in the lime kiln which killed nobody.

About 100 civilians were injured and a dozen or more have so far been found killed. The army was immediately called in to dig for victims. Poor little Frankie is getting rather nervous after all these raids, and once last year she got concussion when the next-door house fell into her bedroom in the Close. Today raiders came over here again and bombed Starcross. Our guns were all going off and the bombs made our windows shake a good bit, but it rather frightened my little sergeant friend after her nasty experiences …

Friday 15 January

The heaviest rainstorm for eight years has lashed the Straits of Dover for the past twenty-four hours. Thousands of seagulls were driven far inland. Buses plying coastal roads between Kentish seaside towns have travelled axle-deep through lakes of rain.

Monday 18 January

Big Russian forces are being used to blast into submission the remaining German divisions in the Stalingrad pocket. Hungry, without the slightest chance of rescue, the Germans are fighting on to the end and in this snow-swept expanse of steppe. The commander, von Paulus knows that he can never be relieved.

Tuesday 19 January

The London area had its third Alert within twenty-four hours last night.

Wednesday 20 January

The news that Leningrad has been relieved after 500 days of siege and unheard of suffering is the greatest event since the salvation of Stalingrad. In the popular mind, it ranks second only to the decisive victory at Moscow in December 1941.

Thursday 11 February

Madge got the four dozen raspberry plants planted in the space next to the violets facing west. He also moved the damson to a place near the lilac where it can grow without being clipped back at all. He then put the half dozen red and half dozen black currants into the bit of ground under the bank, loganberries at the back to grow up the bank. On Tuesday he is going to put in three young gooseberry plants with the currants to fill in the plot of ground.

For myself, I have been busy in the flower garden. I began in the middle of January and have so far pricked over the two big herbaceous beds on each side of the drive, the delphinium bed, iris beds, lily pond surround, all round the conservatory, half the rockery and I have tidied up the clay bed by the front door, it is too wet at present to dig it at all. Have raked the sticks off the lawn and cleared away all the rubbish under the north wall. Now I must finish the rockery and clean up the terrace under the windows. The pear trees are in bud, also the peaches, extraordinarily early and let us hope there will <u>not</u> be severe frost after this wet winter. It rained more in January than it had for forty years. In Exmouth we had six inches during the month.

Sunday 14 February

I went for a short walk with Dolly and Shandy; Domino and Sam did so love it. They look forward every Sunday to their nice country walk with Domino's 'girlfriend'.

Betty and Frankie came to tea. Betty is on a week's leave. Frankie rushed in here before lunch, wondering where they lived; she could not find the house and had forgotten the address. Betty Casels and Robert also came to tea. They fed the hens with me first, as Robert loves the hens and would not miss feeding them for anything. Joan could not come as Michael was so tired after the air raid last night and she thought he had better stay at home. However, Joan had a party after tea which she invited me to, so up I went with the other two (Betty and Frankie). It was great fun and we all enjoyed ourselves hugely. One of the Royal Marine officers was most amusing and kept us in fits.

Tuesday 16 February

Betty and I met at the bus leaving here for Exeter at 10.35. It was a cloudless day so we very much enjoyed our day. First we shopped. Betty found a beautiful pair of fur-lined boots at Charles and Charles. They only had five pairs in the shop. We then went round doing a few little jobs and things until we went along to the café to meet Frankie for lunch. After lunch we went back to Frankie's flat where we had a smoke and ate sweets while Frankie showed us her wardrobe. At about 1.45 we tootled off to the film, *Bambi*, another of Walt Disney's, it was charming and in colour, but rather terrifying for small children I thought. After that we had a frightful American picture which was one of the most uninteresting and blithering films I have ever seen. The news was good. Lord Louis Mountbatten addressing the cadets at Sandhurst 'passing out' parade was quite devastating!

Saturday 20 February

This was the day when I should <u>not</u> have been amused! Mr Barber and Madge had arranged to cut down one of our fir trees with the help of Mr Barber's gardener, Avery by name. Madge and Avery began sawing and axing the tree until they were both hot and tired, then they arranged trunks and boughs lying on the lawn for the tree to fall on without damage to the grass. Mr Barber himself arrived for the seats in the stalls just before the performance was due to begin. Mrs Pile and I, both busy spring cleaning in the drawing room, craned our heads out of the window for the show. Suddenly, an awful heave! The tree fell with terrible crashing, tearing noises – but not on the logs on the lawn – on the top of the next tree, one we particularly valued for its use in shutting out Mrs Barber's house from our vision. The two gardeners were speechless and Mr Barber stood there with his mouth wide open, then he scuttled home without a word! After a while I went out and laughed at poor Madge, who looked a bit sick but said he could take being laughed at! Another hour went by while they scrambled about cutting out branches from the tree the fir fell into, before Maimie, furious, went out and told Madge what she felt about it and he also completely lost his temper and they had a real old row on the lawn.

Sunday 21 February

I'm getting on with the garden. Have been weeding and digging the big south herbaceous bed and bank behind. I started it last Monday and still have another day before it is finished. I'm then going to hoe the path from the wicket up to the KG. Then the rose beds, but I wish I could prune the roses before forking over the beds but am afraid it is too early yet in case we should get bad frosts before the real spring. Last week we picked our first daffodils from the garden and today I have picked a second bunch for Maimie's room. I'm longing to do the paths as they are beginning to let the garden down badly; they seem to be covered with baby grass plants, how it seeded in them is a mystery to me. The bulbs are all up now and in big bud. Meg is coming home next month so I hope the garden will look pretty for her, but we are amazingly early this year owing to the wet, warm winter. The soil has dried up better than for several months; it is doing it good to get the sun into it where I have been able to dig it over. The garden is getting really thrilling at this time: even the big hyacinths are in big fat bud. The whole garden smells of violets because I have planted them everywhere, they love our soil and grow wild under the trees, in the rocks, crazy paving, even in the KG.

Thursday 25 February

Maimie does not seem up to much, her eyes are now giving her trouble as well as everything else. I was busy all day: cooking and housework all the morning and hoeing the long path past the south border during the afternoon. The dogs of course helped me in the garden, poor Domino barking at all the planes overhead. He is a silly old dog, so fearfully excited by the planes. Sammy sat near in his basket; he is not allowed to sit about on the ground since his illness. The cats are getting very lazy; they both so love lying on Maimie's bed all day purring, naughty little things.

The garden is looking prettier every day. The primroses, daffodils and crocuses are looking lovely everywhere. In fact, somehow when in the garden the rest of the world and the war seem very far away. The climbers up the wire are all shooting and looking very well after their move in the autumn to their new positions. The lilies under the Italian cypress are just coming up as well and the whole thing is very thrilling. The roses in the rose beds are shooting so quickly, I am determined to prune them next week; it is such an early season this year. At this rate the garden will be very tidy by the time Meg comes on 18 March, but one never knows what may happen before then.

Friday 26 February

Domino, Sam, Rusty and I were all quietly polishing the pretty little nick-nacks on the ornamental table in the drawing room (the last job of the spring-clean) when suddenly I heard the unmistakable sound of machine-gun fire, rather deep-throated but it came nearer – nearer still. Domino rushed out in the garden before I could stop him. The noise now was terrific. Four German fighter-bombers raced across our lawn at tree top height, machine-guns rattling as hard as they could. Domino rushing madly round the lawn below them barking furiously. I thought he would be killed for certain. I had Rusty in my arms and little Sammy frightened, crouching at my feet. Then before one had time to think the bombs had begun to rain down as well. The house swayed, the windows shook, the German guns spattered and roared. Some frightened children gathered round the gate into the lane so I called them in. They were very excited and talked without stopping. One had seen a bomb actually falling! He was thrilled! The four planes vanished as quickly as they had come, but, over the town, bombing as they went. The devils. Anyway, after lunch I heard that another four came in from another direction and two American fighters brought two down over the sea ...

Saturday 27 February

Had some details of the raid yesterday morning. A bomb, dropped outside the amusement place in The Strand, jumped past Lloyds Bank into the shops next to it. It completely demolished the tailor's, shoe shop, stationer, jeweller and fruiterer. The shoe-shop man and young daughter were killed. Mr and Mrs Boyce in the jeweller's were saved, so was the fruit shop, Pratts. The tailor was rather badly hurt. Near the gasometer a whole row of rather nice houses were demolished. Up Hulme Road in Philips Avenue a house had a direct hit, killing three women; the damage done there is very bad. Near us, in Raddenstile Lane, the White House had a direct hit killing poor Mrs Thornton and her two maids; poor Colonel Thornton was working in Exeter at the time. Mrs Tindall and a friend were killed while crossing the road in the town to catch a bus and poor Miss Harrison had a leg broken by blast while walking up a road and is in the hospital now. Once again the Beacon was hit when a bomb fell on a house near the poor dear little Misses Thomas … Exmouth is getting her share of blitzing and no mistake. But we must expect it here on the coast I suppose … Altogether, so far, twenty-one people lost their lives yesterday and twenty-eight were sent to hospital injured, but they are still digging …

Sunday 28 February

Maimie up again today. Her eye a bit better and she seems more herself after a week in bed. The dogs and I picked flowers to decorate the house in the morning. We chose daffodils and narcissus for one big bowl in the drawing-room, laurustinus and pyrus-japonica for another and for a third we had some branches of forsythia. In the hall we put a big bowl of laurustinus and pyrus and the dining-room table had a mixed bowl of floating flowers. The drawing-room is at last completed, having had the chimney swept on Monday. Mrs Pile and I have been up to our eyes in cleaning it ever since. I cleaned the windows, picture frames, cut glass ornaments and glass lamp shades with some wonderful new stuff I bought at the ironmonger. The result is simply marvellous; everything shines and glitters all round the room. We have decided to live in the dining-room for the rest of spring as the fire makes such a mess in the newly spring-cleaned room and the Otto stove in the dining-room is very cosy and warm. The wood and coal fire in the other room will also save Madge's time, he had to cut wood for hours every week to keep the fire going and now he wants more time for the garden. We have the big sofa from the drawing room so it is quite comfortable to sit in for the time being until the weather is warmer.

Tuesday 2 March

Frankie rang me up to tell me of her narrow escape on Sunday afternoon when she was walking in the country. Suddenly an RAF fighter plane dashed through the hedge a few feet from where she was standing – it then dashed across a field and crashed into a bank. She ran for help but when she, with several friends, got to the plane, much to their joy the pilot walked to meet them, quite unhurt. He was a

Rhodesian and was one of the pilots who shot down one of the German planes which attacked Exmouth on Friday. By the way, the death roll here is now thirty-one. Poor General Price was killed in his car when it was turned over in the town when they bombed it. I shall miss him.

Sunday 7 March

Fighter pilots who won renown in Spitfires are now flying the fast, still secret, Typhoons and find the Typhoon faster than any plane the Germans have flown, so far. These fighter planes equipped with the Sabre engine, have become the terror of the tip and run raiders. Every time the raiders set out for the English coast the Typhoons are waiting for them over the Channel. They are faster than the Focke-Wulf 190 (this latter plane was the type that blitzed Exmouth on February 26).

Thursday 11 March

Dolly and her spaniel, Shandy, met me, Domino and Sam at the bus stop, where we boarded a bus for Budleigh, getting out at Landsdown. We walked along the East Budleigh road for about half a mile before turning up the lane which leads up onto the common. The day was perfect for a good tramp, the sun brilliant, the wind cold, the air crisp and keen. When we got to the big pond, in a field by the tiny lane which we came to by climbing up a steep knoll under a clump of fir trees, then crossing a ploughed field with a glorious view and another with roots, the two spaniels went mad with joy, plunging into the water, barking and grunting with delight. They swam round, turning they looked lovely with their ears lying on the water, their swimming so graceful. We then walked along the top of two fields with splendid views before diving over a hedge into a huge wood which was carpeted by bluebells with cascades of honeysuckle hanging over all the saplings. The spaniels got up a pair of pheasants in the middle of the wood. We eventually came out by the Royal Marine Camp where they were firing on the range, so we made ourselves scarce, getting over a bank into the road which runs past Raleigh's Farm. Outside the farm a young sheepdog played with the dogs while a carthorse looked on with a man loading up mangolds from a big heap. Raleigh's house, called Hayes Barton, could be a heavenly home if the garden was remade. It is a sweet place and only two minutes ride from the heather-covered common. We continued down this road until we came to East Budleigh, where we climbed up a steep bank and sat down on some ancient steps leading to the churchyard and had our tea with the three darling dogs sleeping at our feet. This bank was really the side of an old orchard which had huge clumps of golden double daffodils under the old apple trees. The sun where we sat was hot enough for May – glorious. After a half-hour sit down we started our walk home. The dogs got quite tired but they kept on well. We walked past Snow's nurseries, where I paid a bill, then on along the road for another mile before turning up a small lane which brought us out by the big Georgian house, Tidwell, where Lord Clinton's agent lives. Then along another mile or so until we arrived back at Landsdown where we started from. Here we waited for a bus to take us home to Exmouth. The little dogs as happy as they could be, Sam rather weary …

Sunday 14 March

Frankie and I walked down to the Maer Bay Hotel to see some friends of hers, Mr and Mrs Gastrel, delightful old pair, Maimie would like them. They are living there for the duration; their house was taken by the military with ten days notice to get out. In the afternoon we slept in deck chairs on the terrace in the blazing sun with Maimie with a parasol up. It really was heavenly and so warm. The garden was much admired by Frankie. It is looking nice. I have mowed the lawns now and cut the edges except round the fruit trees. The hyacinths in the round bed are glorious just now. The primroses in clumps up the new south border are pretty, my choice denticulata primula is out too. The narcissus in the two borders by the front drive are a picture, so are the anemonies round the four iris beds near the lily pond. The big trumpet daffodils all along behind the loganberries are beginning to flower now. They are a sight. The spring is a very beautiful time and no mistake. The polyanthus are lovely as well, so are wanda and several mauve aubrietias – I can never remember the flowers so early before, it is so lovely having this early spring after a wet winter and it cheers one in the blitzes.

Thursday 18 March

Maimie not able to make the effort, so I went alone to Ambrose's wedding. The day was brilliant, not a cloud in the sky so the run to Topsham by bus was very pleasant. Arriving at the church door, I met Joan Ashford and Mrs Longridge so sat with them in the church. The bride was late. Bammy looked awfully nice, his mother charmingly dressed in a coloured brocade dress with black hat and coat. The best man was nice, a lieutenant in RA. Dr and Mrs Morton were very jolly and gay, their little girl very sweet. Joan Ashford looked pretty in brown and fawn. Miss Chesnutt and Mrs Vernon very sweet and pleased to see me. Mr Tucker a splendid host and Alice rather amusing. The vicar and his wife very nice. Mrs Barnes very chatty about Penelope and Ralph (the latter doing very well in his job in London). Miss Symons was at the church but not at the reception so I had no talk with her. Bammy was so pleasant and himself. He thanked me more than once for the silver salt cellars, which he liked tremendously.

Friday 19 March

Meg arrived yesterday, having taken exactly twenty-four hours getting here from Belfast. She got home at 6.45 in nice time for supper. She looked very well and wore a very smart navy hat. She had a good journey down after a quiet crossing when it was rather foggy but not enough to delay the boat more than a few minutes …

Today Meg, Domino, Sam and I went down shopping in the town. We paid the books and bought quite a few odd things for the weekend. We then had coffee at

Clapp's Café, hoping to see someone we knew but we arrived late and the place was nearly empty. Esme rang up last night to say she was coming on Monday for a little visit. It will be delightful to see her again; it has been years since she has actually stayed with us. In the afternoon we all lounged in the sun in the conservatory where it was quite hot. I clipped baby Sam again as he is getting a bit smelly and so hot in his huge coat. The darling little dog was as good as gold and moved in any position I wanted him so amiably, it took me an hour and a half to finish him.

Sunday 21 March

Frankie rang me up to tell me that Alex has been killed. I am terribly sorry. He was in private life a Count in Poland and died a squadron leader in the RAF. His deeds and exploits are some of the bravest I have ever heard of. He was the best pilot in the Polish Air Force and was given especially daring jobs. Some time ago he was flying over occupied countries dropping British spies, and returning two days later to pick them up again. After escaping from Poland, Alex did sabotage in France, spied in Germany and France. Among other things, he personally blew up one important factory. As a squadron leader and before that, he shot down quite a number of enemy planes and I well remember one day at the Exeter Airport he shot down two German planes in one day. He was piloting a Beaufighter when he was killed. He crash landed near an airport in the north of England. He was wounded after a fight and I can only think he must have lost consciousness before landing. He had full honours at his funeral. So ends a gallant life, fighting with faultless courage for his country and its liberty. His charming sister, Majer has only recently been sent to the Middle East, she adored him, poor girl. His wife and two small sons are hiding in a forest in Poland. God help them …

Monday 22 March

Meg went down to the town to meet Esme at the station, where she fetched up after a journey of about six hours from Lynton. Esme in very good form, although she said she felt awfully tired and finds her work at the hospital rather wearing, however she looked much better than when I last saw her at Topsham. She seemed fatter. After she had tea, Meg and she went down to see a play, *The Blue Goose*, at the Savoy, in aid of the Lifeboat and produced by the Exmouth Amateurs. Esme liked it very much and thoroughly enjoyed the show, she is living a pretty dull life now at Lynton, I fancy.

Tuesday 23 March

In the morning Meg, Esme, Domino, Sam and I went for our usual weekly walk up to Littleham to pay the milk book and leave Miss Price some eggs. The wind was bitterly cold and Esme and I both thought our colds would not be improved! We went home along the fields with the dogs – the hedges and lanes are getting so pretty and green – got home just in time for lunch.

After an early tea I rushed down to the station in a taxi in the pouring rain to catch the Exeter train to spend an evening with Frankie, who was a bit quiet for her after hearing of the death of a <u>third</u> friend this last week, killed in action. Life is sad nowadays, I must admit. Never mind. The only thing is never to think of the day ahead, just live for <u>today</u>. We went to a very exciting war film, about a lone British bomber, flying over Germany, bombing the target, being shot down and the survivors of the crew escaping. Really very thrilling indeed … Had a drink and a gorgeous duck egg supper at Frankie's flat before returning home in pouring rain and only too thankful that I had a taxi anyway to bring me home dry and warm with my cold none the worse …

Wednesday 24 March

We three and the dear dogs went down shopping and had coffee at the Sunlit Café, we expected Mrs Everett but she did not turn up after all. We shopped also. Meg bought me a glorious book for my birthday at Boots. After lunch we looked at my wardrobe and I gave Esme my biscuit-check linen coat and skirt. She liked it and we spent the rest of the day altering it to fit and suit her, the result will be awfully nice. I also gave Esme my funny little hat from Madeira, with its little tail sprouting from the top! It suited her very well and goes with the suit. I also put in the blouse that goes with it, so it is quite nice for her for the summer. It is nice to get rid of clothes that one is tired of on unfortunate friends, because in these days of clothes rationing, one simply cannot throw anything away if it is in good condition. I also got rid of my beautiful (but very old) shoes I got from Frankie who got them made for her in Austria years ago. They were much too big for me and I had completely given up wearing them and Meg got into them quite easily. I am pleased about that as well as shoes are always so useful and so wasted in the cupboard if one does not wear them …

Sunday 28 March

Frankie arrived in good spirits in good time. She looked very nice in her well-cut paleish tomato coat and skirt her mother gave her. We had poor Henny Penny for lunch; she was delicious in spite of being four years old. I had boiled her very gently <u>all</u> day yesterday on the Ideal and this morning I poured over her plenty of thick white sauce full of parsley sauce. The girls all said she was excellent.

After lunch I went for a dog walk with Dolly and Shandy, we only went to the meadows, where the two spaniels swam in the brook. On our return we found the family all fast asleep in the sun on the terrace. Marjorie had an early tea before catching her bus for home; she has to work tomorrow morning. Frankie suddenly decided to rush off to catch a bus to Exeter before supper, she does not like the blackout and Mary was out so she dashed back in daylight. Spent the evening cleaning up and trying to go to bed early, after yesterday night, when we sat up playing Rummy in a new way until after 1 a.m. Marjorie's way is the best I know and makes the game really interesting, so we sat up nearly all night watching Meg win easily as usual. She always won at cards!

Friday 2 April

Feel quite thrilled with the thought of going out in the car again with Maimie for shopping, we are both getting clothes which is always thrilling! The dogs and I went down to the town this morning, doing the usual dull things one has to do, pay books etc. On our return home Domino and I cleaned the car and started her up. She looks lovely and dear Domino sat next to the driver for nearly an hour watching me and feeling so excited, poor darling, he will have to keep watch at home with Sam instead of shopping I am afraid. The dogs are too much of a good thing when it comes to buying clothes.

The garden looks prettier every day, the daffodils, narcissus, hyacinths, grape-hyacinths, primulas, primroses, almond, forsythia and viburnum carlesii are glorious, the bees getting very busy and every corner seems to be singing as I walk by. I do love our beautiful little garden in the spring, summer and autumn, it is always gay with glorious flowers and peaceful with the songs of birds and cooing of the darling wood pigeons. Must stop writing now and Domino and I must go out to polish all the chromium on the car before we start for our shopping expedition.

Wednesday 14 April

Another day like heaven, really warm, sunshine and blue sky. The garden is getting very dry now, that is the only disadvantage of the long unbroken spell of dry weather; it has not rained since the first week of February. Domino, Sam and I all paid the dairy at Littleham, took half a dozen eggs to Miss Price and walked home across the fields, it was so perfectly lovely, the elms quite green everywhere, the blackthorn going over but still pretty, the buttercups and daisies beginning to colour the green fields. While we were wandering up the tiny lane towards home the siren howled out a warning, but the peace was only broken by the guttural purr of a few German planes flying very high along the coast in the misty sky. No bombs disturbed the birds singing and wood pigeons cooing all round. Once, one of our coastal machine-guns gave a short rat-a-tat as if to remind the offending Germans to fly a little further away!

Yesterday Esme sent me a large book token, so very sweet of her; she said she thought it was about my birthday time. Maimie and I went down in the town and to my intense satisfaction I was able to get Axel Munthe's *Memories and Vagaries* and for another I chose *Laughing Odyssey* which is about Russia …

Saturday 17 April

Another perfect day. Maimie and I are both in summer clothes and hot in them. It is just like a June day, not a cloud in the sky all day and warm, brilliant moon all day. I do hope some people will be able to enjoy this really glorious spell of weather and not be too busy to be able to spend any time out of doors in this heavenly sun. Yesterday evening Dolly and Shandy fetched us out for a walk in the fields, the dogs nearly went mad with excitement, they ran, barked, fought, begged, paddled and swam. They enjoyed every second of their time. We collected Dusky from next door and he played with them and was much more normal and less nervous, poor little dog; he is getting used to the crazy party now and is not too scared to run with them all, he is taking to the water, goes in and absolutely wallows with Dom and Shandy. Sam is too French and Parisian to bathe or run wildly, he picks his way and only runs when the ground in front is clear, he does not rush madly through all the undergrowth like the three spaniels do. We did not get home till nearly seven o'clock and were rather late giving the hens their supper, the two broody pullets furious at being shut up!

Sunday 18 April

Woke up to a brilliant morning, the sun sending gleams of gold through the early misty atmosphere, which seemed to hang over the trees like a filmy veil. This wonderful spell of summery weather to herald spring is indeed too good to be true almost. The winter has passed so quickly, we have really had only four months of cold winter days this season, now summer seems to be here again. The trees are now pale green right up to the top-most twigs, the undergrowth has been green for the last fortnight, they look simply lovely, you can just see the blue hills of Haldon behind them before the leaves grow too big to see any view through. The early purple irises are all out everywhere, the laburnum trees and the lilac. Tulips make all the duller corners bright and the mauve perpetual candytuft and white daises round the house are a blaze of blossom. It is all so lovely. The stocks in the 'long' bed are out, also the cheiranthus vivid golden. All the seeds are flourishing in the conservatory. The fruit is beginning to set on the peaches, gooseberries, greengage, pears and the black currants are a mass of flower, so the garden is looking nice in every corner. The hens are laying well, two pullets are broody and the three fattening cockerels putting on weight quickly …

Tuesday 20 April

A wonderful day again, the dogs and I paid the dairy at Littleham, took half a dozen eggs to Miss Price and then walked down to Littleham village where we posted some letters before turning up the lane to the meadows past Green Farm. The cows were grazing in the fields and the birds singing as we walked past the thatched old house and along the lane by the stream until we came out in some more meadows. There dear Domino bathed in the deeper water of the brook running at the bottom. The dogs always love this walk. On our way home we met Betty Weippert, who has been for several bathes at Sandy bay and says the water is as warm as it often is in August. Amazing to think of! This evening I am going to mow the big lawn, I want to get them all done for Easter as the grass is growing fast now in spite of no rain, but we are getting pretty heavy dews at night. I do hope the new moon will not bring awful weather. After this perfect month, it would be so trying …

Tuesday 27 April

The poor dogs were very sad because I left them alone when I dashed off to catch the 11.30 bus for Exeter where I met Frankie outside her office before walking to Tinley's Café in the Close, where we met Patience Thesiger, my old company commander, and her father and mother for lunch. It was awfully nice to see Patience again, I had not seen her for about two years and hardly recognised her in mufti, as I rarely saw her in anything but uniform. She looked very young and cheerful, thoroughly enjoys life I think. We all talked about old times in the old company of course. She says Betty is very well in Didcot and they did some shows in Town recently, which was fun.

After lunch Frankie and I went back to her flat for a few moments before catching my bus for home, I was fortunate enough to get into the Budleigh one leaving Exeter at 2.05, which brought me up to Hospital Corner, most convenient; I must try and always get that one. On my return home, after a terrific welcome from all four animals, I began potting up my young tomato plants in the greenhouse. A great thrill, it really is getting quite like summer at last. Madge must make up the hot bed for marrows ...

Wednesday 28 April

Domino, Sam and I fetched Dusky out to walk him up to Littleham with us. He thoroughly enjoyed the walk but was scared of the large force of fighter squadrons which went over our heads, very low, in the direction of France. Poor little dog, he shrank from them. On our way we took the Misses Clay four Easter eggs. Miss Clay seemed very pleased and is coming down to see Maimie soon again. On the way home we took the field path where Dusky unfortunately found some farm hens to run after; next time I must keep him on the lead when we pass the farm.

Sunday 2 May

Maimie and I went to church. We started early to get a seat as the church was packed to overflowing to hear the Archbishop of Canterbury, Dr Temple, who preached the sermon. This is the first time in the history of Exmouth that it has been visited by the Archbishop. His sermon was long and very fine; I came away with the impression that he is a man with a very tremendous faith. It was indeed a thrill to see and hear him. It took me back to 1939 when I was in the congregation of St Peter's, Rome and saw the Pope. What an extraordinary contrast. The two heads of two great Churches but such different men. Our vicar, Mr Shelmadene, was taking the service for the last time. He is going to Silverton this week. He looked rather sad, but it must have been a triumphant day for him – not many vicars have the Archbishop of Canterbury to preach their goodbye sermons for them on their last Sundays!

Monday 3 May

An April heat wave, during which the maximum temperature never fell below seventy degrees, provided parts of the South of England with the warmest spell at this time of the year in the present century.

Wednesday 5 May

Poor Frankie just rang up to tell me Eugene has been killed. Her mother wrote and told her that his friend wrote to tell her. Presumably he was still flying a Lancaster bomber and was in one of the recent big raids. It is too beastly for anything. Eugene was the last airman I knew still alive and now he has gone. Every friend and acquaintance I have had in the RAF have been killed now. Poor Frankie is in an awful state about her dear Pole, Eugene. He was so nice. I am mad about it. What will become of Poland? All the officers seem to be dying, certainly all the aristocrats, like Alex and his good-looking friend with the impossible name!

Yesterday, when I was lunching with Frankie, I was horrified when she told me to read a letter she slipped into my hand. It was from David, her naval friend's father, writing to tell her that he was killed at Aden in 1942. So little Frankie is in the depths of despair now, hearing the death of two great friends in two days has been a frightful shock to her …

Exeter was looking rather lovely in the brilliant sunshine as we sat in Frankie's window overlooking the Close and beautiful cathedral; we also saw lots of delightful British officers and some fat Americans outside the Clarence.

Tuesday 18 May

With a single blow the RAF has precipitated what may prove to be the greatest industrial disaster yet inflicted on Germany in this war. Early yesterday morning a force of Lancasters, with crews specially trained for the task, attacked and destroyed the great dams on the Mohne and Sorpe rivers, tributaries of the Ruhr, and also the dam on the Eder river. Today the waters of the Ruhr and Eder are sweeping down the valleys carrying everything before them. Railways and road bridges are broken down. Hydro-electrical power stations are destroyed or damaged and a railway marshalling yard is under water. The effect of the destruction of the three dams is incalculable. Some idea of the flood of water released by the destruction of the dams can be judged from the fact that the 202,000,000 tons capacity of the Eder reservoir would have been enough to supply the whole of London for 150 days even in peacetime. The Lancasters used mines to blow up the dams. Wing-Commander Gibson personally led the attack on the Mohne dam. After dropping his mines he flew up and down alongside the dam to draw the fire of the anti-aircraft from the planes following him. They attacked from almost '0' feet in face of terrific anti-aircraft fire …

Wednesday 19 May

The floods loosed by the RAF breaching of the Mohne, Sorpe and Eder dams continue to spread havoc and destruction through the Ruhr and Weser valleys.

Thursday 27 May

I collected Dusky and with Domino and Sam we met Dolly at the Hospital Corner bus stop, boarded the Budleigh bus and saw Barbara in further up the road. We went as far as the turning for East Budleigh and Ottery, got out and walked up the road, then along the lane to the fir copse where the view was, as ever, lovely, we then continued on until we came to the pond. The spaniels all made a wild rush for the water. They swam and they swam round and round, up and down. It was lovely to see them. Dusky is a beautiful swimmer he does not seem to move, he just floats along. They were so good while we lunched – all sat round as good as gold. Barbara loved them all.

Friday 28 May

I had a lovely picnic at Sandy Bay with Barbara. It was such fun. The three dogs enjoyed every minute of it. We tried to climb round the cliffs but could only get a short distance as the sea was too high, but the dogs adored it. They came into deep water, when we got up on the rocks Domino and Dusky dived in and out, the water was about 4ft deep, they loved the party, nearly went mad with joy and Dusky did not seem to mind the salt water in the least, I thought he might hate the taste. Sammy was rather tired and during tea he dug a little hole in the sand to lie in under a rock in the shade. By the way, Sam also swam. He came after me in deep water; I was beginning to think I should have to go back to the shore to fetch him when I found him bravely following me, splashing, swimming and jumping among the rocks. He is a dear little dog. He naturally does not like the water but today he evidently thought we would leave him behind. During tea they were all very good and only sat up and begged for food after we called them. By way of amusement Domino tore up and down the beach barking at any gull or jackdaw he saw, they flew overhead laughing at him, he gave himself no end of exercise chasing them …

Saturday 29 May

I sold quite a good number of 'buttons' in Exeter Road and saw the parade, which was very good – for Exmouth! The Royal Marines with their faces painted for commando work looked very fine. They were all armed to the teeth with various weapons but what struck me as most pathetic was that directly behind these 'Commando' Marines was their Red Cross unit carrying stretchers etc, also with their faces blacked. One contingent of Royal Marines wore gas masks and made queer noises while they passed. The march was finished by about a dozen tanks, armoured cars etc, very interesting I thought. Of course the greatest thrill was the first man in the whole parade. A tall, dark and handsome naval lieutenant carrying his sword and behind him a unit of ratings marching as one man. I got home in time for lunch. After lunch Dolly came up for a walk but I could not very well go so she stayed to tea. Frankie also came for her weekend; we all had tea on the lawn with the three dogs.

After tea we all went up to Woodbury to see Mrs Mitchell and her goats. She was awfully nice and showed us her three B Alpine kids, before going into the paddock where the other four were running loose. We immediately fell for the two brown ones and eventually bought them both. One is in kid now and the other is giving milk.

Sunday 30 May

We got up frightfully late, spent the whole day talking goats and half the night. I am in a thrill. We are getting a carpenter to convert the big tool shed into a goat house. It is already tiled on the floor with a good drain, so we only have to make a loose box, two stalls, three racks, two windows and cut the door so the top opens separately, quite easy for a carpenter I think. The difficulty would have been the flooring but fortunately that is all ready. We are fencing in a tiny little yard for them outside so they can come out in the air on wettish days, if they want to. I am thinking of making a pen for them in the chicken pen as it would be nice to put them loose somewhere occasionally, also the kids must have somewhere to play in. These goats we have bought are called Susie and Nicholette, rather sweet names. Dolly says Nicholette is Maimie's goat; she is like a little bird, soft brown with darker markings on her back, head and legs. She is a small goat. Susie is larger, a pale fawn with cream coloured markings, but it is difficult to judge her as the kids have made her figure enormous for the time being. I think Susie is a Togenburg but they are neither pedigree goats as I came to the conclusion that I do not know enough to risk buying pedigrees …

Monday 31 May

Torquay had another bad air raid yesterday afternoon. The siren went here about three o'clock while we were in the garden. St Mary's Church at Babbacombe got a direct hit and so far twenty-one children have been dug out dead. A children's service was in progress at the time. I hope Aunt Margaret is okay. One of the hotels was hit on the front. The children bathing were machine-gunned and the shopping centre bombed. One of the four raiders was shot down in a street, doing a lot of damage; the other three were brought down by fighters and ack-ack guns. Fifteen planes came over altogether, so the percentage destroyed was v. good – 4 out of 15 …

Friday 4 June

Yesterday evening Dolly and I biked up to Marley to milk Nicholette. I was so afraid I was going to be a failure, as it is many years since I did any milking and then it was cows at Greenhouse. Anyway little Nicholette quite enjoyed me doing her, she nestled up against me and chewed her cud all the time which Mrs Mitchell said was a very good sign as it showed that she liked me. A man once tried to milk her and he frightened her, so she quite refused to stand quiet while he did her, he had to give it up in the end … The evening was great fun and we so enjoyed it. Dolly milked Nic too – Nic's little kid was a funny little thing. She did not approve of me in the stall and eventually took a flying leap on to Nicholette's back which rather upset things. Susie was very friendly as well, poor little goat, she is still very fat and full of kids. I am longing to see her after they are born, it will be fun. Dolly is so kind and is trying to find a man to help build the goat stable. I went down to the blacksmith's to ask him to make me a couple of iron stakes for tethering and told him the trouble I was having finding a carpenter, he promptly volunteered to come up tomorrow afternoon to help me – wasn't it nice of him.

Saturday 5 June

The blacksmith arrived after lunch and we solidly worked on the house until five o'clock. He filled up one doorway with another door from one of the attics and he put down a division between the loose boxes. I am to buy a hundredweight bag of cement from Heywoods yard on Monday and we are going to do the floor on Tuesday evening. There is a double door to be fitted at the shed entrance and hay racks to be made. But taken on the whole we are getting on very well with it, much to my relief!

Of course, there is to be a tiny yard outside (to be enlarged later) then the job will be finished. I think I shall be able to have Susie and Nicie next week, won't it be thrilling! I have got a couple of tethering ropes, and two chains coming next week, so that part of it will be done. Must order some hay on Monday and get another big dog collar and two swivels from Otton.

I am really getting fearfully excited now by all this terrific excitement! A dairy has always rather fascinated me and two brown goats looking almost exactly like deer does appeal to me frightfully. They will be so sweet on the lawn …

Sunday 6 June

Dolly and I took the four dogs up to the Littleham fields, where they had a lovely time bathing in the brook at the bottom of the fields. They did enjoy themselves. We gave Dusky some lessons in retrieving a ball; he is getting quite good at it and more obedient every time we take him out. Domino got terribly excited and Shandy very jealous of Dusky's lessons. They are a funny troop of dogs to walk – all so original and such good friends. Domino and Shandy are both awfully good with the pup, in fact they are teaching him to do the right thing! Sam is still a bit growly with Dusky. He pretends to be such a grand little dog all the time while the spaniels laugh at him.

After an early supper Dolly and I biked up to Marley again to milk Nicholette. She <u>was</u> a darling. I went into her stall all by myself with the stool and bucket and told her to stand in her usual corner to be milked which she immediately did. I very laboriously milked her, it took me ages and she stood there as good as gold chewing her cud and nestling up against me all the time. She looked prettier than ever today, just like one of the Powderham deer with her dark line down her back and marking down her legs, her little eager face too, was sweet …

Monday 7 June

I'm very busy today buying all the things for the goats etc. I have to order some hay for them and get a bag of cement to do the floor tomorrow. Dolly has a man coming up to help me tonight. We must do the main door and the fence outside. I am rather wondering about the hay racks in each loose box and may be able to start making one this afternoon perhaps. I wish I was really good at carpentry but have always been a fool with the hammer.

Poor old Domino is terribly cross and sulky today. I believe he thinks Dolly and I went for a walk last night with Shandy and left him behind, he is so aggrieved! I'm now wondering when the boy will bring the new hen house. He is hoping to get the men to haul it one day this week and hope he succeeds as I always like to get on with things. Mrs Mitchell is bringing Susie and Nicholette next Thursday morning. I am in a thrill about it all! I do hope they will be happy here, but of course they will not be in the perfect conditions that they are kept in now; they run loose there in a lovely little fenced up paddock, which I have not got, alas! Uncle Snuffy wrote today saying he is letting his house and wants to come near us, if he can …

Thursday 10 June

The two little brown goats arrived safely, Maimie and I in a tremendous thrill. Mrs Mitchell brought them herself in the trailer, she had an awful job to get them in, Susie took them nearly an hour before she would walk up the plank into the trailer. Mrs Mitchell was delighted with their surroundings and the house. She seemed quite pleased with everything but very sad at parting from her two pets. After their former owner went away, the two were a bit strange and nervous, they ate practically nothing all day and refused water, but on the whole they seem wonderfully at home, not frightened of me in the least which I think is very sweet of them, considering I have only seen them three times before. Susie quickly chose for herself the stall especially allotted to her (which was lucky) and Nicholette took the other one. They butt at each other if they go into the wrong one! After supper Dolly came up to help me milk Nicky. She was wonderfully good and chewed her cud standing very quietly all the while except once when the dogs frightened her by their persistent barking. Domino is, so far, very silly about them. He cannot understand what they are and barks at them through the bars of their little pen outside the house.

Monday 14 June

The blacksmith came up after breakfast with the rope tethers complete with rings and swivels also two pairs of pegs. We put Susie and Nicholette on their new tethers which rather pleased them as the dog chains tied together were a bit short. They are dear little goats. Nicky is full of life and ready for anything. She is very affectionate as well. Susie also is a perfect little pet. She is very gentle. They will not be left a minute by themselves and cry directly I take one in and not the other. This evening I took Nicky into their house to milk her, with the intention of taking her back when I had finished. Meanwhile Susie was in such a state that Maimie had to go out to her, she was crying and pulling at her tether quite frantically as we did not immediately return. We took them both out on the lead in the lane and spinney outside our gate. They loved it and ate up the ivy up the trees. Nicky climbed as high as she could up one of the chestnut trees, trying to eat the leaves and young shoots. Mrs Marshall is hoping for some goat's milk in the winter to help her husband along. She finds the rations rather a problem, especially now Mr M. is so unwell. People are difficult to feed if they are off colour …

Sunday 20 June

Miss Price came to tea yesterday and told me that her cat, the mother of Rusty, had just produced six kittens. I am fearfully thrilled and am going to have the eldest, if all goes well! We are going to name him Ruffles. He is orange with long hair. His brothers are white and orange and his two sisters tortoiseshell. I am wondering what Rusty and Ming will think of him. I expect they will both be very annoyed with a kitten; cats are funny jealous things, and usually dislike small kittens. Miss Price is going to let me have some gooseberries for jam and I am going to put a few pounds of prunes with them, they make a delicious flavour I believe. Our gooseberries are poor this year, after a bumper crop last summer. Joan and Mrs Marshall sold me several pounds for bottling last week and I am hoping to have some raspberries when they are ripe for jam. This war makes me frightfully domesticated, find myself thinking about food all day. Darling little Nicholette is supplying me with lovely milk and I made a little Devon cream of some today. I was not sure that you could do it with goats milk but have proved that it can be done. The bees seem to be alright at the moment.

Saturday 26 June

Marjorie arrived in time for tea after a slow journey, if compared with the time in one's own car! The Exmouth bus was too full to board so she had to wait for the next, which was a pity, but she got here by 4.45. So delightful to see her again, looking so nice in navy blue hat, dress and shoes with a putty-coloured short furry coat. She looked very well and cheerful. She is really rather thrilled because Evelyn has gone overseas after a week's embarkation leave. Tropical kit, so we all imagine she must be going to India or somewhere. I do think it is wonderful for her to be really <u>doing</u> something for England with no mistake. Evelyn must look charming in her uniform and such a sweet nurse. I envy the men who get her when they are ill or wounded.

Marjorie loved the goats. She milked Nicky after supper and did it very well. She has never milked before and little Nicky was so good while she did it. Marjorie would very soon learn if she tried often.

Sunday 27 June

Another wonderful day, blazing sun with no clouds anywhere. It is glorious to have this summer weather at last after so many dull, coldish days. After breakfast Marjorie came out with me to milk Nicky – she did not get on quite so well, but she only needs practice. After that Marjorie picked strawberries and turned the hay. She loves country life with its varied occupations to keep one busy from morning to night. Frankie rang up during the morning to say she had a headache or sore throat or something so she is not coming with her American gunner officer after all. I am not surprised! She keeps her men friends entirely to herself always. It is a pity as it spoils her, but some women are like that! Marjorie had to leave by the 4.50 bus to catch the six o'clock from Exeter, so we had tea early and when I was starting to walk to the bus with her Domino had an attack of hysteria so I had to turn back and put Domino to bed in the house, poor old dog, it is his third attack in four days. I must get Mr Norrington to come and see him tomorrow; it is getting nasty as he has them so often. Dear Domino, his nose is so terribly out of joint because of Susie and Nicholette; their arrival has made him mad with jealousy, I do believe …

Sunday 4 July

Dolly and I took the four dogs down in the Littleham fields to play in the stream. Domino found a young rook in the hedge and chased it so much that we had to put him on the lead; the poor bird did not seem able to fly very well. We then walked down the stream till we came to the ford and foot bridge where the spaniels had a lovely little swim. Shandy and Dusky enjoyed it tremendously. When we got back we fetched Susie and Nicky for a drink. By the time we got them in, Frankie, with a Canadian sergeant, had arrived. She looked fit and quite well again after her bad throat. She is going on leave next week which will be nice. Her home in Dorset must be glorious at this time of year. Frankie is fearfully thrilled because she has had news that Eugene is a prisoner of war in Germany, not killed after all. I dread to think what will happen to him. He is a spirited kind of man and a Pole and I hate to think of him in the hands of the bloody Germans. Frankie's Canadian was a nice chap, thoroughly patriotic and said he was so proud to wear the King's uniform and would not wear mufti for anything. He gave up a very good job with Ford's to join up and has been in this country for nearly two years. I was delighted to meet a soldier from Canada.

Friday 9 July

I went down to the town to do some shopping as usual – I generally find Friday a good day for it – and when I came back, Nicky jumped up the fence of their little run, shouting and beating her hoofs in the air. I rushed up to her to see what was the matter and heard a strange noise! It was surely a kid! I went in and Nicky nearly knocked me down to show me Susie's twins. One snow white and the other pale fawn. They had been born at last! What a thrill! Nicky carefully washed the white one which was obviously the elder, while Susie licked the latest arrival. They were so proud. I thought Nicky was sweet to be so excited with Susie's babies. She was so gentle with them and had been doing midwife beautifully while I was out in the town. I am glad to get hold of 14lbs of groats today; they will do Susie good, she looks rather weary and thin now the event is over. Took Nicky out in the compound while I cleaned the stable out, they were born in her loose box, so I carried the babies back to Susie's and cleaned out Nicky's. Mr Norrington came later, said Susie was well and the kids both boys!

Sunday 11 July

Another deplorable day, so dark and dismal, looks like rain but so far it has not begun. After milking Nicky I took her up to the club to tether her in a nice new place, but she wouldn't hear of being left here alone; directly I went away she began calling as loud as she could, so I fetched her onto the lawn until after lunch when we carried the kid and took Susie to join Nicky in the compound for half an hour. The baby played about, he climbed up the bank and once fell over on his little side. He is the sweetest thing you ever saw, the same pale colour as his mother. His tiny brother, a snow-white, like father, was taken away yesterday by poor Mr Norrington, who loathes the job of killing kids, but I cannot keep the billies. It does seem tragic but it cannot be helped. Poor darling Susie. I am afraid she will be terribly upset when this lovely little thing goes, she loves him. She did not seem to notice the loss of the white one because she still had the fawn one. Dolly came in for a walk with the dogs, so we took them round the meadows towards Littleham where they had their usual bathe coming home like wet doormats …

Wednesday 14 July

After a certain amount of preparation for 'The Girls', as Maimie calls them, I walked down to meet their train at 3.15. Was quite anxious at first because so many people got out of the train and I failed to see my two aunts until at last, at the end of the multitude, I suddenly saw them coming towards me. It was so delightful to see them again and they both looked so well and nicely dressed. I thought nobody would ever guess that Aunt Beeloo is about eighty. She had on a very smart navy blue hat put on at exactly the right angle, with blue dress and coat to match. Amamy had a very pretty grey dress and coat with black hat which was also very smart. We got a taxi up and arriving at the house Aunt Beeloo, when she saw Maimie cried out, 'Why, it's Emily coming to meet us'; she said she was awfully like Aunt Emily but as time went on she found Maimie's voice and way of talking exactly like Amamy, so much so that she was always mistaking them for one another. It was nice for the three sisters to get together, it is a long time since they met, for this reason: Devon is rather a trial; we never see any of our relations as they congregate chiefly in and around the Home Counties, Devon is too far away.

Thursday 15 July

Amamy woke up with a terrible idea in her head; she decided that whatever happened, I was to be photographed! Of all things on earth! So after a late breakfast with a good deal of chat between Amamy and myself (Aunt Beeloo, much against the grain, was made to have her breakfast in bed). After a late milking of little Susie and Nicky and a late ordering of dinner, we eventually set out for the town. No bus appeared, so we walked and I hope Amamy was not getting too tired. We made an appointment for the photograph before doing a little shopping. Among other things, Amamy very kindly got a beautiful bath seat for Maimie to sit on in the bath, now she cannot get in and out of her tub. We were very fortunate to find one, but after much hunting the 'fat man' in Otton's produced an old and dirty seat from behind the scenes. After a scrub at home we put it over the bath and it looked splendid for Maimie, who is quite looking forward to using it tomorrow. Mrs Everett came in to tea. She looked very charming in her black coat with flowered dress, it is my favourite 'get up' of hers. Amamy loves the kid and we have decided to keep him. Aunt Beeloo has christened him 'Sandy', because of his own colour and after General Alexander of the African campaign.

Friday 16 July

On arrival, Amamy and Aunt Beeloo decided to stay till Saturday. They are quite enjoying themselves with us I think. They laugh and joke all day. Amamy spends a lot of time playing with the animals. Sandy spent an hour asleep lying on her lap the other evening with Susie quietly grazing nearby on the lawn. The joke is though – Aunt Beeloo has '<u>pretended</u>' never to like animals. Well. Whenever I go near her room she not only has both the dogs on the bed but the two cats as well. Not what I call an animal hater! She adores everyone. Sam and Domino thoroughly enjoy the adoration as they live for it and usually get it, but I never thought they would achieve such a complete victory over Aunt Beeloo!

Aunt Beeloo is in the big spare room and Amamy in the small one. I put a second mattress on the bed because I was not sure if the one on it was lumpy, being a flock one, they get full of lumps which want renewing or remaking every few years to keep them comfortable and this one has had nothing done to it for years. I do hope they are both comfy in their rooms, anyway they seem quite happy and cheerful. Most amusing about the Maternity Home they are staying at in Looe, it has twenty-one inmates, chiefly old men, all wanting the one lavatory at once!

Saturday 17 July

In the morning we said goodbye to 'The Girls'. It was sad that their tiny visit had come to an end. The time flew by so very quickly. I hope they will have a decent journey back to Cornwall; the trains are packed by all accounts which is an awful bore for old people. I think they are very brave to travel at all in these days but usually someone is kind, as they say, and they get a seat somewhere, at their age they simply cannot stand for ever, especially in a moving train. Amamy insisted on giving me a £1 note on our way down to the station which was nice of her, very kind indeed, but she is naughty to give me anything. After a little shopping I returned in time for lunch and then to get things ready for Bea and Marjorie, who are coming for the night from Torquay. At tea time they duly arrived, but unfortunately I got hopelessly late with tea and the poor things had to sit and wait until nearly six o'clock while I ran about with Ridler, who is fixing up the goat pen really strongly. Then Mr Norrington came to see Susie, who is not picking up quite as quickly as she should after the birth of her twins; then Mr Barber came in with a basket of beans for the goats and last but not least, Dolly came round for a walk with the dogs. She stayed and helped me get tea which <u>was</u> a joy as it was after 5.30 by this time!

Sunday 18 July

Began the day by a late breakfast and a lengthy discussion on the political situation of England now and in the future. I quite forgot the time and by the time we had finished it was getting very late and the goats had to be milked! I left Nicky for Marjorie to milk while I did Susie. But that wicked little goat thought otherwise; she was most indignant with the idea of being milked by Marjorie. I listened (so did Susie) for any signs of milk production such as splashing in the bucket or squirts across the straw – nothing, not a sound until at last a soft thud and there was Marjorie sitting in Nicky's bed with the stool collapsed under her! This pleased Nicky tremendously. She simply grinned with delight and proceeded to dance, jump and kick. Susie, Marjorie and I laughed too at the ridiculous scene but in the end Nicky had her way and I had to milk her after all! We then took them all up to the club to graze before getting on with indoor jobs. Susie's doctor came with the pills and we successfully gave her one in soft bread, she did not know anything about it. The kid playing all over the place is getting naughtier every day, he is <u>such</u> a pet. The girls tried to catch a bus down to the town after tea, but it was full so they had to walk with huge suitcases.

Monday 19 July

The house seems very quiet with one person in it. Maimie is having her day in bed. It will do her good after all the recent excitement, but she is looking all the better for seeing Amamy and Aunt Beeloo. She loves her relations and so seldom sees any of them, such a pity. But she is doing well this year as Uncle Snuffy is coming down for a fortnight next month, so she will have seen them all.

I am busy doing the washing and ironing of two weeks as I was too busy to do it last week and in the evening I have got to go to a Housewife thing right up at Withycombe, which is a hell of a nuisance with supper to get and the goats to milk etc. These evening affairs are almost impossible for me! I hate going out. It means I do not get to bed until nearly midnight by the time I finish all the jobs. Susie and Nicky have been in their stable all day as it has never stopped raining hard the whole time, they are quite happy eating hay and pea pods. Poor pets, they were so thirsty at lunch time when I took the bucket into the shed, although it was only away from the door, they did not drink anything as they did not want to get wet in the rain. The baby is bored stiff lying in a heap of hay watching the rain …

Friday 23 July

Had a very disturbed day. The first event was when one of the gardeners from the allotments arrived after lunch to tell us that the boys were bullying our goats. They had been running after Sandy and tugging at Susie's and Nicky's ropes. We tore out and while Maimie talked to the children I went up to speak to the goats. Maimie and I then walked down to the Roman Catholic school to complain to the headmaster, a good looking man. When we got home, I began bathing Sam when who should come in but Mrs Cox, having left her poodle bitch with the poodle dog up the road to be mated. We had a very amusing chat until she had to go to pick up the dog to take it home. Then we had tea and I was just bathing Domino when Dolly arrived to teach the kid to walk on a lead. I finished Domino, who soon dried rolling on the lawn with Shandy and Sammy. Ridler then turned up to scythe the lawn. Dolly and I then walked both goats up and down the lawn with Sandy tied to Sammy. Both on a dog lead. Sam soon taught him to run along and not pull against the lead.

Sunday 1 August

Dolly and her mother came in to tea. I really think Mrs Smith rather liked all my animal family. She professes to dislike animals but mine softened her heart because of all their winning little ways. After tea (when we ate Alpine strawberries and goats cream which Mrs Smith said she thought delicious), Dolly and I collected the little goats and tied Sammy on to Sandy with a dog chain, they gambolled round the lawn while I took their photograph. Sandy is already a good bit bigger than Sam, who is such a tiny dog really, however they got on very well together and Sam even tugs at his end of the chain to make Sandy go in the right direction, usually the kid quite overpowers him! Susie and Nicky must have their photographs taken one day, they are so pretty and would look lovely in the camera, but, films being almost impossible to get now, I am most particular what I take and hardly dare use the camera at all. This is the first time I have used it since the war actually but then we have not had anything so exciting as a kid before!

Monday 2 August

I spent the day in the garden but he noise was terrific. The Royal Marines band playing all the afternoon and early evening in the cricket field. Then a very deafening loudspeaker arrangement screaming all the late evening. If this is what bank holiday is like in the middle of the greatest war in history, what will the armistice be like (when it comes)! It was nice to hear the row really. It reminded me of my Oxford summer, when the gramophones play on the river all the summer evenings and everyone is gay all the day and night. Incidentally, I did get a certain amount of work done in the garden. I got the beds each side of the drive tidied and the lily pond lawn mown also the edges round the rockery, round bed rose bank and sundial mown, so now I have the 'orchard' to mow and round the hives and across along the tennis lawn wire. The grass has grown a good bit lately owing to the persistent wet days but the ground is in much better order for a little wetting. It was deplorably dry and the things had begun to flag piteously, now they have quite picked up and everything is flourishing in the sun and damp.

Wednesday 4 August

Maimie and I took the car down to meet Uncle Snuffy and Aunt Fancy. I was half afraid of being asked by the police what I was using petrol for, fortunately there were none about. Uncle Snuffy looked very ill, old and completely done by the journey; Aunt Fancy older and tired, also very exacting looking. Well, the enormous luggage was the next trial. I could not possibly get one bag near the car, the other two were fairly big ones but I got them on somehow but Aunt F.'s particular trunk was out of the question. We eventually had to get a taxi which followed me to Prattshayes, where we had a difficulty to get it upstairs (I mean the trunk, not the car!). However, at last we got them both settled and Lady Chetwynde gave us a lovely tea after which I helped Aunt Fancy unpack while Maimie talked to Uncle Snuffy. I do hope they will be alright and like it at Prattshayes. There is no washing stand in Uncle Snuffy's room, which may upset him I am afraid. He is old-fashioned, quite naturally at his age, and expects hot water in his room, which is a luxury you never get in these days.

It came on to rain in torrents, so Maimie and I had to return to take in the dear goats, I had to dry them all down in towels, they were soaked …

Friday 13 August

I met Betty in the town and we had coffee at Clapps before lunch. Sylvia, her friend, came as well. Betty was rather quiet I thought; she seemed to be thinking. She did tell me that she is going overseas for two years with the army of occupation. It should be a wonderful experience and she will love it, I feel sure. Sylvia is going home tomorrow.

Maimie, Uncle Snuffy and I went to tea with the Claytons. Mrs C. wanted him to thoroughly look at her bees. He is selling her a colony in the autumn so she wanted his advice as to the position for the hive etc. They had staying with them a very charming Polish army officer. He was in the Polish Cavalry during that fearful attack on Poland by Germany and Russia and was taken prisoner by the Russians, who ill-treated him shamefully. He was so weak for want of food that he could hardly stand. However, he was eventually sent to Persia to join the English and has been in England two months. He likes it here and seems quite happy. He told me that he thinks he will be back in Poland by this time next year and that Germany will be beaten by then!

Uncle Snuffy had an interesting talk with Colonel Clayton and was extremely interested in his life when he was Military Attaché in Warsaw before the war.

Monday 16 August

A lovely bright, hot and sunny day for the family birthday, which went off quite well. First of all, Maimie had a letter from Cousin Cally, a bottle of whisky from me. Then after breakfast I tore down the town on the bike and told Clapps I wanted a nice cake, so they let me have two nice ones, which was delightful of them in these days. Then I got a bottle of bath salts for Rusty to give her. While I was out Miss Price called with a huge bunch of beautiful great magnolias, the scent of which is exquisite. After lunch we went out to look over a house for Uncle S. but it will not suit Aunt F., I feel sure! Before tea Uncle S. came to spend the rest of the evening with us. Of course Aunt Fancy would go to Exeter for the day, today! After tea I found in the letterbox a parcel from Meg and a letter from Amamy and one from Aunt Beeloo, so now Maimie has heard from all her family. Then after supper Dolly came up with a lovely basket of delicious white grapes. By the way, Uncle Snuffy brought with him from Exeter a basket of purple grapes and nectarines, so really the birthday has been a real success, which is such a good thing because Maimie loves birthday tokens of affection.

Sunday 22 August

Just been round the garden looking at everything. Have picked the 'Merryweather' damsons and the greengages. Yesterday we picked the peaches off 'Royal George'. Today I also picked all the red outdoor tomatoes, they are doing very well this year and I must make some tomato sauce this week. It has begun to rain now and I am thinking of my poor little goats out in it on their tethers. I hope after the war is over to be able to live somewhere where I do not have to have them tethered at all, but loose with a shed to run to in bad weather. Mr and Mrs Barber have each lent me a book about the Lake District, that is where I intend to go to live, a wonderful environment and one which cannot be completely spoilt by this fearful 'New' England which is to come according to the Communists in this country under the cloak of 'Socialism'! I am quite thrilled by the idea although I do not want to leave our present home, I am very fond of it, but the expenses of Devon will frighten all poor folk like us away after the peace has been won. Besides if one lives in the real wild country one could keep a horse to ride as well as have the goats loose on the fells. Cumberland is a perfect country in itself ...

Sunday 29 August

Yesterday evening I went on a pub crawl with Joan and Frankie. We went to one or two Hotels, the first we tried was closed as they had no beer, we had to laugh! The next was very full but they had beer and whisky, so we were well away. We finished up with the Cranford, which had a dance going on where all the 'young things' were dancing, we all felt very aged as we watched; all the girls and boys we had looked upon as children seemed to be there. The evening was great fun and we all enjoyed it tremendously.

This morning I once more joined the girls and we visited our old friend 'The Beacon' before lunch. There was nobody there we knew but they had real pink gin – my favourite drink – so I was in heaven. Got home a bit late. After lunch Dolly came and we took the four dogs and little Sandy out for a walk towards Littleham in the fields. He was naughty going out and yelled a lot but on his way home he was a very good kid. Everyone loved him and he was not a bit afraid of passing people.

Miss Price came to tea, bringing with her a huge armful of raspberry plants to fill in gaps where mine failed.

Wednesday 8 September

The Italian armed forces surrendered unconditionally to the United Kingdom, America and Russia, officially today. It was signed in Sicily on Friday really, but for reasons beneficial to the Allied cause, it was not official until today.

Wednesday 15 September

Maimie went shopping in the morning. This is the first time she has been out in the town in the morning since her illness last year. We got very nice grey wool for her to knit a coat and some fine grey for stockings as grey ones have gone off the market, except for the services, so now Maimie is well stocked in knitting, which will last her some time. While we were shopping we ran into Mrs and Miss Everett, so we fixed up to go to Budleigh for tea on the beach and do a little shopping there at the same time. It will be great fun …

Later we had a delightful tea sitting on the beach at Budleigh with our backs against a fishing boat, which kept the very high wind off us – fortunately we also took rugs and cushions as well as food, so were a pretty comfy party by the time we settled. I took with me Sam and he behaved so well. He was frightfully pleased with himself for being chosen out of all the animals to come, just like a child. He thought a visit to Budleigh a great treat and soon found a little Aberdeen to play with. This will be the last time we go to Budleigh in the car until the war is over, unless we sell her before, which we are thinking of doing. The wind was high and it was very cloudy, no sun at all while we were on the beach. The sea was grey-green …

Friday 1 October

Having spent much valuable time in thinking about our personal financial situation, we have come to the conclusion that there are cheaper places to live than Exmouth and cheaper homes to run than ours, so we rang up Messrs Haynes about selling etc. and Miss Brown today sent up her representative to measure the rooms and generally value the house, which she said is worth £3,250. It seems to me a queer time to contemplate moving house, no help and labour extremely expensive as well as practically nil. I shall be very sorry to leave the garden because I have spent a lot of time on it and put in many hours improving it all round. The situation is unique they tell us: in the country and yet so near the town. Now I keep goats, I should like a paddock for them to run in off their tethers. Here I have the use of the tennis club grounds for them but of course they have to be tethered, poor little tiny things. It is so awful that Rowley is <u>not</u> for sale, it was built by my family in Queen Elizabeth's days and could be made perfectly wonderful in every way, but never mind. We must find some other beautiful old relic of England's past history to plant ourselves …

Saturday 2 October

Tore round to make everything nice for Meg, wish I had a little more time, as Mrs Pile is away with her husband and it takes me all my time milking the goats and cooking. The house is getting rather dusty. Never mind. The war will be over some day, I hope! Then perhaps we will be able to get an all-day maid. Meg arrived in nice time for supper, we hoped she had had a nice crossing, but it was rough in the Irish Sea and she was sick and still felt washed out I could see. It is very brave of her to make so little fuss. The boats they use now are only old rolling ones from Dublin. When the war is over I hope it will be nicer for her in nice boats and of course she will have Tim with her; two people are never quite as bad as one, you can talk and think of something else if you have a companion. Anyway, Meg, except for a certain seasick look, was in the pink and had obviously put on weight, which is nice as she was too thin. It is nice to be the three of us again and people talking about the house instead of silence except when Maimie and I talk to each other. Two people in a house are really too few. I always like about four to laugh and joke, it is easier to get amusement from remarks not always ones own.

I think Meg is going to have her usual good weather!

Friday 8 October

Bombs fell at several points of London last night, when the capital had its fourth alert of the week. It was the longest warning since the raid on 20 May.

Monday 11 October

Today Dolly and I took Shandy, Domino, Sam and Dusky in the bus to Otterton, where we got out and had one at the Crown before walking back to Budleigh Salterton by the banks of the Otter. It was a glorious walk and the day perfect for it. We proceeded along some lanes out of the village until we came to a lane leading to a gate under huge beech trees. Here the river ran softly down to the marshes on one side and by the parkland on our side. As we walked pheasants got up, moorhens called while they scuttled about in the river and wood pigeons cooed in the trees above us. We came to a lovely glade where we sat on an old fallen tree trunk to eat our lunch. The dogs all sat up round us begging for the 'shapes' I had put in with my buns. After we finished Domino and Dusky ran down to the water barking for us to come immediately! We joined them on the river bank and threw them sticks while they swam across and round in circles, playing with one another like the moorhens. Shandy of course swam with them. The water was deep and clear and the dogs adored it. At last we got them out to dry and warm in the sun as we went on our way. I can never remember the three spaniels enjoy a day as much, they put up pheasants, bathed, hunted until they were so excited that they became most unruly. However, by the time we caught the bus they had quieted down.

Tuesday 12 October

The navy, using a new weapon, has broken the back of the German Fleet. The great battleship *Tirpitz*, sister ship of the ill-fated *Bismarck*, is seriously damaged. The *Tirpitz* is probably the most powerful battleship in the world. She will not be able to take part in operations for a considerable time. The navy decided to attack her in harbour using midget submarines with specially selected crews. These tiny craft were sent to the sheltered Alten Fjord, over 250 miles within the Arctic Circle in the most northerly division of Norway. The attack was made on 22 September. Three of the midget submarines have so far not returned; the Germans claim to have captured prisoners.

Sunday 14 November

Dolly very kindly came in to help me cut sandwiches for a bit of a party. She cuts them particularly well, very thin and straight, I am bad at it. We made some of Meg's filling, patum and cheese. I also provided sweets and chocolates, for Frankie instead of smoking! It was quite good fun. Dolly came, also Wilfred Davis, who is home after five years overseas; it only seems yesterday that he came to an Easter party I gave, how time does fly! He is home from Malta and looks rather thin after his experiences. He has a very hairy job to do with electricity, which means he often goes to sea in naval ships. It is obviously a very interesting job indeed as he has already been to Uganda and Kenya, Australia, Ceylon, Bombay and Malta in five years. Next came Joan and Frankie, full of beans. Then the battery, which consisted of the colonel and major and three subalterns. Last of all came Mr Edwards – sub in the HQ battery up the road. I hope everyone enjoyed it. They have all come from the Shetlands where they saw very little life I fancy, nothing except birds. One of the subs was a Russian and a real charmer, he is a huge fellow, perfect manners and full of fun, I liked him awfully.

Saturday 20 November

Frankie came for the weekend. She was going up to town but put it off, so she arrived for lunch and afterwards we rang up a taxi and Keith Barling, one of the RA subalterns, and off we three went to Woodbury, where Mr Putnam still owns some land. Unfortunately we had no dogs so it was a blank in the big wood, which obviously was full of pheasants but they just lay still. One just must have a dog for a wood like that, one cockbird did get up; unfortunately, he chose a moment when Keith was climbing up a bank. However, while we were rather sadly strolling along the road waiting for the taxi, who should come along but a lonely bird, he flew straight into the gun, I watched him get up in a field, he was flying back to the wood to roost. Anyway he brought him home in triumph instead! Poor old bird! It was fun for me and Frankie, we enjoyed the afternoon no end but I am afraid it was a bit of a blank for Keith, who is a first-class shot. Got home late and tore round milking etc before Joan came along for the evening. We all drank gin and ate chestnuts by the fire until the small hours; we seemed to find a lot to say! It was a quiet, cosy and really chatty evening and we were all quite happy. Betty comes on leave tomorrow, I hope she will not stupefy Joan and me, she is so superior!

Friday 26 November

Spent the afternoon gardening. I cut off the untidy phloxes and Michaelmas daisies in the new long bed going down to the door into the lane. The garden looks perfectly frightful, leaves everywhere and under them weeds. I am in despair about the place, it all looks so awful and such a lot to do. Madge is getting on with clipping the top of the hedge; it will tidy things up a bit when the job is done. I find I have so little time in the garden, I seem to spend so long doing the little goats, they take me all my time, milking, feeding, cleaning, taking and fetching from their tethers, etc. They are such darling little animals, but I have so little time I only wish I could find a way out. After the war I would like a boy to come in and look after them either morning or evening, but of course I shall never be able to afford even that small luxury, so don't let's think about it, it is too grim to bother about anyway! The dogs got a certain amount of exercise running up and down from the club with the goats which saves me a bit but I wish the days lasted longer and one was never tired, then I could take them for more walks, poor tiny things, they find life very dull I am afraid, with nothing but the garden to run in half their time, poor Dusky next door, we never seem to take him out now ...

Saturday 4 December

Frankie came for the weekend and I did like seeing her, life here is a bit depressing with Maimie in bed, in an awful after-flu state of mind, and nobody to talk to at all. Frankie is always so gay and makes life appear much more inviting with her cheery laugh and lively conversation. I had my fire fighting practice, after an early supper of very delicious fish Frankie brought with her. It went off quite well and after an hour we were all allowed to go, which was one great thing. While we were standing around in the cold we watched over a dozen searchlights playing above us, they were picking out planes, which at intervals appeared like tiny silver butterflies. Frankie and I dashed down to the Maer Bay for a bit of drink at nine o'clock, after putting Maimie to bed etc. The place was packed with American officers and our own naval ones. The Americans, needless to say, were completely tiddly and amusing themselves by giving drinks galore to three fur-coated shop girls. It was amusing to watch! Towards closing time a lot of 'other ranks' came in, also American. They were rough and very noisy. A fat and elderly blonde staying in the hotel kept dishing out drinks to the 'boys'. Frankie and I thought they (there were two of them) must be well-to-do London tarts on holiday!!

Tuesday 7 December

The three Allied leaders: Mr Churchill, President Roosevelt and Marshal Stalin have held a meeting at Tehran, capital of Persia, which lasted four days. They established their plans for defeating Germany by attacks from the East, South and West, and reached an understanding on their policies for peace on a basis that will banish war for generations to come. The discussions opened on Sunday 28 November. One of the outstanding incidents at Tehran was the presentation by Mr Churchill to Marshal Stalin of the Sword of State, the gift of King George to Stalingrad, in honour of the city's heroic resistance …

Saturday 25 December

We had a very pleasant Christmas Day. We could not go to church because we were too late ordering a taxi, but as Maimie has only just recovered from her attack of 'flu'. We were unable to know if she would be fit to go until a day or so before. I spent the entire morning cooking the lunch. We had my best cock, bread sauce, bread crumbs, Christmas pudding, made by Robertson and very good, with brandy sauce, mince pies and goats' cream. Whisky to drink. Mrs Everett said everything was well cooked and the sauce the best she had ever eaten, so I feel very proud! We did not wash up afterwards, but sat round the fire in the drawing-room, listened to the King, he was splendid. At tea time the Clays came in, Miss Clay brought me some cigarettes, which was very nice of her. We had Christmas cake, made by myself, hot buttered toast and bread and butter. They all admired my decorations in the centre of the dining-room table. It does look very cheerful I must admit– also the holly Joan gave me, which I have stuck on top of the pictures, gives the house a cheery look. When everyone had gone we washed up the things in the pantry – it took quite a long time and I was thankful we had not ruined the afternoon by doing it. The day was very pleasant, though quiet I suppose …

Tuesday 28 December

The Admiralty announced that the German battleship *Scharnhorst* has been sunk by units of the Home Fleet on 26 December in the Arctic. The *Scharnhorst* was using her great speed to escape when four destroyers – three British and one Norwegian – steamed ahead of her and, practically unsupported, attacked and slowed her down. The bigger ships, which included one battleship – *The Duke of York* (35,000 tons), flagship of Admiral Sir Bruce Fraser, C-in-C home Fleet – then closed in for the 'kill'. The destroyers attacked with torpedoes and after the *Scharnhorst* was hit the cruiser HMS *Jamaica* delivered a final torpedo attack after which the *Scharnhorst* sank north-east of the North Cape.

six

1944

Invasion Barges in the Docks, Sad News from Normandy

Saturday 1 January

I went to a sherry party in the morning given by Wilfred Davies before he goes to Bermuda later this month. In the afternoon I took the dogs and the kid for a walk in the fields. The Allied air force over the house all day on their way to France.

Sunday 2 January

Maimie and I took a taxi and went to the second service at Holy Trinity. Mrs Everett came in to tea, afterwards she and Maimie visited Mrs Fletcher. Mrs E. was very amusing about the other people at Mansfield! Colonel Cowel called to wish us a happy New Year.

Monday 3 January

Both the Misses Clay came in to see us. They were very chatty and quite cheerful. After tea I went down to see Mrs Fletcher at Mansfield, the room full of old people.

Tuesday 4 January

We got a taxi and took Maimie to the dentist. Madge and I started cutting down the dead fir tree. Dolly and Marjorie came in after tea. M. is on leave from Edinburgh.

Wednesday 5 January

Ruffles very unwell, so I rang up Mr Norrington, who came almost immediately and gave him a pill. He improved during the day. I spent the afternoon gardening in the blazing sun to the music of a US band playing during a troop review.

Thursday 6 January

We dug up the old lily bed and replanted the best crowns in a new bed. Picked prim-roses, violets and coronilla.

Friday 7 January

A spring day which I spent pricking over the front flower beds; the bulbs are all up half an inch.

Saturday 8 January

Maimie and I walked up to Mrs Everett for a tea party. After supper Joan and I went and had one at the Maer Bay: enjoyed it.

Group Captain Frank Whittle has invented the new jet-propelled plane – The Gloster Fighter.

Sunday 9 January

Dolly and Marjorie came for a walk with the four dogs. The animals thoroughly enjoyed it; they had not been for a decent run for some time. Mrs Smith joined them at tea and afterwards we played Newmarket until supper time.

Monday 10 January

Maimie had a day in bed, I gardened all the afternoon.

Wednesday 12 January

Esme coming. She arrived after tea, looking well, a bit thin but then she is so fearfully busy in the hospital, to say nothing of the family shopping every morning and the various visitor dogs she still has when the owners go away.

Thursday 13 January

In the afternoon the dogs and I took Esme down to the docks to see the thirteen invasion barges. She had never seen any before, so was extremely interested in them. They were all there. We walked back across the golf links. The whole trip took us nearly two hours.

Friday 14 January

We went down to the town all the morning to do some shopping. Esme found a few things she wanted. After lunch we took all four goats for a walk and after tea went to see Mrs Fletcher on our way for a drink at the Maer Bay.

Saturday 15 January

Sam and I saw Esme off on her train; she had to get back before Monday. I shall miss her as she is fun and it is nice to have someone to go round with sometimes. I hope that she will be able to come and see us again, but she has a lot of friends waiting for her.

Sunday 16 January

Dolly came up in the afternoon and we took the dogs for a walk in the fields. She is better again, and had not had 'flu' at all! I began sewing together a new overall and hope it will be alright as I have never made one before.

Monday 17 January

Mrs Mitchell came very kindly and trimmed the goats fur for me. She did the job beautifully and the little people were as quiet and good as they could be, even Alexander and he had never had his feet done before; he stood as still as a mouse. Dug in the garden.

Friday 21 January

I took the two dear dogs down the town for my weekly shopping and enquired the price of ash bins. The last sold for 35s! Dolly came up and we fetched Mrs Fletcher up in her chair for tea. I think she enjoyed coming, but was a little frightened when we lifted her and her chair up and down the steps.

Sunday 23 January

Frankie for lunch. She was full of beans after her leave when she had a very good time and thoroughly enjoyed it.

Tuesday 25 January

Maimie and I go to the oculist …

Wednesday 26 January

Fire fighting …

Friday 28 January

Dolly came with Shandy and we all walked up to Marley, where we went in to see Mrs Mitchell, who insisted on giving us a delicious tea and the dogs a huge bowl of milk. Her goats looked in the pink. She laughed when we arrived with our four dogs and Sandy the kid.

Monday 31 January

Fire fighting 7.55. Shampooed goats on Saturday. Washed mine and Maimie's hair yesterday, also brushed and defleaed both dogs.

Regarding the above, I really do feel that I am moderately clean at all events, which goes some way to making the world go round.

Wednesday 2 February

I caught the 11.05 bus for Exeter, where I brought some feeding tins for the goats before meeting Joan, Betty and Frankie at the Clarence. They ran into some other friends so it was fun. B. and J. came on to lunch at Colsons before I caught the 2.05 for home.

Friday 11 February

Dolly, the dogs and I with Sandy, walked up to Marley to give Mrs Mitchell back her basket, we had kept it a long time. Mrs M. told me she had sold a broody hen this morning; just the thing I wanted for the sitting of duck eggs I have ordered.

Saturday 12 February

Dolly and I fetched Mrs Fletcher up in her chair, also all her belongings in relays. She is very thin and I do hope she will like being with us and get fatter quickly. She is going to live with us which will be delightful as she will be such a companion for Maimie.

Sunday 13 February

Marjorie came yesterday for the night. Today we all sat round the fire talking. Mrs Fletcher had a good night and seems better although she looks tired still. She has a very small appetite but I must feed her up on goats' milk and eggs.

Monday 14 February

Ruffles not well so we had to ring up Mr Norrington who came in the morning. He says he has ruptured himself and he will always be a delicate cat. Unfortunately there is nothing to be done, but he may get rid of it as he is so young.

Tuesday 15 February

Wireless gone wrong so I had to get Ellis to come up, he took its insides away. Got some fish for the cats, which they loved. Mr Norrington says they must not have any bread or horse meat, so it is difficult to feed them for the time.

Thursday 17 February

Bernard and Pauline came over to see Mrs Fletcher. They arrived in time for lunch looking very fit. I had not seen him for nearly ten years or Pauline since the war. It was fun their being able to see us before Bernard goes off to Washington on a military mission.

Friday 18 February

Dolly and I took the four dogs and Sandy for a run round the lanes, the fields seemed too wet and deep in mud. We put Dusky on a short lead with Domino, who kept him back well …

Wednesday 23 February

Two naval officers who took their midget submarines *X6* and *X7* through fifty miles of mine-guarded fjord and inside the last defence of anti-submarine nets to strike at Germany's 41,000 ton battleship *Tirpitz*, have been awarded the VC. The attack was on 22 September 1943.

Friday 3 March

Mrs Fletcher very concerned at the idea of losing Miles, who has been offered a job as ADC to the Governor of Barbados. She wanted him to settle in England, but the Colonial Office has more advanced ideas as to his future.

Sunday 5 March

Minnikin had twin sons born at six o'clock after tea today. It is awfully disappointing as I had hoped for nannies and Mrs Mitchell is ready to receive one as a gift and now I shall have to disappoint her also. They are lovely kids and exactly like their father, Westward Knight …

Monday 6 March

The two poor little kids had to be taken away by Mr Norrington and killed. He so loathed doing it. I must admit, if I had been him, I should never have had the courage to take up the work of vet, he hates killing all animals so much.

Thursday 9 March

Meg arrived from Belfast looking cheery and well. She had a good journey, came from Scotland to London and down. She arrived in the middle of supper, we waited some time for her but she missed the Exeter connection.

Friday 10 March

Did nothing special. We all went shopping in the morning and Miles mowed the untidy rough piece of lawn all the afternoon, it looks lovely now but it has been an awfully hard job for him.

Saturday 11 March

Meg went to tea in Topsham with Reggie and Lexy. Miles and I went to a drinks party with Joan and Frankie. Two rather peculiar samples of Royal Marine officers and a rather nice American colonel were there. We laughed a lot at the two Marines. The American was very quiet.

Monday 13 March

Meg went to Torquay to see Aunt Margaret. She said she found her aged and very blind, but she does not feel up to having another operation at her age and so I fear will get worse, poor dear old Aunt Margaret. Her two nieces are looking after her well, that's one good thing.

Friday 17 March

Meg came in while I was getting breakfast to tell me the exciting news. Nicky has a baby nanny kid, born about seven o'clock this morning. She is a lovely British Alpine like her father. This is the first nanny kid I have had. Isn't it thrilling! I went to tea in Dawlish.

Saturday 18 March

Nicky's little kid perfectly adorable, being a warm sunny afternoon I put them down in the compound to play. The baby played about all over the place, jumping and skipping all over the lawn. Nicky loves her.

Sunday 19 March

Meg's last day with us. I think she enjoyed her visit but the time went all too soon. She got on so well with milking the goats, they all love her and she can do anything with them. I believe she rather loves them!

Monday 20 March

Miles escorted Meg as far as London where she met Amamy and Aunt Beeloo, while Miles met the Governor of Northern Rhodesia. The animals and I miss Meg; she was so busy with them all and spoilt the little people. Nicky's kid still progressing.

Tuesday 21 March

Washed my hair and had it cut in the morning. I also did some shopping for the 'farm', doing very well in my black-market! The shopmen tell me I must get a few extra things for the invasion, because when we start that, the transport will be very limited.

Thursday 23 March

I rang up for a sitting of Indian Runner duck eggs. Mrs Cardwell has kindly offered me one of her broody hens, so now I am in a great thrill waiting for the eggs to arrive.

Sunday 9 April

My birthday. Had a pleasant day. Meg gave me a length of very pretty material for a skirt, a beautiful book of the Psalms, cigarettes and a bar of chocolate. Domino gave me a huge zinc bath for the ducks and £1. Dolly gave me a lovely cigarette lighter and Shandy a bar of soap.

Sunday 16 April

The Archbishops of Canterbury and York having issued today week a Call to Prayer, we have ordered a taxi, fortunately we got one – they are in such demand now. Frankie spent weekend with us and Miles back today from London.

Monday 24 April

Miles left us to stay his last week, before embarking, with his mother in Torquay. We find the house quite empty without him, he is such a companionable man and so cheerful. He left his hat in the hall so I rushed it down to the ferry on my bike and arrived just as the boat was leaving.

Thursday 27 April

The Buff Rock hatched out six chicks, one caught its foot in the coop door and died and the seventh egg got broken a week ago but was fertile, so all Mrs Mitchell's were good. I only had seven eggs to fill up with four duck eggs.

Friday 28 April

Dolly and I went for a glorious walk along the beach to Sandy bay, a lot of soldiers bathing. Sandy came with the dogs, he was very brave about climbing down the cliff to follow me onto the sand, poor darling was frightened but would come.

Saturday 29 April

Four white and fawn Indian Runner ducklings hatched under Snow White. I fancy she has not kept up enough heat. These eggs were under the buff rock hen until her chicks came out on Thursday, when I moved them under Snow White.

Sunday 30 April

I put the ducklings on the lawn, two white and three fawns. Mrs Everett came in to tea to see them and the chicks, pullets and the kid. The latter is growing quite big; she already jumps in and out of her stall over the door with the greatest of ease.

Thursday 4 May

Maimie in bed with a bad back. We think it must be a bit of lumbago, an awful nuisance for her and very painful. I got on with weeding the south flower bed; it is completely smothered by pink campion from the hedge along the back.

Sunday 7 May

Had tea with Joan and Betty, who is home on sick leave. Frankie was there and said she had been to see her brother in hospital. He mentioned two other submarine officers there, one is dying of starvation because he thinks his tummy has been blown away, the other feels very ill because he thinks he is going to have a baby.

Monday 8 May

Dolly coming up to take Sandy and Patsy for a walk, she has not been out yet alone with Sandy. After we are having tea with Miss Barber. Rusty has worms so I rang up his doctor. I mowed the lily pond lawn and Riddler is coming to do the rest.

Wednesday 10 May

We put the baby chicks into the big run with their mother and coop. They are beautiful birds now, just beginning to get feathers. We gave the ducklings a big bath to swim in but they got cramp because the water was too cold.

Friday 12 May

Did some shopping, I have a longing now for clothes, a despairing craving in these days of coupons! However, I got an overall, a vest and material for a grey skirt and next week, when I go to Exeter, I hope to get a blouse. For Maimie I got four yards of vyella for a nightie; it took twelve coupons!

Friday 19 May

Cassino, the last fortress of the Gustav Line, was stormed by the Eighth Army yesterday. After seven days of fighting over 1,500 of the crack 4th Parachute Regiment were taken prisoner. Many more Germans were killed. Great quantities of stores and equipment were captured. The final assault was carried out by British troops while Poles took the monastery.

Monday 22 May

I took Sandy, Dusky, Sam and Domino up to Littleham to take Miss Price her three eggs. Domino was in a naughty mood. Sandy as good as gold. He made friends with an American, then further on, a British sergeant. They both wanted to walk with him. The young sergeant was wearing a ribbon.

Tuesday 23 May

I biked down to the docks with Dolly to have a look at all the invasion barges and other craft waiting for our attack. The estuary is full of it, wonderfully hidden away on the far side of the river under the woods of Powderham; they hardly show.

Wednesday 24 May

Miss Landon talked to me about Plymouth; the last air raid was bad, killing a number of people. The Sound is a mass of shipping; some of the troopers take 2,000 men.

Sunday 4 June

We went to church, being Trinity Sunday, listened to ducks quacking outside which was a peaceful sound. The dogs, cats and ducklings were all overjoyed at our return, poor little things, they do hate it when we lock up the house.

Monday 5 June

I was kept awake in the night by guns in the Channel and wave upon wave of heavy aircraft overhead.

Tuesday 6 June

D Day. Allied armies landed in France early this morning. The greatest invasion in history has begun. General Montgomery commanded the Allied armies. General Eisenhower is Supreme Commander.

Saturday 17 June

The King visited the beaches in Normandy yesterday. It is four centuries since a reigning sovereign of England last set foot on Norman soil to visit his armies in Calvados ...

Sunday 18 June

The Germans are attacking London and the southern counties with their 'secret weapon', the pilotless plane – a jet-engined monoplane. They send them over during daylight and night and they fly so far, then burst and explode, demolishing anything that may be in the area underneath.

Saturday 24 June

My darling little baby kid Patsy has died. I just cannot get over it. Mr Marshall told me, so Dolly and I rushed up to the club. There she was, lying quite still. Her little neck was broken the steward told me afterwards. He buried her in our garden. The sweet tiny thing. She jumped too far for her beastly rope and it got her neck.

Thursday 29 June

Mr Norrington came in to see Minnie, we think she has worms. she is rather thin and whimpery. He said it was not my fault that my darling little Patsy died. He said she must have jumped up too high for her tether and she died instantly without knowing anything about it. I shall never put another kid on a tether. Never ...

Friday 30 June

I looked at my bees and found they all had their queens and there was honey in the supers, eggs and brood in the brood combs. So now I have two hives with this year's young queens and the third hive a last year's queen, so all are splendidly young and fertile.

Monday 3 July

Dolly and I went over in the bus to Drewsteignton to see Silkhouse. It was a darling old place, the walls 3ft thick, white outside, with half tiled and half thatched roof. A goat house of thatch and stone in the garden; a rill running through and a wood at the top of the property.

Monday 10 July

Mr Wilson lunched with us. He owns Silkhouse and came to talk business and to see Maimie. He liked our furniture and agrees it will look nice there in the old house. He also suggested planting anything in the garden that I liked to bring over, which is fearfully thrilling.

Sunday 16 July

Marjorie arrived at tea time yesterday until after tea today. She is very interested in the new house and loves the name, and all I say about it seems to appeal to her. She is going to help us more after the war.

Tuesday 18 July

I carried the hay and made quite a little stack under the roof.

Thursday 20 July

I went into Exeter and bought a Hepplewhite mahogany wardrobe for my new room at Silkhouse. The old corner washstand arrived this morning, so I am getting on with the furniture. I'm selling my present modern walnut suite by auction here; I hope it will fetch a lot of money.

Friday 21 July

German Staff Officers attempted to kill Hitler yesterday. The Nazis claim that the leaders of the plot have been wiped out. Colonel Count von Stauffenberg, who placed the bomb designed to kill Hitler, came from an old southern German family.

Sunday 23 July

Maimie and I spent the day doing pictures; we are throwing away or selling a number of frames, altering some of our pictures ready for Silkhouse. Dolly came in and told us the sad news that Bill Meredith has been killed in Normandy. He was in the Dorset Regiment; poor Betty was so devoted to him.

Monday 24 July

Dolly and I went to see Silkhouse, we took baskets of bulbs and rock plants, but only had time to plant some of them ourselves. Mr Wilson gave us lunch. We loved the house, it is sweet. After supper my two ducks arrived. Dolly and I fetched them from Exmouth station after supper.

Wednesday 2 August

Mr Rowland wrote telling us that he heard yesterday that dear Jappy had fallen in action in Normandy on 19 July. It seems too awful to be true that such a priceless jewel as he should be killed; he was perfect in every way – brilliant, happy, kind and ever charming. I would rather anyone had gone but Jap.

Saturday 5 August

Frankie came for the holiday weekend. They have had a murder in her company. An American soldier knifed an ATS girl in one of the hostels. The girl (although married) was 'one' with the boys.

Sunday 6 August

We lazed about on the lawn all day, glorying in the beautiful sunshine.

Wednesday 9 August

Field Marshal von Witzleben, Generals von Hase, Bernardis, Hoepner and Stieff, Captain Klausing and Lieutenants Count Yorck von Wartenburg and von Hagen were all hanged by the People's Court of the Greater German Reich as traitors in the plot to kill Hitler. The field marshal and Hoepner asked to be shot but it was refused. Their estates will be confiscated by the Reich.

Wednesday 16 August

Maimie's birthday. She quite enjoyed her day in spite of being in bed still. The doctor says she must stay there for a month and keep quiet. Jappy being killed was the last straw; I thought she would be ill. She loves all those Rowland boys like nephews.

Thursday 24 August

Mr Wilson came over to exchange our landing carpet for his stair carpet. He had tea with Maimie in her room, Miss Price came in also; it was quite a nice party for her. Afterwards Miss Swinton called and I saw her also. Madge says I can take any of our fruit trees I like, so I am thrilled to death with the prospect of not leaving our best fruit behind.

Saturday 26 August

Sandy had his first day at serious work. June Eggleston took him up to a fete in Littleham, where he collected 5s 2d for the Exmouth animals dispensary. June said he behaved very well and looked such a pet with his tiny basket tied to Miles' Sam Brown which he wore as a girth.

Sunday 27 August

Paris surrendered, after General Leclerc, commander of the French Armoured Division, had sent the German commander an ultimatum telling him to cease fire. General de Gaulle entered the city at 7 p.m.

Friday 8 September

I went down to see Phyllis Rycroft and her goats. The temptation was too much for me and I decided to buy her nanny kid. She is a beauty, her great grandfather being Champion of the World. Her mother gives a gallon a day. Her pet name is Primrose.

Tuesday 12 September

Germany invaded. American troops have crossed the German border.

Thursday 14 September

Had a letter and a charming photo of Henry. He hasn't altered one little bit in all these years. I was delighted to have a photo at last! He has been walking and climbing in the mountains near Simla and has been up among the chain leading to Tibet. Oh, how thrilling.

Wednesday 20 September

The spearhead of the British Second Army is believed to have contacted the airborne troops dropped at Nijmegen, heavy fighting is going on. In their sweep to the north of Holland. British columns linked up with airborne troops at Eindhoven and at Weghel.

Thursday 21 September

Allied airborne troops are fighting fiercely for the river crossings in the Arnhem area. More airborne troops were landed in Holland yesterday.

Sunday 24 September

British tanks, which drove north from the bridgehead across the Rhine at Nijmegen to relieve the British airborne troops west of Arnhem, are reported to have been checked four miles away. Even a German war reporter paid tribute to the dogged paratroops in a broadcast last night.

Thursday 28 September

The survivors of the British First Airborne Division, after holding the Arnhem bridgehead against overwhelming odds for eight days and nights, were withdrawn to the south bank of the Lower Rhine during Monday night.

Wednesday 4 October

Primrose arrived. I fetched her across the golf links, Mr Rycroft came all the way with me. Phyllis was taking her mother by train; she was bought by a man in Somerset. Primrose is perfectly sweet, so gentle, but my goats are already jealous of her.

Monday 9 October

Little Primrose is settling down very well, she is so docile and sweet natured but Minnie is fearfully jealous of her, butting her whenever possible, Susie is kind, Sandy rather flirtatious! She is a beautiful little lady, I am so delighted with her.

Wednesday 18 October

Mr Norrington came to vet Susie and Rusty. He said Susie was getting on well, but the goats were out of condition owing to the hay shortage which is simply awful. Rusty's ear is not very nice – he thoroughly cleaned it out. Maimie in bed resting before Meg's visit. She hopes to arrive tomorrow night.

Saturday 21 October

Meg and I bussed to Drewsteignton to see Silkhouse. Meg loved the place. She liked the house and garden, also the view from the wood. She found a beautiful beech tree in the orchard hedge. Meg really was delighted with my idea of a home.

Wednesday 25 October

The day has arrived that I have planned for since we decided to buy Silkhouse. Meg and I went in a lorry, with two men and all the fruit trees and shrubs, to the place and spent the day planting like mad all over Silkhouse garden. I do hope they will do well.

Saturday 28 October

Dolly and I bussed over to Silkhouse to plant the few remaining shrubs and to look at all the other ones in case any of them were left un-planted. It looks very nice and we both long to see it in the spring. It rained a good deal so we saw the place in bad conditions, but it looked sweet in spite of the weather.

Sunday 29 October

The Home Guard is to stand down on 1 November.

Thursday 2 November

Meg returned this morning, in so far as catching the morning train up to the north Midlands, but she does not anchor off Ireland until tomorrow morning. Her visit has been a great success; she so loved Silkhouse and helped us so much with ideas etc.

Wednesday 8 November

British and Canadian First Army troops marched into Middleberg yesterday evening. Twelve years ago I was there on holiday!

Monday 13 November

Scenes of great enthusiasm are marking Mr Churchill's visit to Paris. Tens of thousands of people gave him one of the greatest welcomes ever seen in the French capital on Saturday when he drove through the streets with General de Gaulle. The mystery of Hitler's whereabouts, or whether he is still alive, has deepened. Himmler, Gestapo chief, is reading all the Fuhrer's speeches now.

Tuesday 14 November

The 45,000 ton battleship *Tirpitz* has been sunk by RAF Lancaster bombers in Tromsoe Fjord, North Norway. One of the twenty-nine bombers did not return. Britain's coal situation is worse. As the demand for coal becomes more imperative production drops. Miners keep on striking.

Monday 27 November

I met Betty for a coffee. She is on leave for ten days. I also posted off three Christmas airgraphs.

Friday 1 December

Yesterday I began getting up leaves going along the front drive to start with. They are all down at last and I must get them up as soon as possible when the weather permits. Fortunately they are so heavy with wet that the wind has no effect on them.

Thursday 7 December

Had my hair cut, shampooed and set. Started feeding goats on roots.

Wednesday 13 December

Nicky and Minnie in season.

Saturday 23 December

Mr Norrington operated on Blackie, who has been taken very ill.

Sunday 24 December

A very busy day, iced the cake in pink and white, got all the things arranged for tomorrow. The cockerel is ready to cook, the plum pudding is waiting, the goats have their swedes to cut up. Got the parcels all done up and took some of them up the road. Blackie very ill, second operation this morning.

Monday 25 December

Christmas Day. Poor little Blackie was our first thought. They rang up after breakfast to tell us he was better and I could fetch him, so the dogs and I set off after lunch, feeling very fat having eaten and drunk well! Dolly and I went to tea with Mrs Everett and her family, after we played games and I thoroughly enjoyed the evening.

Tuesday 26 December

Blackie better today. The goats bored because I have had no time to take them out for a walk in the lanes. Dolly and Mrs Smith came to tea and enjoyed the Christmas cake very much. Tomorrow we are going to take the goats and dogs, including Dusky, for their walk.

Goodbye to Cranford Avenue

Saturday 1 January

Maimie in bed with a bronchial cough and cold, I also have a heavy cold. I took all the goats and dogs for a quick walk down the lane. Dolly came in to see us after tea. Mrs Everett asked me to go to the cinema, but I declined. In the morning I cleaned out the nest boxes in the fowl house.

Tuesday 9 January

Vice-Admiral Jonas Ingram, Commander in Chief U. Atlantic Fleet, has warned America that New York and Washington may expect an attack by V bombs next month.

Wednesday 10 January

The Battle for Luzon has begun. General MacArthur has landed in the Philippines with a huge force of troops. According to the Japanese the Allies have a huge number of warships and troop carriers steaming along the Luzon coast.

Saturday 20 January

Three inches of snow. June came and we took all the goats for a run, also dogs, in the fields. They loved it. We had snowball fights with them; Sandy put his head down to receive them each time. June's dog, Vicky, being half sheepdog, is learning to herd the goats for us; she fetches them back if they run away.

Sunday 21 January

June came after breakfast, so we took the goats out again in the snow, sheet ice in places. Nicky lamed herself somehow. After lunch Dolly came over for a walk with Dom and Dusky, we left little Sam at home as he had enough exercise this morning in the cold. Snow lying everywhere, lawn deep still.

Thursday 25 January

I took Minnie over to Newton Poppleford, in the train, to be mated. She was as good as gold all the way, not so nervous as Susie. She liked the billy. The journey rather fun; the country looked beautiful in the snow. Sidmouth has six inches, so everywhere round is dazzlingly white. We found the roads slippery owing to the snow being frozen like ice.

Saturday 27 January

June came up to take the goats for a walk. When we got out on the roads we found the surface was two inches thick with sheet ice. We could not stand up. The lane was <u>awful</u>, the ice inches deep, but fortunately we had no falls and all got home safely.

Sunday 28 January

South Wales has had its worst blizzard since 1878. Britain has had its heaviest snowfall since before the war. Dartmoor had 10ft. Bodmin Moor 6ft. Bristol several feet. Brighton snow ploughs in use. In Suffolk hundreds of birds are lying dead in the fields. Many hundreds of sheep are buried all over the country.

Wednesday 31 January

Exeter had its coldest night on Sunday since 1813 with twenty-four degrees of frost. 100 Devon schools were closed owing to deep snow. Skating in progress on the Exe. Here in Exmouth bottles of milk froze on doorsteps. At Topsham mails were delivered by sledge.

Saturday 3 February

June came up after lunch and we took the goats and dogs for a run in the lanes and fields. We made them jump the brook at the bottom by Prattshayes. The birds sang, the rooks cawed and the wood pigeons cooed, it was a real spring day and so hot rushing about.

Sunday 4 February

June rode over with Pixie, who I got on to. She is lovely to ride and I have decided to give up smoking and have one ride a week instead. Dolly and I took the dogs in the fields. It was a lovely day although not as sunny as I had hoped it would be.

Thursday 8 February

The long-awaited meeting of Churchill, Roosevelt and Stalin is now taking place in the Black Sea area. They have reached complete agreement on joint military operations for the conclusion of the war against Germany. Discussions have begun on problems of the peace.

Sunday 11 February

June and I took the goats and dogs for a walk in the meadows. They enjoyed it tremendously as usual, but not quite as much as yesterday when we were out longer and Domino ran after a rabbit round and round the field and was in such a fuss when it got away through a gap in the hedge.

Tuesday 13 February

I tethered the goats out in the club, this is the first time the weather has been fit for them since Christmas. I also began my spring gardening by starting to cut the hedge along the road in the front. The flowers are blooming and the birds are singing so everything is lovely.

Thursday 15 February

New kinds of memorials were proposed in the House of Lords. They suggested having a beautiful garden in London filled with trees and shrubs <u>given</u> by the people of England and at one end a shrine to the men who fell. Another suggestion was a huge hedge and another, a college like All Souls, Oxford, 'where men could be taught to love beauty again'.

Saturday 17 February

I went for my first ride for about eight years. June came too on Pixie while I rode Prince. I did enjoy it and had forgotten how glorious riding is. We did nothing spectacular today, just trotted along the seafront. Pixie was very nervous after the gunfire last time she was down there.

Thursday 22 February

We have arranged by phone to occupy Silkhouse on 12 April. After waiting for eight months it all seems so sudden, but it is very thrilling really, although being wartime things are difficult to fix up with rations and no car etc. It will be lovely in the summer.

Wednesday 28 February

It was overcast today but still no rain, so the soil is nice for digging and the grass dry, so I machined the front lawn and finished digging over the rose bank, the garden is beginning to look tidier at last and the daffodils, crocuses, primroses and stylosa iris all in bloom and very lovely.

Saturday 10 March

June and I went for a glorious ride over Woodbury. The horses loved it and the day was lovely so everything was wonderful. Pixie was very good, only shying sometimes at objects she saw but invisible to the rest of us.

Thursday 22 March

We sold this house today. So now No. 3 is sold. In many ways it seems very sad. I have been very happy here and am very fond of the house. I have done so much in the garden and love all the plants like personal friends.

Saturday 24 March

Mr Loram brought the car over for us to see. It is a nice one, quite racy in its way. A Crossley, ten horse power, fawn and black, old, but always owned by a careful old parson [*sic*].

Sunday 25 March

Maimie and I are both going to tea at the Devoncourt with Uncle Snuffy and Aunt Fanny. It is a glorious day (the temperature in London yesterday was seventy-three degrees p.m.). The baby chicks are well and feeding well, but I wish I could have them loose but I am afraid of the cats and I am too busy to watch them myself.

Monday 26 March

Got the new car insured, I now have to get the licence and some petrol, only hoping they will let us have some by the 12th. I washed the two sheepskin rugs, an awful job but well worth it as they were filthy and are now gleaming white.

Tuesday 27 March

I went into Exeter to do some shopping ready for our move. I got a crowbar for 19*s* 6*d* and various other things. I am glad the day is over. I loathe shopping, the smell of buses and the noise of all the traffic is awful, and I longed to be home in our garden. Had lunch with 'Baby' Davidson.

Saturday 31 March

June and I rode up to the football field on the common where we gave the horses a canter, the wind was high and the view exquisite. The horses both enjoyed their time out with us. Prince had been resting all the week ready for this morning.

Wednesday 4 April

Spent the morning shopping and at the dentist, then doctor after lunch, and the rest of the afternoon putting linen away and clearing cupboards, chests etc for the move. After supper I fetched the hoover from Mrs Everett, who kindly lent it me to thoroughly clean all carpets.

Sunday 8 April

We spent the day packing up like mad ready for the move and Maimie's visit to Mrs Everett while the actual removal takes place. Colonel Cowel came in to say goodbye. June came in to take the goats for a walk. Dolly came very upset about her mother who cannot live long now.

Monday 9 April

I spent the day digging up the garden, got up the pet rockery plants yesterday and today dug up various bulbs and herbaceous plants. It is so awful to leave my lovely little plants behind, so I am taking all I possibly can to put in Silkhouse garden. Henry wrote from Cambridge, so he is home after nearly five years in India.

Tuesday 10 April

Got Maimie ready to leave 3 Cranford Avenue for her future home. Meg and Tim arrived from Northern Ireland; they have come especially to help in this fearful house move. I was glad to see them as I feel very tired and muddled by this time.

Wednesday 11 April

Cullen Bros, the Exeter removers, arrived after breakfast to pack up the house, they went on until evening while Meg and I shopped and Tim got down the wire netting round the tennis lawn and goats shed in the compound, which I am going to use for the ducks.

Thursday 12 April

Meg rushed off to catch an early train and to meet the first van of our furniture in Exeter. June arrived and we packed the fowl house, fowls, chicks, ducks, bees, cats and goats into a cattle truck with Tim. Then June and I with Domino got into the last van, to arrive at three o'clock to see Meg and Sam at Silkhouse with the first van unpacked, waiting for ours to come up.

Friday 13 April

Woke up in our new home. Another brilliant, hot day. We had all slept well. June and I got the livestock fed while Meg got breakfast. Tim a godsend, he is so good at carpentry jobs. Maimie arrived at three o'clock with Mrs Everett and Dolly. Maimie likes the little place very much.

Saturday 14 April

We all unpacked all day, still a hell of a lot to do of course, it will take weeks to get everything fixed up. Meg and I undid eight huge crates of china and glass today, ready for Cullen to fetch when he brings another load of outdoor stuff this afternoon.

Sunday 15 April

Up to our eyes in work all day, it will be nice when it is all finished and we can sit down and enjoy life to the full. Tim got the new wireless he made for Maimie up in the drawing room. Meg and I started planting some of the boxes of plants I brought with us.

Monday 16 April

President Roosevelt has died suddenly. June had to go home so Tim and I went with her to Exeter, where Tim shopped and I fetched the Crossley from Pinhoe. The car works all right but the engine seems rather powerless. It is a joy to have a car on the road again after so long. We took half an hour to get over here from Paul Street.

Tuesday 17 April

I shall have to keep the goats tethered until I have been able to buy some sheep netting to keep them out of the kitchen garden, they are quite happy here but will be more so when they can be loose in the little field anyway. Uncle Snuffy came for the day; he liked the little place I think.

Wednesday 18 April

I biked over to Chagford in the morning; it was very pretty but awful hills. I introduced myself to the grocer, butcher and bank so I feel that I have done quite well for myself in one day. There seem to be quite good shops there, rather to my surprise.

Friday 27 April

Henry and I took the car up to Post Bridge where we walked up the Dart to Cut Hill, it was a long drag, the cold wind was awful but the view the best of any I have seen from Dartmoor. Even Henry thought it quite extensive. I should like to take Meg up there one day.

Saturday 28 April

I motored Henry into Exeter to the station; he has got to go back today I do miss him awfully. I then went on to Exmouth to collect the pots of greenhouse flowers from 3 Cranford Avenue. Found my visit most depressing. The historic announcement that US troops have linked with Russians in Central Germany was made simultaneously in London, Moscow and Washington.

1941

Household Accounts and Roses, Bushes, Fruit Trees and Shrubs Ordered for the Garden at 3 Cranford Avenue

January
Cash Account and Bill Book

Debit					Credit			
2	Car Licence	15	–	–	1 New Year gift	–	10	–
2	Madge	–	8	–	3 Army Pay	1	8	7
2	Cigarettes & Lunch	–	2	5 ½	3 Billeting	1	3	11
3	Batsford Book	–	7	6	10 Army Pay	1	8	7
3	Lunch and garage	–	2	1	10 Billeting	1	3	11
6	5 gals Petrol	–	10	2 ½	10 Xmas Gift	–	7	6
8	Sutton seeds	1	5	11	17 Army Pay	1	8	7
8	Dentist	1	10	–	17 Billeting	1	3	11
8	Bobby	5	8	–	24 Army Pay	1	16	–
8	Taylor Yendell	–	15	–	24 Billeting	–	16	–
9	Garage etc	–	7	6	31 Army Pay	1	8	6
11	5 gals Petrol	–	10	2 ½	31 Billeting	1	3	11
16	Madge	–	8	–				
17	Batsford Book	–	7	6				
21	5 gals Petrol	–	10	2 ½				
23	Leather for car	–	3	3				
23	Chemist	–	2	2				
24	Petrol	–	10	2 ½				
24	Hair dresser	–	6	6				
28	Linoleum	–	1	6				
30	Madge	–	8	–				
31	8 gals Petrol	–	16	4				
31	Stamp album	–	8	6				
31	Stamps	–	12	6				

February
Cash Account and Bill Book

	Debit					Credit			
6	Stamps	–	8	–	7	Army Pay	I	8	7
6	Madge	–	8	–	7	Billeting	I	3	II
7	Face Powder	–	7	II	14	Army Pay	I	8	7
7	5 gals Petrol	–	10	2 ½	14	Billeting	I	3	II
13	Stamps	–	8	6	21	Army pay	I	8	7
13	Stamp album	–	8	6	21	Billeting	I	3	II
17	Madge	–	8	–					
17	5 gals Petrol	–	10	2 ½					
18	Chemist	–	2	I					
20	Stamps	I	4	–					
20	Stamp album	–	8	6					
21	Madge	–	8	–					
21	5 gals Petrol	–	10	2 ½					
24	Motor Macs	2	6	5					
24	Car oil & greasing	–	4	6					
25	Madge's son	–	3	6					
26	5 gals Petrol	–	10	2 ½					
27	Stamps	–	10	–					
27	Madge	–	8	–					

March
Cash Account and Bill Book

	Debit					Credit			
I	Dog biscuit	–	9	–	7	Army Pay	I	8	7
10	Mrs Hearn	–	2	3	7	Billeting	I	3	II
10	Lunch	–	2	6	14	Army Pay	I	8	7
II	Madge's son	–	4	–	14	Billeting	I	3	II
II	5 gals petrol	–	10	2 ½	21	Army Pay	I	8	7
II	Lunch	–	2	6	21	Billeting	I	3	II
13	Car wash	–	2	6	28	Army Pay	I	8	7
13	Oil & grease etc	–	6	II	28	Billeting	I	3	II
14	Oatmeal 5lbs	–	I	5 ½	28	Credit Money	2	5	–
14	Lunch	–	I	6					
14	Madge	–	8	–					
14	5 gals Petrol	–	10	2 ½					
14	Fan belt	–	4	–					
14	Pills for dog	–	I	2					
17	Cherry Blouse	–	10	II					
17	Mrs Hearn	–	2	3					

18	5 gals Petrol	–	10	2 ½
21	Groceries	–	8	–
24	Mrs Hearn	–	2	3
25	5 gals Petrol	–	10	2 ½
26	Fancy flowers	–	3	11
27	Scent	–	8	6
27	'Make up'	–	9	6
29	8 gals Petrol	–	16	4
31	Beatrix Potter book	–	2	6
31	Batsford	–	7	6
31	Lunch	–	2	–

April
Cash Account and Bill Book

	Debit						Credit			
1	Iron-monger	–	6	–		4	Army Pay	1	8	6
1	Lunch	–	2	2		4	Billeting	1	3	11
7	3 gals Petrol	–	6	1 ½		9	Present	3	–	–
8	Batsford Book	–	7	6		11	Army Pay	1	8	6
8	2 lunch	–	4	–		11	Billeting	1	3	11
9	3 gals Petrol	–	6	1 ½		18	Army Pay	1	8	6
16	5 gals Petrol	–	10	2 ½		18	Billeting	1	3	11
16	Ink etc	–	4	1		24	Army Pay	1	8	6
17	Madge	–	8	–		24	Billeting	1	3	11
17	Mrs Hearn	–	2	3						
17	Dog biscuit	–	7	6						
20	5 gals Petrol	–	10	2 ½						
24	5 gals Petrol	–	10	2 ½						
24	Madge	–	8	–						
24	Lunch	–	2	–						
24	Book (Salop)	–	7	6						
24	Bay Rum	–	2	7						
24	Glasses	–	2	–						
26	Dog biscuit	–	12	–						
29	5 gals Petrol	–	10	2 ½						

May
Cash Account and Bill Book

Debit					Credit			
1 Madge	–	8	–		2 Army Pay	1	8	6
3 Dog biscuit	–	7	6		2 Billeting	1	3	11
3 5 gals Petrol	–	10	2 ½					
5 Bath Salts	–	4	6					
5 Wedgewood bowl	–	13	6					
7 Hair Perm	1	5	–					
7 Mud pack	–	1	–					
8 Madge	–	4	–					

Veitch's Sunray Collection A Roses

Christopher Stone	Scarlet	Mrs G A van Rossen	Crimson
Comtesse Vandal	Salmon	Mrs Sam McGredy	Salmon
Crimson Glory	Crimson	Phyllis Gold	Yellow
Golden Dawn	Yellow	The Bishop	Crimson
Mme Butterfly	Salmon		
McGredy's Ivory	White		
Mrs Barraclough	Carmine		
Mrs Edward Laxton	Rose		

Bush Roses Picked by Myself

Angela Pernet	Orange-apricot	Betty Uprichard	Pink-carmine
Duchess of Athol	Orange	Emma Wright	Orange
Independence Day	Yellow-copper	Lady Barnby	Glowing pink
Lady Sylvia	Salmon pink	Los Angeles	Salmon
McGredy's Sunset	Yellow-scarlet	Mrs Henry Bowles	Rose pink-salmon
Ophelia	Salmon	Picture	Glowing pink
President Hoover	Carmine-gold	Shot Silk	Cherry pink
Souvenir de		Sweetness	Apricot
Madame Boullet	Coppery yellow		

Polyantha Roses

Orange Triumph	Scarlet-orange	Paul Crampel	Orange-scarlet
Rhododendron	Pink Pearl		
Azalea			
Kentish Cob (1)		Nuts and Filberts	
Red Skinned Filbert (2)		ditto	
Davidson's Eight (½ doz)		Black Currants	
Seabrook's Black (½ doz)		ditto	

Fruit trees ordered from Veitch, 20 January

Bramley Seedling	(K)	
Charles Ross	(D)	
Lord Derby	(K)	Apples
Ellinson's Orange	(D)	
Lanes Prince Albert	(K)	
Newton Wonder	(K)	
Laxton's Superb	(D)	
Bellissime d' Hiver	(K)	
Doyenne du Comice	(D)	Pears
Louise Bonne of Jersey	(D)	
Lancer	(D)	Gooseberry
Belle de Louvaine	(KD)	Plum
Laxton's Gage	(D)	ditto
Early Alexander		Peach
Royal George		ditto
Angler	(D)	Gooseberry
Crown Bob	(D)	ditto
Keepsake	(K)	ditto

Rose Trees (Rambler and Climbers) from Veitch

Allen Chandler	(Pillar)	Vivid scarlet
Blush Rambler		Rich blush
Carmine Pillar	(Pillar)	Crimson
Lady Hillingdon		Deep yellow
Madame Butterfly		Pink, apricot and gold
Crimson Conquest		Bright crimson
Emily Gray		Yellow
Mermaid		ditto
Princess of Orange	(Pillar)	Brilliant orange-scarlet
Tausendschon	(Pillar)	Peach pink

1943

Household Accounts

January
Cash Account and Bill Book

	Debit				*Credit*
1	60 Cigarettes	–	6	–	
1	Dog meat	–	1	–	
1	Shoe polish	–	–	7 ½	
1	Glass cut	–	–	3	
5	Dog meat	–	1	–	
8	Dog meat	–	1	–	
8	2 Dog Licences	–	15	–	
8	60 Cigarettes	–	8	–	
8	Dog biscuits	–	2	–	
13	7lbs Ceiling White	–	1	9	
13	1lb Blue undercoat	–	1	9	
13	1lb Dog meat	–	1	–	
13	40 Cigarettes	–	4	–	
16	40 Cigarettes	–	4	–	
16	Dog meat	–	1	3	
20	60 Cigarettes	–	6	–	
20	Dog meat	–	1	–	
22	Dog meat	–	–	10	
22	Chemist	–	2	10	
22	Clipping Sam	–	6	–	
22	Snow (Trees)	–	16	–	
22	Veitch	5	–	6	
22	1 cwt Potatoes	–	16	–	
29	60 Cigarettes	–	6	–	
29	56lbs seed Potatoes	–	12	6	
29	1lb Dog meat	–	–	10	
29	Shoe laces	–	–	3	
29	Chemist	–	1	–	
29	Dog biscuit	–	2	–	

February
Cash Account and Bill Book

	Debit					*Credit*
4	Fare to Exeter	-		1	6	
4	Brassiere	-		2	7 ½	
4	2 pr Stockings					
5	40 Cigarettes	-		4	-	
5	Weed Killer	-		5	6	
5	Dog meat	-		-	10	
9	Cod liver oil (Hens)	-		1	6	
9	Dog meat	-		1	-	
9	Air mail	-		1	3	
9	Dog biscuits	-		1	3	
9	Fare to Topsham					
11	1 cwt Potatoes	-		16	-	
12	Cigarettes	-		4	-	
12	Dog meat	-		1	-	
16	Fare Exeter	-		1	6	
16	Cinema	-		2	6	
16	Lunch	-		2	3	
18	Dog meat	-		1	-	
18	Dog biscuits	-		1	6	
24	Dog meat	-		1	-	
24	Cigarettes	-		4	-	

March
Cash Account and Bill Book

	Debit					*Credit*
1	Boots Tonic Wine	-		5	6	
1	Cod liver oil	-		2	3	
1	Pills	-		-	5	
1	Dog meat	-		1	4	
1	Dog biscuits	-		1	4	
1	Cigarettes	-		2	-	
1	Sweets	-		3	6	
5	Dog meat	-		1	5	
5	Cigarettes	-		4	-	
5	Dog biscuits	-		1	4	
8	Dog meat	-		1	-	
8	Cigarettes	-		2	-	
12	Cigarettes	-		6	-	
12	Dog meat	-		1	5	